DATE DUE

APR 06 2015		

THE LIBRARY STORE #47-0207

MAN, MYTH, AND MAGIC

MAN, MYTH,
AND MAGIC

The Seasons: Natural Rites and Traditions

Cavendish
Square

New York

MAN, MYTH, AND MAGIC

Published in 2015 by Cavendish Square Publishing, LLC
243 5th Avenue, Suite 136, New York, NY 10016

Library of Congress Cataloging-in-Publication Data
Maple, Eric.
 The Seasons : natural rites and traditions / Eric Maple.
  pages cm. — (Man, myth, and magic)
 Includes index.
 ISBN 978-1-62712-678-6 (hardcover) ISBN 978-1-62712-680-9 (ebook)
 1. Seasons—Folklore. 2. Seasons—Mythology. I. Title.

GR930.M37 2015
398.21—dc23

2014002048

Editorial Director: Dean Miller
Editor: Amy Hayes
Art Director: Jeffrey Talbot
Designer: Jessica Moon
Photo Researcher: J8 Media
Production Manager: Jennifer Ryder-Talbot
Production Editor: David McNamara

Photo credits: Cover photos by: File:Maasai Youth/Anita Ritenour/Flickr/Wikimedia Commons, File:Maasai Youth/Anita Ritenour/Flickr/Wikimedia Commons, File:0100727 Nikko Taiyuin Fujin 6080/Jakub Hałun/Wikimedia Commons; DeAgostini/Getty Images, 1; DEA/A. DAGLI ORTI/De Agostini/Getty Images, 2–3; Mexico, 14th century - according to the prophecy, the Aztecs founded Tenochtitlan in 1325, in the place where an eagle devours a snake perched on a cactus (oil on wood), Mexican School/Museo de la Ciudad, Mexico/De Agostini Picture Library/A. Dagli Orti/The Bridgeman Art Library, 5t; DeAgostini/Getty Images, 5c; Ainu Bear SacrificeCirca1870/PHGCOM/Wikimedia Commons, 5b; Masterson Station Park Tree/Wikimedia Commons, 7; File:Full double rainbow gotland/Niklas Tyrefors/Wikimedia Commons, 8; File:Jarai tomb (guardian spirit sculpture)/Rdavout/Wikimedia Commons, 9; DeAgostini/Getty Images, 11; File:Piglet carrier Louvre CA86/Marie-Lan Nguyen/Wikimedia Commons, 12; File:US Navy 041219-N-9047Q-033 Command Chaplain Cmdr. Michael L. Schutz baptizes a young child on the flight deck of the conventionally powered aircraft carrier USS Kitty Hawk (CV 63).jpg/U.S. Navy photo by Photographer's Mate Airman Raul Quinones/Wikimedia Commons, 14; File:Guy Fawkes effigy by William Warby from Flickr/William Warby/Flickr/Wikimedia Commons, 15; File:Artos2/Lunyo/Wikimedia Commons, 17; Mexico, 14th century - according to the prophecy, the Aztecs founded Tenochtitlan in 1325, in the place where an eagle devours a snake perched on a cactus (oil on wood), Mexican School/Museo de la Ciudad, Mexico/De Agostini Picture Library/A. Dagli Orti/The Bridgeman Art Library, 18; File:Modern timber framing in pritzenhagen germany 003/Sebastian Wallroth/Wikimedia Commons, 19; Der Samstag (Saturday)/From Jewish Art/Wikimedia Commons, 21; File: Honorius/Hopsee/Wikimedia Commons, 23; File:Total solar eclipse on 22nd July at Varanasi,India/Manoj.dayyala/Wikimedia Commons, 25; File:Berlin Goethe-Gymnasium Reliefs Uhlandstraße Feuer/Andreas Praefcke/Wikimedia Commons, 26; File:Hanus Schwaiger - Water Gnome - Google Art Project/Hanus Schwaiger/Wikimedia Commons, 28; File:Herbert James Draper - Halcyone (1915)/Herbert James Draper/Wikimedia Commons, 31; File:Ainu Bear SacrificeCirca1870/PHGCOM/Wikimedia Commons, 33; File:Cihuacoatl statue (Museo Nacional Antropologia)/Madman2001/Wikimedia Commons, 34; Paul Strawson/Alamy, 35; File:Venus-de-Laussel-vue-generale-noir/photo 120/Wikimedia Commons, 36; File:Andrea del Sarto - Il sacrificio di Isacco (Prado)/Andrea del Sarto, Colección Real/Wikimedia Commons, 39; William Thomas Cain/Getty Images, 40; File:Endoxyla Leucomochla/Mdekool/Wikimedia Commons, 41; File:PANDEMUERTO/Luis VG/Wikimedia Commons, 42; CharosetIngredients/Jonathunder/Wikimedia Commons, 44; File:Lord's Table/John Snyder/Wikimedia Commons, 45; DEA/A. DAGLI ORTI/De Agostini/Getty Images, 47; File:First Thanksgiving cpb.3g04961/Jean Leon Gerome Ferris/Library of Congress/Wikimedia Commons, 48; ROMEO GACAD/AFP/Getty Images, 49; RDImages/Epics/Getty Images, 50; Grandma's Hearthstone, 1890 (oil on canvas), Haberle, John (1856-1933)/Detroit Institute of Arts, USA/Gift of C.W. Churchill in memory of his father/The Bridgeman Art Library, 52; File:La maison des Vestales (Forum Romain) (5983789754)/dalbera/Flickr/Wikimedia Commons, 53; File:Hortus sanitatis 1491 Mandrake/Jacob Meydenbach/National Library of Medicine/Wikimedia Commons, 55; File:Lajkonik/Kpalion/Wikimedia Commons, 57; File:Antique english dollhouse/Paul Keleher/Flickr/Wikimedia Commons, 59; John Scofield/National Geographic/Getty Images, 60; File:Gilded bronze door knocker/BabelStone/Wikimedia Commons, 61; Daesin manura (natural pigment on silk), Korean School/Gahoe Museum, Jongno-gu, South Korea/The Bridgeman Art Library, 62; File:Taksin Memorial Spirit House/Rlevse/Wikimedia Commons, 63; Education Images/UIG/Getty Images, 65; Horizons WWP/Alamy, 67; PhotoStock-Israel/Alamy, 69; File:Cú Chulainn & the Bull/Karl Beutel 2003/Teufelbeutel/Wikimedia Commons, 70; File:MV - Handschuh/Wolfgang Sauber/Wikimedia Commons, 71; DeAgostini/Getty Images, 73; A boy reading the Torah during his Bar Mitzvah (photo), ./Photo © Zev Radovan/The Bridgeman Art Library, 74; File:Maasai Youth/Anita Ritenour/Flickr/Wikimedia Commons, 76; File:Exterior of Carthage Jail by C.C.A. Christensen/Carl Christian Anton Christensen/Wikimedia Commons, 78; File:Diwali (Festival of lights) November 2013/peddhapati/Flickr/Wikimedia Commons, 79; Sephirot Tree of Life, 1617 (engraving), Fludd (Fluctibus), Robert (1574-1637)/Private Collection/© Leemage/The Bridgeman Art Library, 80; File:Icon between tombs/ACOR Cannes/Flickr/Wikimedia Commons, 81; Werner Forman/Universal Images Group/Getty Images, 82; File:AF Mlm Berbedak/Jerome wong c j/Wikimedia Commons, 83; File:Pieter Bruegel the Elder - Peasant Wedding - Google Art Project 2/Pieter Brueghel the Elder/Wikimedia Commons, 84; Universal History Archive/UIG/Getty Images, 86; Dan Porges/Getty Images, 87; John Tlumacki/The Boston Globe/Getty Images, 89; File:dendera relief/Bernard Gagnon/Wikimedia Commons, 92; File:Bronze statuette of Cybele/Peterjr1961/Wikimedia Commons, 93; File:Anahita in Maragha/Unknown/panoramio/Wikimedia Commons, 95; DEA/G. DAGLI ORTI/De Agostini/Getty Images, 96; File:Lippo di Vanni - Vierge à l'Enfant en majesté/Lippo Vanni/Ophelia2/Wikimedia Commons, 97; File:McCutcheonNY1905/John T. McCutcheon/Wikimedia Commons, 98; File:Central Dragon/J Bar/Wikimedia Commons, 99; File:Stories of beowulf grendel/J. R. Skelton/Marshall, Henrietta Elizabeth/Wikimedia Commons, 101; Ola-ola/Shutterstock, 102; Bruno Roiff/Shutterstock, 103; Patryk Kosmider/Shutterstock, 105; Harold M. Lambert/Lambert/Getty Images, 106; Jean-Christophe Huet/Getty Images, 107; Morocco, North of Meknes, Volubilis, House of Dionysus and Four Seasons, Dionysus and Allegory of Four Seasons, Spring, 3rd century ad/The Bridgeman Art Library/G. Dagli Orti/The Bridgeman Art Library, 109; File:Imst - Roller/James Steakley/Wikimedia Commons, 110; File:Águia da Portela (6932934731)/Leandro Neumann Ciuffo/Águia da Portela/Wikimedia Commons, 111; File:Mardi Gras Parade, New Orleans, Louisiana, Highsmith/Carol Highsmith/Library of Congress/Wikimedia Commons, 113; Matt Cardy/Getty Images, 115; File:Supraśl Muzeum Ikon 03/Andrzej Otrebski/Wikimedia Commons, 116; File:The Story of the Three Bears pg 20/Leonard Leslie Brooke/archive.org/Wikimedia Commons, 118; File:Schadow Grabmal Alexander 2/Johann Gottfried Schadow, photo Andreas Praefcke/Wikimedia Commons, 119; File:Dali Clocks (5836924514)/Salvador Dali, photo by Tony Hisgett/Flickr/Wikimedia Commons, 121; File:Wheel-of-fortune-time-death-bnf-fr-1358/Unknown/Gallica/Wikimedia Commons, 122; Egyptian - Ba Bird - Walters 571472/Anonymous/Walters Art Museum/Wikimedia Commons, 123; File:Naked lion-headed (leontocephaline) statuette of Parian marble entwined by a serpent and carrying two keys, from the Mithraeum at Sidon (Colonia Aurelia Pia, Syria), Louvre Museum (9365098940)/Carole Raddato/Flickr/Wikimedia Commons, 125; Dinodia Photos/Alamy, 126; File:Ignaz Günther Chronos BNM img02/Ignaz Günther/Wikimedia Commons, 128; The British Library/Robana/Getty Images, 130; File:0100727 Nikko Taiyuin Fujin 6080/Jakub Hałun/Wikimedia Commons, 131; File:Tlaloc (Sala Teotihuacan del Museo Nacional de Antropología e Historia)/El Comandante/Wikimedia Commons, 132; File:GOES-13 2 Jan 2014 1745z satellite/National Oceanic and Atmospheric Administration/Wikimedia Commons, 133; File:Imbolc Festival February 3rd 2007/steven earnshaw/Flickr/Wikimedia Commons, 136; File:Vasnetsov Snegurochka/Viktor M. Vasnetsov/Scanned from A. K. Lazuko Victor Vasnetsov, Leningrad: Khudozhnik RSFSR, 1990, ISBN 5-7370-0107-5/Wikimedia Commons, 137.

Cavendish Square would like to acknowledge the outstanding work, research, writing, and professionalism of Man, Myth, and Magic's original Editor-in-Chief Richard Cavendish, Executive Editor Brian Innes, Editorial Advisory Board Members and Consultants C.A. Burland, Glyn Daniel, E.R Dodds, Mircea Eliade, William Sargent, John Symonds, RJ. Zwi Werblowsky, and R.C. Zaechner, as well as the numerous authors, consultants, and contributors that shaped the original Man, Myth, and Magic that served as the basis and model for these new books.

Printed in the United States of America

Contents

A Reader's Guide to *Man, Myth, and Magic: The Seasons: Natural Rites and Traditions*

Part of what makes this world so mysterious is the way in which customs, relationships, and understandings of the world around us echo throughout the variety of cultures in the world. Commonalities exist between the stories and traditions of Europe, Africa, Asia, and both North and South America. Even as each culture has its own initiations rites, spring festivals, and harvest rituals, civilizations are inundated with people's desire to interact with the natural world, celebrate milestones of success and growth, and mark the passage of time. Upon examination, what we are left with is a rich variety of rites and celebrations to compare and examine across continents.

Man, Myth, and Magic: The Seasons: Natural Rites and Traditions is a volume devoted to pursuing an understanding of this variety. It is, in brief, a study of different rites and cultural understandings of the world around us. This book attempts to look not only at natural phenomena but how humanity has reacted to it, explained it, and even created dogma from it. Each article gives an in depth look at several different cultures' traditions surrounding important events. From superstitions surrounding rainbows to building rites to the concept of time, *Man, Myth, and Magic: The Seasons: Natural Rites and Traditions* examines celebrations and rituals, no matter how apparently small, to give the readers a better understanding of the human condition.

Objectives of *Man, Myth, and Magic*

Each volume of the *Man, Myth, and Magic* series approaches individual topics from an unbiased position. In *The Seasons: Natural Rites and Traditions*, presenting rites of passage without editorializing commentary allows readers to best form their own opinions and understandings on the variety of rituals. The comprehensive coverage of different seasonal traditions, as well as the major deities and religions related

Man himself, it appears, would be an elemental spirit of Nature, but for the divine element in him.

to these traditions, for example, can aid students researching faith, particularly in a comparison of faiths from around the world.

The Text

An impressive lineup of expert contributors have created articles arranged alphabetically, and the depth of coverage varies from short entries defining a singular subject through multipage contributions providing far-ranging discussion of complex issues. From Animism to Winter, key traditions, concepts, and faiths are profiled, with articles focusing on how the development of different civilizations and cultures viewed these natural events as either benevolent or evil.

Not only is the text informative, but the work is highly illustrated, with beautiful images of traditional artwork as well as informative pictures that present abstract concepts, such as time, with striking simplicity. Subjects of major interest are provided with individual bibliographies of further reading on the subject at the end of each article, making *Man, Myth, and Magic* a preliminary resource for any avid researcher.

The past century has seen a powerful revival of interest in these subjects at both the scholarly and popular level, making works like this possible. There has been a flourishing revival of popular interest in ancient civilizations, mythology, magic, and alternative paths to truth. This interest has shown no sign of diminishing this century; on the contrary, it has grown stronger and has explored new pathways. At the same time scholarly investigation of our subjects has continued and has thrown much new light on some of our topics. The present edition of *Man, Myth, and Magic* takes account of both these developments. Articles have been updated to cover fresh discoveries and new theories since they first appeared.

With all this, *Man, Myth, and Magic* is not intended to convert you to or from any belief or set of beliefs and

A typical tree in the fall with leaves turned red symbolizes the customs of change that are inherent in cultures around the world

attitudes. The purpose of the articles is not to persuade or justify, but to describe what people have believed and trace the consequences of those beliefs in action. The editorial attitude is one of sympathetic neutrality. It is for the reader to decide where truth and value may lie. We hope that there is as much interest, pleasure, and satisfaction in reading these pages as all those involved took in creating them.

Illustrations

Since much of what we know about myth, folklore, and religion has been passed down over the centuries by word of mouth, and recorded only comparatively recently, visual images are often the most vivid links we have with the past. Similarly, taboos that are often not spoken of can breach the world of art. As such, illustrations are an essential part of understanding culture and the evolution of civilization. They give us a feeling for things we cannot know and speak the words we cannot say.

The wealth of illustration in *Man, Myth, and Magic: The Seasons: Natural Rites and Traditions* is invaluable, not only because of the great diversity of sources, but also because of the superb quality of colour reproduction. From a modern colour photograph of a bonfire on Guy Fawkes Day to representations of deism, rituals, ancient myths, sacred paintings, and texts, all are recorded here in infinite variety, including tomb and wall paintings, and artifacts in metal, pottery, and wood. Examples of artwork from countries around the world are represented.

Index

The A–Z index provides immediate access to any specific item sought by the reader. The reference distinguishes the nature of the entry in terms of a main entry, supplementary subject entries, and illustrations.

A full double rainbow in Gotland, Sweden

Skill Development for Students

The books of the *Man, Myth, and Magic* series can be consulted as the basic text for a subject or as a source of enrichment for students. The additional reading at the end of many entries is an invaluable resource for students looking to enhance their studies on a specific topic. *Man, Myth, and Magic* offers an opportunity for students that is extremely valuable; with text that is both multidisciplinary and interdisciplinary; a wealth of fine illustrations; a research source well-suited to a variety of age levels that will provoke interest and encourage speculation in both teachers and students.

Scope

The *Man, Myth, and Magic* series lends itself to a multi-disciplinary approach to study. As well as being an asset to social studies teaching, the book provides students from a wide range of disciplines with a stimulating, accessible, and beautifully illustrated reference work. Students interested in math and geometry will be fascinated by the positioning of Chichen Itza and the Pyramids, which take into account the sun's height at the vernal equinox. Readers excited by the sciences will be delighted to discover the deep cultural ties to the success of crops, the progression of environment,

and the astronomical positioning of the stars. Furthermore, the great excerpts of texts from *Alice in Wonderland* to Aztec Prayers will stimulate the imagination of any student of literature. In summation, the work is one that can appeal to any person eager to learn.

Conceptual Themes

As students become involved in the work, they will gradually become sensitive to the major concepts emerging from research. Students will begin to understand the role of the different belief systems and how they communicate and understand the world around them.

The concepts discussed in this book appear in religions and mythology all over the world. *Man, Myth, and Magic: The Seasons: Natural Rites and Traditions* celebrates the customs of change and the importance differences that separate humans from the rest of the animal kingdom. The progress of the seasons the rising and setting of the sun the importance of fertility—all are fundamental concepts universal to civilizations, and understanding the methods that these civilizations used to incorporate the stories and myths centered around each makes for a keener understanding of history. This volume and other title selections in this set enable students to broaden their understanding of the world.

Animism

Animism is the belief that all things animate and inanimate, all the phenomena of Nature, are possessed of an individual spirit or soul. It is the view of the world, to quote a famously eloquent passage in *The Golden Bough*, 'that peopled with a multitude of individual spirits every rock and hill, every tree and flower, every brook and river, every breeze that blew and every cloud that flecked with silvery white the blue expanse of heaven . . .'

The word comes from the Latin words *animus* and *anima*, which could mean 'breath' or 'life' or 'soul' and were essentially connected with the concept of the life-breath (and animism must be clearly distinguished from animatism, the belief that a single lifeforce is present in all the phenomena of the world).

It is doubtful whether any single religious belief has been more widely and tenaciously held than animism. In Greek mythology there were the nymphs—the spirits of springs and rivers, trees and hills and caves, imagined as beautiful young girls. Running water, streams, and wells, were the province of the Naiads, while the Dryads and Hamadryads were the spirits of trees. Nymphs attended the great goddess Artemis in mountain and meadow, and in the waves of the ocean frolicked the Oceanides and the Nereids, one of whom was the mother of the great hero Achilles.

British folklore, similarly, is full of local country spirits—brownies and boggarts, and the knockers who held sway in Cornish tin mines.

Animism, however, is far from dead. In Africa, New Guinea, and the Pacific, to this day, the spirits of animals and trees, thunder, and lightning, wind and rain, still retain much of their ancient hold on human esteem, and their displeasure can provide a convincing explanation of otherwise inexplicable misfortune.

In Burma the minor spirits called *nats* can cause bad luck if they are unwisely neglected. The house nat has his respected shrine in each home, bamboo nat shrines stand by the roads and among trees, and the blossom in a Burmese girl's hair does due honour to the nats. And even the biggest and brashest Western-style hotels in Thailand have unobtrusive little shrines to the local spirits called *phis*.

The permeation of everything by spirits means that there is a complicated network of relationships between different spirits and between spirits and mankind. Human beings, if they are wise, move with care and caution in this dangerous labyrinth.

It makes good sense, for instance, to apologize politely to the spirit of a tree before felling it, or propitiate the spirits of a mine before extracting its ore. In the silver mines in Peru today a little figure of El Tio ('Uncle') stands close to the shafts, and miners give him offerings of cola leaves and put lighted cigarettes in his mouth to provide him with a propitiatory smoke, just to keep him sweet.

From Animism to Monotheism

So widespread and persistent is this belief in a multitude of spirits populating the world, that animism was put forward in the nineteenth century as the minimum definition of religion and the explanation of its origin. In his influential book

Statue near a Jarai village in the central highlands of Vietnam

Primitive Culture (1871), Sir Edward Tylor, who was Professor of Anthropology at the University of Oxford, argued that animism was the earliest stage in the development of religion.

Thinking people, he suggested, were early impressed by two groups of questions. What makes the difference between a living body and a dead one, and what causes sleep, trance, disease, and death? And secondly, what are the human forms that are seen in dreams and visions? By pondering on these matters, early philosophers probably drew the obvious inference that every person has both a life and a phantom, both of which are connected with the body. Life enables the body to feel and act, while the phantom is its image or second self. Both can leave the body during sleep and unconsciousness, and at death.

Tylor went on to argue that primitive man assumed that the life and the phantom were manifestations of the same 'soul.' From this emerged the idea of the soul as a ghost or apparition, and this concept in its turn produced the idea of the personal soul or spirit, which could leave the body and did leave it at death. Once this was realized, Tylor suggested, early man would have gone on to conclude that, since human beings had souls, so did all natural phenomena—trees, streams, rocks, clouds, and the rest—have souls that animated them and gave them life.

In the next step, according to this theory, people began to think of a god of the winds in general, instead of, or in addition to, a spirit of each individual wind, a deity of the woods as well as the spirit of each tree, and so on. Great gods and goddesses emerged from the multitude of lesser spirits. In this way, it was argued, animism gave way to polytheism, the worship of many gods, from which some more enlightened peoples in time advanced to monotheism, the worship of one solitary deity.

The Modern View

The theory had a long run, but more recent study approaches the origin of religion along different lines. The Egyptian *Pyramid Texts* (c. 2400 BC),

> *On the contrary, they regard a human being as a compound of a physical body and various psychic elements, of which the soul was only one.*

the earliest written records of religion, do not reveal any notion of a clear-cut division between soul and body in human nature. On the contrary, they regard a human being as a compound of a physical body and various psychic elements, of which the soul was only one.

Similar, though less elaborate conceptions were held by many ancient peoples, including the Mesopotamians, the Hebrews, and the Homeric Greeks. Tylor's dualistic idea of the soul as the inner essential self, independent of the body, did not emerge until sometime later in India (c. 700 BC) and Greece (c. 600 BC).

The origin of the idea of deity is also far more complicated than Tylor supposed. The evidence of archeology indicates that the earliest form of deity was the Mother Goddess, the deification of the female principle, which expressed man's need for fertility and new life.

S. G. F. BRANDON

Baptism

Baptism is known generally as the rite of initiation into membership of the Christian Church. Most people probably regard it as originating from the baptism of Jesus by John the Baptist, an incident that is graphically recorded in the New Testament and frequently depicted in Christian art. But ritual washing or immersion in water was already an ancient and widespread practice before that time, and various meanings were attached to it.

To understand the full significance of Christian baptism, it is necessary first to appreciate the varied symbolic roles of water in religion.

In the creation myths of many peoples water is the substance out of which the world, or the creator of the world, originally emerged. The ancient Egyptians imagined that in the beginning there was only a featureless expanse of water, called Nun. Out of this the primeval hill first emerged, followed by the creator god Atum, who stood on it to begin the work of creating the universe. In Babylonian myth the first gods are produced by the intercourse of the salt waters (Tiamat) and the fresh waters (Apsu). Later, the Babylonian god Marduk slays Tiamat, which is conceived of as a great monster, and fashions the universe out of its body.

In these ancient traditions water was regarded as the source of life, a belief which was strengthened by the fact that man and all other living creatures need water to maintain life. The idea of water as a life-giving substance has found expression in many religions in the idea of a mystic 'water of life' or 'fountain of life.'

Opposite page:
The Baptism of Christ painted by El Greco (1541–1614) found on the Modena Triptych, a portable altarpiece

The cleansing property of water also acquired religious significance as a means or symbol of ritual and spiritual purification: thus in Psalm 51 the petition is made to God: 'Wash me thoroughly from my iniquity . . . purge me with hyssop, and I shall be clean: wash me, and I shall be whiter than snow.'

The Salvation of Pharaoh

It is not surprising, therefore, to find in the earliest religious writings so far known, the *Pyramid Texts* of Egypt, which date from about 2500 BC, that water has both a revivifying and a purifying role. These texts are concerned with the mortuary ritual practiced to ensure the resurrection of the dead pharaoh to a blessed and eternal life, and they illustrate the ideas and beliefs of the Egyptians at this time. Several of them refer to a lake in the next world in which the sun-god Re revivifies himself each morning, and in which the dead king will also bathe and be revivified. The texts also show that ritual lustrations (washings) were frequent during the ritual of embalming, their purpose being both to purify the corpse from the contamination of death and to revivify it. The ritual was patterned on the rites believed to have been performed by various deities to raise the dead god Osiris to life again. The dead pharaoh was ritually identified with Osiris, in the belief that the reenactment of the rites would similarly resurrect him to a new life.

The ancient Egyptian evidence is especially important because it presents so graphically the two aspects of water combined in a single ritual process of salvation. The water cleanses the body of the deceased from the corruption of death and also revivifies or regenerates it for a life of eternal blessedness. This twofold process for the achievement of a blessed immortality is not found again until the emergence of Christianity. However, ritual ablution as an initiatory rite or for spiritual rebirth was practiced in the mystery religions of the Graeco-Roman world, and there are interesting comparisons with Christian baptism.

Washing the Pig

As a purification rite only, bathing in the sea was an important part of the initiatory ritual of the Eleusinian Mysteries, the oldest mystery cult of ancient Greece. On the second day of its Greater Mysteries initiates hastened down to the sea, each carrying a small pig. They washed both themselves and the pigs in the sea as an act of ritual cleansing. The pigs were subsequently sacrificed, their blood being considered a potent purificatory agent against demonic evil.

It is in the mysteries of Cybele and Attis that we meet the most savage form of a regenerative bath. The rite was known as the *taurobolium*. The initiate descended into a pit and was bathed in the blood of a bull, sacrificed above him. (There is mention also of a *criobolium*, which involved the slaughter of a ram.) The first documentary evidence of the rite dates from the second century AD.

The rite seems sometimes to have been primarily a sacrifice for well-being of some kind; but its regenerative function is shown by certain inscriptions that use the word *renatus* (reborn) of the initiate or refer to the day of the taurobolium as his birthday. Some of the ideas that underlie this rite would seem to be obvious: the bull has ever symbolized strength and virility; and its blood is its life-substance. However, in what manner the bull was associated with Attis, a 'dying-rising god,' and in what sense the devotee was reborn or rejuvenated by the taurobolium is not clear.

Ritual washing for various purposes was an ancient custom among the Hebrews; after being healed of leprosy, for instance, or after touching a corpse. Jesus is reported to have healed

A piglet carrier of the Eleusinian Mysteries, a cult of ancient Greece

a blind man by sending him to wash in a pool, after anointing his eyes with clay (John, chapter 9). These examples show the belief in the power of ritual washing to remove ritual 'uncleanness' and in the curative property of water. But more significant as a forerunner of early Christian baptism was the ritual bath that had to be taken by converts to Judaism. This rite was essentially a purification from heathenism, in preparation for membership of the holy people of Yahweh, the God of Israel. An essential requirement was the total immersion of the candidate.

The Baptism of Jesus

The discovery of the Dead Sea Scrolls, and the excavations at Qumran of the settlement of the community that owned them, have shed much light on the nature of the baptism of Jesus. The Qumran Covenanters, who regarded themselves as a holy community within Israel, would admit a new member after public repentance and baptism. A passage from the scroll known as the *Manual of Discipline* says 'that his flesh will be cleansed by the sprinkling of water for impurity and by the sanctification of himself with purifying water.' The large cisterns, with steps descending into them, found at Qumran indicate that baptism was by total immersion.

Before considering the Christian accounts of the type of baptism practiced by John the Baptist, it is useful to look at the account in the *Jewish Antiquities* of Josephus, the Jewish historian who lived in the first century AD. This is significant in the light of the evidence from Qumran since the area of John the Baptist's activity was nearby.

For John was a pious man, and he exhorted the Jews who practiced virtue and exercised righteousness toward each other and piety toward God, to come together for baptism. For thus it seemed to him would baptismal ablution be acceptable, if it were not used to beg off sins committed, but for the purification of the body when the soul had previously been cleansed by righteous conduct.

It is in this setting of contemporary Jewish ritual ablutions, emphasizing the purifying action of water, which the earliest form of Christian baptism, particularly that of the baptism of Jesus by John the Baptist, is to be understood. This is clear from the earliest account in the gospels (Mark, chapter 1). 'John the baptizer appeared in the wilderness, preaching a baptism of repentance for the forgiveness of sins. And there went out to him all the country of Judea, and all the people of Jerusalem; and they were baptized by him in the river Jordan, confessing their sins . . . In those days Jesus came from Nazareth of Galilee and was baptized by John in the Jordan.'

The disciples of Jesus, under his direction, apparently baptized their converts and, although there is some obscurity as to whether Jesus himself actually baptized, early tradition represents him commanding his disciples to do so. 'Go, therefore, and make disciples of all nations, baptizing them in the name of the Father and of the Son and of the Holy Ghost' (Matthew, chapter 28). This commandment that baptism should be 'in the name' of the three Divine Persons, who were in later Christian doctrine to constitute the Trinity, seems to indicate a later elaboration of the original formula. But the use of the Trinitarian formula soon became established as orthodox doctrine, and it has continued to be regarded as an essential condition for a valid baptism.

This evidence of the original form of Christian baptism, and its close connection with contemporary forms of Jewish baptism, shows that baptism at first was essentially a purificatory rite, which was intimately linked with repentance of sins. It was the essential requirement for admission to membership of the Christian community and it was closely related to the recognition of Jesus as the Messiah of Israel, who would shortly return with supernatural power to establish the kingdom of God. But there is no suggestion that the rite affected some kind of spiritual transformation of the baptized person, such as might be described as 'rebirth' or 'regeneration.'

Ritual Death and Rebirth

It was St. Paul who was responsible for transforming this original form of baptism into the sacramental rite of rebirth that baptism became in the Christian Church. This decisive change is first expressed in the sixth chapter of Paul's letter to the omans, which was written about AD 56 or 57. The passage concerned needs quotation and commentary to bring out its full significance.

'Do you not know that all of us who have been baptized into Christ Jesus were baptized into his death? We were buried therefore with him by

A Baptismal Prayer

Almighty and everlasting God, who of thy great mercy didst save Noah and his family in the ark from perishing by water; and also didst safely lead the children of Israel thy people through the Red Sea, figuring thereby thy holy Baptism; and by the Baptism of thy wellbeloved Son Jesus Christ, in the river Jordan, didst sanctify Water to the mystical washing away of sin; We beseech thee, for thine infinite mercies, that thou wilt mercifully look upon this Child; wash him and sanctify him with the Holy Ghost . . .

The Book of Common Prayer

An Aztec Prayer

From the Aztec ceremony of bathing the newborn:

Merciful Lady Chalchiuhtlicue, thy servant here present is come into the world . . . Wash him and deliver him from impurities . . . Cleanse him of the contamination he hath received from his parents: let the water take away the soil and the stain, and let him be freed from all taint. May it please thee, O Goddess, that his heart and his life be purified, that he may dwell in this world in peace and wisdom. May this water take away all ills . . . wash from him the evils which he beareth from before the beginning of the world.

Bernardino de Sahagun
Historia de las Cosas de la Nueva Espana
(trans. H. B. Alexander)

A child being baptized into the Christian church

baptism into death, so that as Christ was raised from the dead by the glory of the Father, we too might walk in newness of life. For if we have been united with him in a death like his, we shall certainly be united with him in a resurrection like his. We know that our old self was crucified with him, so that the sinful body might be destroyed and we might no longer be enslaved to sin. For he who has died is freed from sin. But if we have died with Christ, we believe that we shall also live with him. For we know that Christ being raised from the dead will never die again; death no longer has dominion over him. The death he died he died to sin, once for all, but the life he lives he lives to God. So you also must consider yourselves dead to sin and alive to God in Christ Jesus.'

This passage, full as it is of esoteric imagery, clearly sees baptism in a very different way from that of the earlier ritual cleansing, which initiated the convert into the Christian community. Instead, Paul presents the rite as a ritual death and rebirth, which simulates the death and resurrection of Christ.

There is a parallelism of imagery between the burial of Christ in the tomb and the burial of the new convert under the baptismal water. In other words, in baptism the Christian is ritually assimilated to Christ in his death, dying to his former self, so that as Christ was resurrected from the dead, the Christian, thus ritually incorporated in Christ, will rise to a new immortal life.

This Pauline doctrine of baptism recalls, in a striking manner, the assimi

lation of the dead with Osiris in the ancient Egyptian mortuary cult. Like the Egyptian rite, baptism for Paul effects rebirth or transformation to a new exalted state of being. Paul's view had a decisive influence and found dramatic expression in the baptismal ritual of the Early Church. Special baptisteries were constructed to allow total immersion. Candidates took off their clothes and descended into the water, thus ritually symbolizing a dying of their old selves. On emerging from the baptismal water, they were clothed in white robes, received a new name, and given mystic food of milk and honey, so proclaiming their rebirth by baptism to a new life in Christ.

Baptism of Babies

In the Early period Church, most candidates for baptism were adults.

Often converts put off baptism until near death, in the belief that thereby they would die purified from sin and spiritually reborn. However, as time went by, the custom of baptizing infants gradually prevailed. It was natural that Christian parents should want their children to enjoy the spiritual benefits of baptism but the practice was decisively affected by the doctrine of Original Sin.

According to this doctrine, a newborn child, though incapable of actual sin, was held to be subject to God's wrath because it shared in the inherited sin of mankind. A baby who died unbaptized was condemned to hell (or to Limbo, a special compartment of hell). The practice of infant baptism led to the introduction of the smaller, elevated font, which replaced the baptistery of earlier churches: and also to the separation of baptism from confirmation, which was originally part of the baptismal ceremony in the Early Church and was regarded as imparting the gift of the Holy Spirit to the baptized through the laying-on of the bishop's hands.

Another important development was that the grace of baptism was believed to be conveyed *ex opere operando*, which means by virtue of the enactment of the rite itself. Emphasis was laid upon the correct 'form' and 'matter:' the Trinitarian formula had to be used, and the water must flow over the candidate and not merely be sprinkled upon him.

The Reformation did not disturb the status of baptism as the essential rite of Christian initiation for Protestants as well as for Catholics. Indeed certain sects such as the Anabaptists and Baptists laid primary stress on its importance; but they insisted on a return to adult baptism by immersion, maintaining that baptism should signify the deliberate acceptance of Christ, which was impossible for an infant.

Today baptism is usually taken to symbolize acceptance of membership in the Christian community, rather than to effect a mystic rebirth, such as Paul taught. The Roman Catholic Church retains the most elaborate baptismal ritual in the West: it includes preliminary exorcisms, anointing with spittle and oil, and the holding of a candle.

S. G. F. BRANDON

FURTHER READING: G. R. Beasley-Murray. Baptism in the New Testament. *(Grand Rapids, MI: Eerdmans, 1973); M. Black.* The Scrolls and Christian Origins. *(New York, NY: Scribner, 1969); A. Carson.* Baptism. *(Grand Rapids, MI: Kregel, 1981).*

Bonfires

In the year's round, many dates are deemed deserving of a bonfire—a blaze that serves as a celebration, a memorial, and even a means of divination. To Britons, 'bonfire night' is synonymous with November 5, the date on which, in 1605, Guy Fawkes and his compatriots failed to blow up London's Houses of Parliament and with it, the monarch, James I. Soon after, it became traditional to light fires on that night, when children would chant the rhyme, as they still do today:

Remember, remember
The fifth of November,
Gunpowder, Treason, and Plot

Guy Fawkes wax model burning on a bonfire in Essex, England

*I see no reason
Why Gunpowder Treason
Should ever be forgot.*

Atop an authentic bonfire there must be a human effigy—a 'guy'—which in the early years was commonly fashioned in the guise of the pope as an anti-Catholic protest in a now Protestant land. The tradition was even carried on by early Puritan settlers in New England who on 'Pope Day' carried effigies of the Devil, the Pope, and Guy Fawkes around the streets before setting them alight.

When Evil Held Sway

Bonfires take on a central role at times of the year when evil is believed to hold sway and witches to roam abroad. Long before Guy Fawkes, bonfires were lit at Hallowe'en, October 31, which today is the eve of All Saints but in pre-Christian times was a pagan festival of both fire and the dead. In Scotland young lads would knock on doors to ask for 'a peat to burn the witches' and as they danced around the bonfire all the children would shout at the tops of their voices: 'Fire! Fire! Burn the witches' then, as the final embers died down 'The Devil take the hindmost' before racing back to the safety of their homes.

The Hallowe'en bonfire was also a site of divination. Once the bonfire was out, the ashes were carefully moved to form a complete circle. Everyone then placed a stone in the circle, near the circumference. If, in the morning, a stone was found to have moved, or even be missing altogether, then it was believed that its 'owner' would not live for more than a twelvemonth. A variation on this theme, common in Wales, was to run through the smoke whilst the fire was still alight, and to drop a stone into the fire as they did so.

At this time of year, the bonfire has yet other purposes. To celebrate Samhain, a harvest, usually dated to November 1, a pagan practice was to burn the bones of animals such as sheep, pigs, and oxen that were slaughtered to be kept for food in the winter months. It is from this cleansing ritual burning of bones that the bonfire or 'bone fire' is named.

Earlier in the calendar, bonfires are lit on Walpurgis Night, April 30,

And he took bread, and when he had given thanks, he broke it and gave it to them, saying, "This is my body, which is given for you. Do this in remembrance of me."

when, as at Hallowe'en, witches are believed to mount broomsticks and take to the skies. Once assembled they are said to convene their sabbats, drinking, singing, and dancing as they commune with the Devil and promise him their allegiance. To mark the night, (which is named for St. Walburg an eighth century abbess from Dorset, England), dispel evil, and at the same time herald the arrival of spring, residents of Germany and Scandinavia still light bonfires on Walpurgus Night, around which they sing heartily. Weeks later, bonfires take centre stage in the celebration of Midsummer.

Eastern Celebration

In northern India, especially the states of Punjab and Himachal Pradesh, the bonfire festival of Lohri is a highlight of the year. Its celebration in mid January marks time when the earth begins to move closer to the sun, heralding the advent of spring and the anticipation of a good harvest in March and April. Before bonfires are lit in the evening children go from door to door asking for sweets as they sing the

praises of Dulha Bhatti, a folk hero renowned for robbing the rich to pay the poor.

As people gather around the bonfires they throw into the flames popcorn and rice, shouting as they do so: 'May honour come and poverty vanish,' in the hope that their wishes will be heard by Agni, the fire god. Then dancing begins, performed by men and, accompanied by the persistent beat of the drums, and carries on late until the night. In a separate ceremony, held in courtyards, women weave their own bonfire dance movements.

RUTH BINNEY

FURTHER READING:
B. Blackburn and L. Holford Strevens. The Oxford Companion to the Year. (New York, NY: Oxford University Press, 2003); David Pickering. Cassell's Dictionary of Witchcraft. (London, UK: Cassell, 2003).

Bread

Because of its vital importance from the cradle to the grave, bread has many sacred associations; it is surrounded by ceremonies and superstitions that derive from its original association with the corn spirit. At one time at the sowing of the corn, the soil was fertilized by sacrificial human blood. The spirit of the wheat, sometimes represented by a human victim bound in wheat sheaves, was ritually killed at harvest time.

Bread has specific meaning across many religions. 'And he took bread, and when he had given thanks, he broke it and gave it to them, saying: "This is my body, which is given for you. Do this in remembrance of me."' The passage from the Bible is well known to any Christian. At the Last Supper, Jesus represents his impending sacrifice on the cross with bread and wine, bread representing his body, and wine his blood. The Christian Communion recalls the sacred metaphor, as worshippers eat bread and drink wine to absolve them of sins and remember the sacrifice of their Saviour.

The theme of the first and last fruits of the field dominates the rites of bread. In northwest India the first of the grain is formally presented to one of the family; in the Russian Volga region it was the custom for the village elder to present a portion of the first bread of the new harvest to each member of the community. A Swedish rite, revealing traces of sacrifice, involves baking the last sheaf into a loaf shaped like a young girl.

Proof of the Loaf

Bread played a prominent role in the primitive European system of trial by ordeal in which accused persons attempted to prove their innocence by eating a piece of bread and butter; if they choked they were considered guilty. In 1619, the witch Joan Flower swallowed a mouthful of bread and butter, declaring that 'she wished it might never go through her if she were guilty,' and dropped dead.

The baking of bread had its special taboos. A menstruating woman was prohibited from participating in the kneading, as it was believed that her touch prevented the dough from rising. Another was the marking of a cross on the dough to prevent it from

falling into the hands of Satan. Bread baked on Good Friday was held to retain its freshness and the woman who baked it was considered highly blessed. The Russians, however, regarded all Fridays as ominous for baking, and Good Friday even more so.

Household bread was equally valued both as a medicine and as a magic charm by wheat-growing peoples. In Belgium stale bread placed in the cradle was thought to protect the baby; in Egypt it was considered a cure for indigestion; in Morocco it was an accepted specific against stammering. In Britain and the United States, bread thrown into the fire is said to feed the devil.

The Sin Eater

There are a number of popular superstitions concerning the magical aspects of bread. A long hole in the loaf portends a death in the household. A curious tradition that it is unlucky to take the last slice of bread on a plate is widespread in Britain and United States. For a single woman to do so means that she will remain an old maid. Also in the United States, it is bad luck to turn a loaf upside down—if one falls that way, it portends a quarrel.

Bread has also figured in the lore of sea and weather. Sailors believe that to cut a loaf and turn it upside down causes a ship to sink. In the belief that storms can be averted, bread is placed on the windowsill in Spain facing the direction of the anticipated outbreak.

A remarkable quality formerly ascribed to bread was its power to react to the presence of a drowned body. It was believed that a loaf weighted with quicksilver and placed in the water would be irresistibly drawn toward the place where the body lay. As recently as 1921, a corpse was discovered after this method had been tried at Wheelock in Cheshire, England.

The artos, or leavened bread, placed on a Orthodox Church altar at Easter time

Bread had an important function in connection with the Last Rites. Until a century ago it was not uncommon for an old man, called a Sin Eater, to be hired to take upon himself all the sins of the newly dead, in return for sixpence, a bowl of beer, and a loaf that had been in contact with a corpse. The idea behind this practice was that it would enable the soul of the dead person to proceed directly to Paradise.

FURTHER READING: Christina Hole. English Folklore. *(New York, NY: Scribner, 1940); Ronald Sheppard and Edward Norton.* The Story of Bread. *(Fernhill, 1957).*

Builder's Rites

Before a building of any type could be erected, it was necessary to propitiate the powers of Nature, because the order of Nature was being interfered with, and particularly the spirit of the earth on which the building would rest. Through every stage of the construction, from the initial selection of the site until the final completion of the rooftop, there followed a succession of magical rites.

In the choice of a site the spirit world was consulted and the entrails of animals examined for signs and portents. A sign of the intentions of the gods might be manifested through Nature itself. In the legend of the foundation of Mexico City, for instance, we are told how the Aztecs, observing an eagle holding a serpent in its talons, recognized this as an intimation from the gods that the city should be established on that spot.

It was the custom in Ireland in the last century to stick a new spade into the earth and only if it had not been removed overnight by the fairies did building operations begin. Another Irish custom, equally bizarre, was that of throwing a hat into the air during a gale and building the house where it happened to fall, since such a site was considered likely to be sheltered from adverse winds. After the land was surveyed, it would be blessed by the priest or magician and thus made safe for occupation.

This fourteenth-century artwork shows how, according to the prophecy, the Aztecs founded Tenochtitlan at the place where an eagle devoured a snake perched on a cactus

The orientation of a building with the sun was of immense symbolic importance. The Temple of Solomon, for instance, had entrance towers facing toward the east, and the Holy of Holies was at west. The altar of a Christian church is usually at the east end. This ancient association with the sun was deliberately flouted by Sir Walter Mildmay, in Puritan abhorrence of superstition, when he built the original Emmanuel College chapel at the University of Cambridge, England facing north and south rather than east-west.

To endow a new building with good fortune and to secure it against the assaults of evil spirits, bread and salt were laid in the foundations. It remained the custom as late as the seventeenth century to build a bottle of water and a piece of bread into the walls of English cottages, as charms to secure the occupant from want.

It was once common practice to sacrifice a human being to the earth deity and it was believed that no building would stand unless its foundations were laid in blood. In the old royal city of Mandalay, men were buried alive under the gates. In Siam victims were crushed to death in a pit. The custom survived into comparatively modern times; for instance, in 1881, the King of Ashanti (now a region of Ghana) mixed the blood of 200 maidens with the mortar when building a new palace. The survival of the custom in the West until Christian times is suggested by the discovery of skeletons in the foundations of old churches, as at Darrington, in Yorkshire, England in 1895 when the church walls were found to be resting on a human skull. It is probable that the recurring stories of nuns and monks immured alive are based upon distorted traditions of this character. The legend that St. Columba buried St. Ronan beneath the foundations of his monastery to propitiate the guardian spirits of the soil may well have a similar basis. In the English fen-

During a topping out ceremony, such as this one in Pitzenhagen, Germany, a wreath is attached to the roof.

lands, traditionally, those who caused flooding by neglecting to keep up the sea walls would be used as living foundations when the walls were rebuilt.

Such practices were followed not merely as a form of psychic insurance for the durability of a building but with the additional aim of providing a ghostly guardian who would prevent the intrusion of hostile spirits, since it was assumed that a human being so sacrificed would haunt the site forever. An example of this superstition came to light in 1966 with the discovery of the skeletons of babies who had been ritually entombed in the Roman fortress at Reculver, England. The tradition persists that the site is haunted by the sobbing ghost of 'a child that had been buried alive by the Romans.'

Shadows for Sale

These rites were replaced over the years by forms of sacrifice less offensive to sophisticated religious taste. A human shadow was used instead of the living person, in places as far apart as the British Isles and Romania; there were even 'shadow traders' who secretly measured a man's shadow and

buried the measurements beneath the foundations.

Puppets or domestic animals later replaced the human being as objects of sacrifice, the blood being poured into the foundations. In the early 1960s during restoration work at Lauderdale House in Highgate, London, workmen found part of a goblet, two shoes, and four mummified chickens that had been built into the chimney breast in the late sixteenth century. More recently a mummified cat was found immured in a cottage wall at Cricksea, in Essex, England where it had been buried alive to protect the house against fire. Coins are frequently discovered cemented into the brickwork of old chimneys; it has been suggested that the motive was to provide 'ransom money for the person who ought to have been there.'

The custom of placing documents beneath foundation stones is extremely ancient. It is recorded that Chaldean kings, interested in antiquity, used to tunnel into the ruins of old palaces for the foundation records deposited by their predecessors. Closer to our modern rites were those performed at Crowland Abbey, Lincolnshire, in 1112 when the Abbot laid the first cornerstone while the citizens submitted written offerings of either money or unpaid labour.

The actual materials used in the work of construction were ritualistically important, particularly in relation to ancient tree worship. This tradition survived among the Ozarks hillmen of the United States in the custom of transferring some of the timbers from an older building to a new one. An English superstition asserts that it is courting trouble if a builder uses tombstones instead of bricks.

In Africa and the East, building operations were often festive occasions, as were those brought to the United States by the early European settlers. No ceremony could have been more light-hearted than the erection of a cottage in Donegal, which used to be a communal undertaking with the neighbours carrying wood and stones to the site to the music of a hired fiddler. Among others, building operations could be far from joyful, however; the Pedi tribe of South Africa, for example, had to maintain a state of continence during the work of construction, and any departure from this, it was thought, would impair the soundness of the completed building.

Topping Out

Within the house the hearth was regarded as a shrine and the door as a barrier against spirits. At Alatri in Italy phallic symbols were carved on the lintel of a postern or passage in the walls of the citadel. In the Channel Islands, however, house builders considerately provided roof ledges upon which witches could rest while on the way to their destinations.

From classical times to the present the completion of a building has been celebrated as a feast. In ancient Rome the contractor, having erected a state or religious building, offered thanks to the Bona Dea, a fertility goddess, who then became its protectress.

The once universal 'topping out' ceremony, in which a barrel of beer was drunk while a tree or wreath was attached to the roof of a completed building, survives today only in attenuated form. It is still observed occasionally, however, as in 1963 when a green bough was nailed to the newly completed dome of Smithfield Poultry Market, London, 'as a means of warding off evil spirits.' The topping out ceremony in its original splendour can still be seen in Germany where a bush like a Christmas tree is positioned after the last timber has been put on. In one such ceremony one of the carpenters gives thanks to God, 'the highest builder in heaven.' Healths are drunk, after which the glasses are thrown to the ground to prevent bad luck.

Little else of the magic of the building trade has survived. And yet public buildings and bridges are still ritually opened, and the first sod of a new site turned with a new spade. There is still the ceremonial laying of the foundation stone, with its inscribed tribute to local dignitaries.

ERIC MAPLE

FURTHER READING: L. Sprague de Camp. The Ancient Engineers. (New York, NY: Doubleday); R. Thonger. A Calendar of German Customs. (Chester Springs, PA: Dufour Editions, 1968); E. E. Evans. Irish Folkways. (London, UK: Routledge, 1966).

The child born on Sunday will be not only 'blithe and bonny, good and gay' but also strong, handsome, and safe from the machinations of evil spirits.

Days and Hours

That Fridays are unlucky is a belief still widely held, and if a Friday falls on the thirteenth of a month it is doubly ill-omened. The worst day of the year for a wedding is Friday 13 May, as May has been generally considered an ominous month for marriage since Roman times.

Unlike the 'Black Friday' sales that go on in the United States the day after Thanksgiving, so called because sales and profits go up and are 'in the black;' in Britain, the term 'black Friday' is now commonly used for any Friday on which things go wrong. The term originally referred to May 10, 1886, when there was financial panic in London, and earlier to the Friday of December 6, 1745, when London heard the news that the Young Pretender had reached Derby in his invasion of England. According to legend, an earlier black Friday still was the one on which Adam and Eve ate the forbidden fruit.

You should not start a new job, call in a doctor, move house, turn the mattress on a bed, begin a sea voyage or, if you are a criminal, come up for sentencing on a Friday. In Ireland, however, it is a good day to die on, provided you are buried on the Saturday and prayed for on the Sunday.

Friday is unlucky because it is the day on which Christ was crucified, and a day of fasting, fish-eating, and general gloom. In the earlier pagan tradition, Friday was the day of the love goddess, a happier association that still survives in the most common version of a well-known rhyme:

Monday's child is fair of face,
Tuesday's child is full of grace,
Wednesday's child is full of woe,
Thursday's child has far to go,
Friday's child is loving and giving,

Der Samstag—a hand-coloured engraving based on a Frederich Campe painting, depicting a Jewish Sabbath (c. 1800)

*Saturday's child works hard for
 a living,
But the child that is born on the
 Sabbath Day
Is blithe and bonny, good and gay.*

There are many different versions of this rhyme (none of them very old) and in some it is Friday's child who is full of woe, which suits the Christian tradition of Friday rather than the pagan one. Two of the other lines fit well enough with the symbolism of the planets for which the days are named. Monday's child is good to look at because of the beauty of the moon, and the lot of Saturday's child suits the toilsome and careworn character of Saturn.

The Ashanti and some other peoples of West Africa gave a child a special name according to the day of the week on which he was born. The habit was exported, with slavery, to the Caribbean and the American South, where black people had such names as Quashee (Sunday), Cudjo (Monday), and Cuffee (Friday).

Sunday's Child

The week of seven days was adopted in Rome somewhere about AD 400, and spread into Europe, but it had been a recognized period of time long before that in the east. It still successfully resists the irritation of tidy-minded calendar reformers, who dislike it because the year does not consist of an exact number of weeks. It was probably chosen to give one day to each of the seven planets known in antiquity.

Our names for Tuesday, Wednesday, Thursday, and Friday come from the Germanic deities Tiw, Woden, Thor, and the love goddess Freyja or Frigg.

Friday, Saturday, and Sunday are the days round which the greatest number of superstitions have clustered.

Friday is generally the unluckiest day of the week and Sunday the luckiest. The child born on Sunday will be not only 'blithe and bonny, good and gay' but also strong, handsome, and safe from the machinations of evil spirits. In Scandinavia he will have the power of seeing spirits.

Although Sunday is the best day to be born on, it is not a good day for doing anything else, except going to church and thinking about the things of God. Nails should never be pared on Sundays or Fridays, nor should you have your hair cut on those days (or on any days except Mondays, Tuesdays, and Wednesdays). It is very unlucky, and hence very rare, to bury anyone on a Sunday. It is also extremely dangerous to leave a grave open over Sunday. 'It yawns for another corpse,' as Christina Hole says in her *Encyclopedia of Superstitions*, 'and a second death in the parish will follow shortly.'

Associations of the Planets and Days of the Week

Sun	⊙	Sunday
Moon	☽	Monday
Mars	♂	Tuesday
Mercury	☿	Wednesday
Jupiter	♃	Thursday
Venus	♀	Friday
Saturn	♄	Saturday

Sunday: Gaining money or support; causing friendship and harmony; finding buried treasure.

Monday: Operations of love; seeing visions; necromancy; inviaibility; operations connected with water, travel.

Tuesday: Operations of death, destruction, hatred and discord; summoning the spirits of the dead.

Wednesday: Obtaining knowledge or discovering the future; theft and deceit, commerce, merchandise.

Thursday: Gaining money, status or friendship; becoming invisible; achieving good health.

Friday: Ceremonies of love, lust, pleasure, and friendship.

Saturday: Ceremonies of death, destruction or injury; summoning souls from hell; obtaining knowledge.

If a grave has been dug and must be left unfilled over Sunday, it should be covered over with planks or turf.

The Sabbath for Man

Sunday has this character in Christian societies, of course, because it is the sabbath, the day that is peculiarly sacred to God. In ancient Babylonia the seventh, fourteenth, twenty-first, and twenty-eighth days of the month were uncanny days, on which the king was not allowed to perform certain actions, including offering sacrifice, pronouncing judgment, changing his clothes, and eating roast meat. Whether this is the origin of the Jewish sabbath is a matter that is still disputed.

The Jewish sabbath (from sunset on Friday to sunset on Saturday) was and is a positively blessed day, both holiday and holy day. It commemorates the last day of creation, on which God rested from his labours: 'and he rested on the seventh day from all his work that he had done. So God blessed the seventh day and hallowed it . . .' (Genesis, chapter 2). The Fourth Commandment instructs the faithful to keep the sabbath day holy and to do no work on it (Exodus, chapter 20).

The prohibition of work on the sabbath was faithfully observed by many generations of Jews and Christians. It was considered so important that when the army of Antiochus IV Epiphanes

attacked the Jews on the sabbath, the Jews refused to fight and were slaughtered unresisting, after which it was decided that in war strict observance of the sabbath must be suspended. Jesus and his disciples evidently took observance of the sabbath for granted. Irritated by what he regarded as tiresome legalistic restrictions on what was allowable on the sabbath, Jesus did make his famous remark that 'the sabbath was made for man and not man for the sabbath' (Mark, chapter 2) but the same comment was also made by Jewish rabbis.

The Christians transferred their sabbath from the last day of the week to the first, the day on which Christ rose from the dead, and the day on which they met for worship. In the fourth century, Gregory of Nyssa said that Saturday was the memorial of God's creation of the world and Sunday the memorial of the Resurrection, but by this time Christian observance of Saturday was in decline. In the year 321, Constantine the Great, the first Christian emperor, who had earlier been a worshipper of 'the unconquered sun,' ruled that the first day of the week, 'the venerable day of the sun,' should be a day of rest. The sun's old association with the first day is responsible for the fact that the Lord's Day of Christianity bears the pagan name of Sunday.

Vampires on Saturday

Saturday is sometimes lucky and sometimes not, perhaps reflecting a mixture of respect for the Old Testament sabbath with hostility to Jews and with the astrological tradition of Saturn's malevolence. Friday night's dreams will come true if told on a Saturday. Traditionally, a couple who marry on Saturday will have no luck at all, but Saturday is now the most popular day for weddings because it is the most convenient. People born on a Saturday are supposed to be able to see ghosts. Down to the nineteenth century in Greece a vampire was believed to rest in its grave only on Saturdays, so this was the day for digging up the body and burning it.

The other days are less important, though in northern England it used to be thought highly unfortunate to meet someone with flat feet on a Monday, perhaps because the flat foot denies the crescent arch that recalls the moon.

Some days, such as Christmas Eve and Christmas Day, are especially lucky to be born on but a singularly unlucky day is Childermas, or the feast of the Holy Innocents (December 28), which commemorates Herod's indiscriminate slaughter of children in the hope of eliminating the infant Jesus. In the fifteenth century Edward IV's coronation was postponed when it was realized that the Sunday that had been chosen for it happened to be Childermas.

Days and Hours in Magic

Astrological considerations have always been important in European magic, and magicians have tried to bring the influence of a planet to bear on an operation by performing it in that planet's day and hour. A list of the operations suitable to each planet is provided by two of the magical text-books, the *Key of Solomon* and *True Black Magic*.

Each planet rules the first hour after sunrise on its own day. The succeeding hours are ruled by the other planets in the order sun, Venus, Mercury, moon, Saturn, Jupiter, Mars. At sunset this progression is interrupted and the first hour after sunset is ruled by the planet fifth in order from the planet that rules the day. The effect is that each planet rules the first and eighth hours after sunrise and the third and tenth hours after sunset on its own day.

Deism

'Natural religion,' religion without revelation, was an important theological movement in the seventeenth and eighteenth centuries. Deism is the belief that the study of Nature and the exercise of reason are better guides to the existence and character of God than the study of sacred scriptures. Deists tended to dislike formal religious observance, ritual, and priests, and to believe that all the major religions contain the same message.

Directions

'I adjure thee, furthermore, by the crown of thorns which was set upon His head, by the blood which flowed from His feet and hands, by the nails with which He was nailed to the Tree of the Cross, by the holy tears which He shed, by all which He suffered willingly through great love for us: by the lungs, the heart, the hair, the inward parts, and all the members of our Saviour Jesus Christ. I conjure thee by the judgment of the living and the dead, by the Gospel words of our Saviour Jesus Christ, by His Saying, by His miracles . . .'

This apparently pious prayer is in fact part of a long incantation in the sixteenth century *Grimoire of Honorius*, intended to summon up to visible appearance one of the most powerful of all demons, Amaymon, King of the North. The *Grimoire* also provides incantations for summoning the demonic rulers of the other three directions: Egym (south), Baymon (west), and Magoa (east).

The belief that each direction has its ruling demon has a long history in Europe. An early list of them is Oriens (east), Amemon (south), Eltzen (north), and Boul (west). Cecco D'Ascoli, the fourteenth century astrologer and magician, said that four spirits 'of great virtue' rule the cardinal points. Each of them has twenty-five legions of spirits under his command. If they are summoned up and given human blood to drink

The *Grimoire of Pape Honorius* (1760) is a textbook of magic claiming to be written by Pope Honorius III. It is unique among grimoires in that it was specifically designed to be used by a priest.

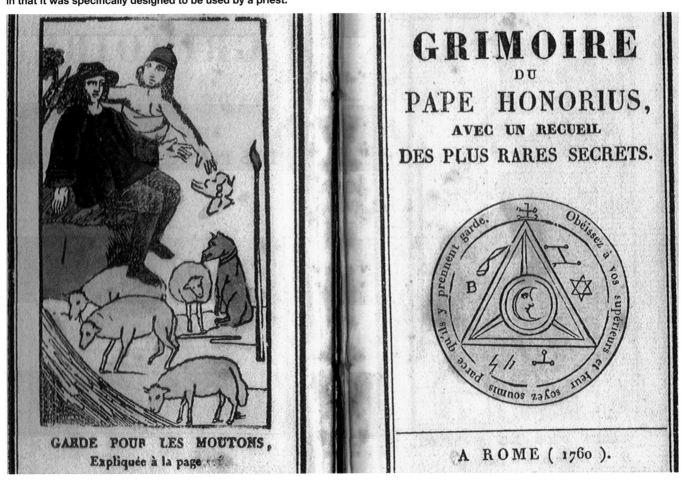

GARDE POUR LES MOUTONS,
Expliquée à la page .

GRIMOIRE
DU
PAPE HONORIUS,
AVEC UN RECUEIL
DES PLUS RARES SECRETS.

A ROME (1760).

and the flesh of a dead man or a cat to gnaw, they will give trustworthy answers to the magician's questions. Their names are Oriens (east), Amaymon (west), Paymon (north), and Egim (south).

Another magical textbook, the *Lemegeton*, says that the kings of the four quarters 'are not to be called forth except it be upon great occasion, but invoked and commanded to send such, or such a spirit as is under their power and rule.' Several centuries later, the modern magician Macgregor Mathers, commenting on the importance of a properly constructed magic circle, said that without one, to summon up 'such fearful potencies as Amaymon, Egym, or Beelzebub' would probably result in the death of the magician on the spot.

In white magic the four directions also have their rulers, the archangels Raphael (east), Michael (south), Gabriel (west), and Uriel (north). The magician appeals to each angel to protect him against evil coming from each direction.

Many Native American tribes—especially those of the southwest—also link spirits and deities with the directions and with colours. The Pueblos see six main directions: north, yellow; west, blue; east, white; south, red; upward, usually multicoloured; downward, black. Animal gods and Nature spirits come into the system, so that Mountain Lion and Oriole (both more or less yellow) are associated with the north. Similarly, the major Aztec god Tezcatlipoca was yellow as ruler of sunrise in the east, blue as lord of the south, red as master of sunset in the west, and black as ruler of evil magic in the north.

The east, being the direction of sunrise, is symbolically the direction of life and light, and to turn to the east is to turn toward the light, toward spiritual illumination, toward God. This is why the altar in a Christian church is almost always at the east end. Some early churches were built the other way round, following the precedent of Greek and Roman temples that usually faced east so that when the doors were opened the rays of the sun shone on the statue of the god.

By contrast, west is the direction of death because the sun 'dies' there each evening. In many prehistoric burials

> *. . . the word 'right' means not only a direction but also justice, virtue, truth, and straightness. The left . . . belongs to abnormality, evil, and the Devil.*

the dead face toward west and in modern Europe people are usually buried with their heads to the west. In Homer the main entrance to the underworld, where the dead live, is in the far west.

The north, on the whole, has an evil reputation. In the northern hemisphere the sun moves through the sky from east to south to west, and the north is the one sector of the sky through which the life-giving sun does not pass. And if you face eastward, the sacred direction, the side on which shadows fall is both the north and the left. But alternatively, instead of taking the east as the point of reference, some peoples have looked to the North Star or Pole Star as the fixed point of the heavens, 'the unmoved mover,' the First Cause. The Etruscans placed the home of the gods in the north, and when one of their seers was about to speak he would face south, identifying himself with the gods. Huehueteotl, the Old, Old God of the Aztecs, lived at the Pole Star, the point on which the whole universe turned.

Evil on the Left
In Europe the left is traditionally the side of evil and the right of good.

Black magic is 'the left-hand path' and to move to the left in magic is to attract evil influences. This is probably because the left hand is normally the weaker and the right the stronger, so that right is the side of God and good: hence the word 'right' means not only a direction but also justice, virtue, truth, and straightness. The left or 'sinister' side belongs to abnormality, evil, and the Devil.

Medieval writers found great difficulty in explaining why the gospel is read in church from the left side of the altar and the epistle from the right (from the point of view of the congregation). This seemed extremely peculiar, since the gospel would be expected to take precedence. The real reason was that the gospel had originally been given the place of honour, the right, as seen from the bishop's chair, but this had been forgotten and ingenious explanations were produced. The epistles, it was said, were the apostles' preaching to the Jews, the chosen people of God (the right side of the altar) but they rejected it. So the words of Christ (the gospels) were offered instead to the pagans (the left side).

Eclipse

Everywhere around the world, since records began, eclipses of both sun and moon have engendered not only great fear but a belief that a monster or creature in the sky has come to swallow these heavenly bodies. Making a great noise, with the voice, and with instruments such as drums, is a universal means of scaring away such evil creatures—and of course are always effective remedies because eclipses, by their very nature, are short lived. Even as recently as 1878, a letter

A total solar eclipse on July 22, 2009, in Varanasi, India

to the *Philadelphia Inquirer* recorded Native Americans throwing themselves to the ground, crying and screaming. 'Finally' read the missive, 'one old fellow stepped from the door of his lodge, pistol in hand, and fixing his eyes on the darkened sun, mumbled a few unintelligible words and raising his arm took direct aim at the luminary, fired off his pistol, and after throwing his arms about his head in a series of extraordinary gesticulations, retreated to his own quarters. As it happened, that very instant was the conclusion of totality.'

For many Native Americans the eclipse-creating culprit was a coyote, jaguar, dog, or a rattlesnake; the Sumu of Nicaragua shoot arrows into the sky at the eclipse, light fires, and furiously beat their drums in an attempt to slay the jaguar responsible. Other theories abound. For native peoples of Alaska an eclipse takes place when the sun receives a visit from his wife, the moon, while Armenians relate the phenomenon to the birth of a pair of dark bodies to a primeval ox, which then place themselves between sun and moon.

With eclipses comes ill luck, particularly to neonates and those not yet born. In the Hindu tradition, children born at the darkest moment of an eclipse are believed to emerge from the womb deaf or mute. The same fate, or the deformity of a harelip, is predicted for unborn children if their mothers-to-be venture outdoors during an eclipse. Cleanliness is also essential at this time, prompting bathing in sacred rivers such as the Ganges and, on the day following an eclipse, the thorough cleaning of homes. In Asia, people also take care to avoid being stung by scorpions or to have accidents that make them bleed. As thanks for being spared from permanent darkness, gifts of food are given to the poor.

RUTH BINNEY

FURTHER READING: Richard Cohen. Chasing the Sun. (New York, NY: Simon and Schuster, 2010).

Elements and Elementals

The theory that all things are made of differing combinations of four basic materials—fire, air, earth, and water—was advanced by the Greek philosopher and scientist Empedocles, who lived in Sicily in the fifth century BC. The theory was taken up by Plato and Aristotle, and was accepted by the great majority of Europeans down into the seventeenth century. It has been reinterpreted by modern occultists to whom the four traditional elements stand for four conditions in which energy can exist: gas (air), electricity (fire), solid (earth), and liquid (water).

The four elements provided a basis for the belief of the alchemists that gold could be manufactured artificially. They were also important in medicine, because they were combined with the doctrine of the four 'humours,' stemming from the famous Greek physician Hippocrates and transmitted into medieval Europe by Galen, the great Roman medical authority of the second century AD. The humours (from Latin *humor*, 'moisture') were the four liquids present in the body whose differing combinations determined each man's temperament and physique. The liquids and temperaments were connected with the elements as follows: fire, yellow bile, choleric (or bilious); air, blood, sanguine; earth, black bile, melancholic; water, phlegm, phlegmatic.

The perfect man, if such a thing existed, would have the four liquids and temperaments in perfect balance in his constitution. Disease was caused by an imbalance of the humours. Too much phlegm caused colds, an excess of yellow bile caused jaundice, and a strongly sanguine person would need to be bled frequently. The infectuous disease cholera was named for its supposed origin in yellow bile and the choleric temperament.

The symbolic meanings of the elements naturally vary very considerably from one writer or artist to another. Fire and air were usually regarded as active, positive, creative, and masculine elements, earth and water as passive, negative, receptive, and feminine. This distinction comes out in the French writer Gaston Bachelard's (1884–1962) summing up of the characteristic qualities of the elements: 'Earthly joy is riches and impediment; aquatic joy is softness and repose; fiery pleasure is desire and love; airy delight is liberty and movement.'

The element of fire tends to be associated with energy, purification, and transformation, passion, and aspiration. Air is connected with breath, soul, speech, with flight as a liberation from the earth-bound state, and so with freedom—'free as air.' Earth is associated with the solid and the practical, with the body, with gloom, and with melancholy because Earthly life is inferior to the life of heaven, with the dead buried in the earth and with hell under the earth, and with riches and material

The dramatic and detailed reliefs of the Goethe Gymnasium in Berlin, Germany, show the element fire

success because it is in the earth that the harvest grows. Water is the fount and origin of everything—the primeval waters of the abyss before the world was formed, 'the deep' that existed 'in the beginning' in Genesis, the unconscious depths of the human mind, unfathomable mystery, and woman.

In the ancient world the whole of Nature was peopled with spirits that lived in every tree and stream, every crag, and cloud. Once the theory of the four elements had been accepted, four classes of spirits were particularly associated with them; the spirits that much later were called 'elementals.' Gnomes and undines are the elementals of earth and water respectively, sylphs and salamanders the elementals of air and fire: minor spirits of Nature, invisible to human beings but never-

theless substantial, and living in the four elements.

The association of the elements with spirits was probably first made by the Neoplatonist, followers of a school of philosophy that arose at Alexandria in the third century AD. The Neoplatonist had a highly developed demonology and their demons (both good and bad) were thought to people the universe, and were the object of religious and magic rites. The Neoplatonist were deeply influenced by Plato, who developed the mystical and religious themes inherent in Empedocles's doctrine of the four elements, and it was an easy step for them to connect the demons with the elements.

The Greek authors do not go into much detail about the demons and spirits that perhaps in the fifteenth

century first acquired the name elementals. For a detailed account, one must turn to the works of the sixteenth century physician, alchemist, traveler, and mystic Philippus Aureolus Theophrastus Bombast von Hohenheim, known to posterity by his adopted name of Paracelsus. He invented the word 'gnome' and probably much of the lore about elementals, though he may also have drawn on legends and superstitions he encountered in his wanderings through many countries, including Sweden, Russia, and possibly even India.

According to Paracelsus, man is made of three substances: spiritual or godly, soulful or astral, and visible or terrestrial. These three substances or elements that go to make up the constitution of man are universal, but whereas man exists in all three, there are other beings that live exclusively in only one of the elements. Various categories of beings are perfectly at home in different elements: gnomes can see and breathe as easily in the earth as undines and sylphs in water and air.

Man himself, it appears, would be an elemental spirit of nature, but for the divine element in him. The elementals proper occupy a position between men and pure spirits. They have flesh, blood, and bones, they propagate offspring, they eat and sleep, and in these respects, and in their physical organization, resemble human beings. However, they can move as quickly as spirits.

The elementals are not immortal, being subject to disease. However, they cannot be imprisoned, and fire and water do not injure them. They dress, talk, and in many ways act like human beings but, says Paracelsus, 'are incapable of spiritual development.' They have reason and language like man— they have minds, but no souls in the spiritual or immortal sense. 'This may appear strange and incredible,' concedes Paracelsus, 'but the possibilities of Nature are not limited by man's knowledge of them, and the wisdom of God is unfathomable.'

He goes on to explain that the undines or nymphs live in water, the gnomes or pygmies in the earth, the sylphs or sylvestres in the air, and the salamanders or vulcans in fire. The four classes of elementals do not mix with each other. Each being keeps strictly to its own element, and to the undines, for example, water is what the air is to us. 'If we are surprised that they are in the water, they may also be surprised because we are in the air.' In their own element—the earth— gnomes can pass through rocks and stones as easily as we can pass through

our own element, the air, and it is the same with salamanders in fire. The sylphs are most like human beings, because they would be drowned in water, suffocated in earth, and burned in fire. Each element is transparent for the spirits living in it: the sun shines through rocks for the gnomes.

The Love of an Undine

In size and appearance, the undines resemble mankind. The gnomes are about a foot-and-a-half tall, but can expand at will to giant size. The sylphs and undines are kindly disposed toward man, the salamanders can neither be approached by nor approach man,

> *If any man has an undine for a wife, he must take care not to offend her while she is near water, as she might be prompted to return to her own element.*

while the gnomes are usually malevolent. On the whole, Paracelsus assures his readers, 'the elementals have an aversion against conceited and opinionated persons, such as dogmatists, inquisitive sceptics, drunkards, and gluttons, and against vulgar and quarrelsome people of all kinds.' What we know of Paracelsus's life suggests that this was a list of his own pet hates. 'But the elementals,' he goes on, 'love natural men, who are simpleminded and childlike, innocent, and sincere, and the less vanity and hypocrisy there is in a man, the easier it will be for him to approach them.'

The elementals have their own manners, customs, languages, and even governments. They have their own houses or palaces, too—at least, the gnomes and undines do. These dwellings are made of special substances unknown to humanity, 'as different from the substances we know as the web of a

spider is different from our linen.'

According to Paracelsus, undines have been known to adopt human shape, clothing, and manner, and to enter into a union with man— a notion that inspired Friedrich de la Motte Fouque's (1777–1843) charming romance *Undine* (1814). Men have also been admitted to communities of elementals.

However, the spirits of the earth, the air, and fire seldom marry a human being, though they may become attached to him and enter his service. They are not, it must be remembered, 'airy nothings,' or merely ghosts or appearances. They are of flesh and blood, only subtler than man.

In a special work on undines, Paracelsus supplies more details about them. If a man marries an undine, and she deserts him, he ought not to take another wife because the marriage has not been dissolved. If he does marry another woman, he will shortly die. The children of a marriage between a man and an undine will be human beings, because they will receive a human soul from the man. The undine, too, receives the germ of immortality through her union with a human being. But 'as an undine without her union with man dies like an animal, so man is like an animal if he severs his union with God.'

Finally, Paracelsus issues a warning. If any man has an undine for a wife, he must take care not to offend her while she is near water, as she might be prompted to return to her own element. In the same way, if anyone has a gnome for a servant, he must be faithful to him: 'if you do your duty to him, he will do his duty to you.'

It would seem that the elementals owe much to the imagination and invention of Paracelsus, and if he drew on any popular fancies, he certainly added many touches of his own. The elementals have not entirely lost their grip on the imagination: the undines have inspired at least one modern theatrical work, and the gnomes of this world are still a force to be reckoned with. Modern occultists also, through concentrated imagination and willpower, try to conjure up 'artificial elementals'—cruel, injurious beings that may resemble toads or snakes, not visible to ordinary sight, but real enough to the person attacked or to a clairvoyant.

DAVID PHILLIPS

Fall

Fall—or autumn—is the season described so evocatively by the poet John Keats as that of 'mists and mellow fruitfulness/close bosom-friend of the maturing sun.' This is the time of harvest and for those of the Jewish faith the time of New Year because, according to the Torah, this is when 'the earth brought forth the green herb yielding fruit according to its kind.'

Despite the glory of its leaf colour, fall was a season of dread in ancient times. According to Richard Saunders, author of the almanac *The English Apollo* first published in the late 1600s, the Greek physician Hippocrates dubbed it 'the Mother and Nurse of deadly diseases' while his compatriot Galen called it 'the most pestilential and dangerous Time of all the Year.' 'Now,' he said, 'the Pores of the Body are opened by a false Spring Heat, then suddenly closed again by Autumnal colds, so that many dangerous Distempers are now ingender'd.' To prevent such ailments as fevers, lethargies, and palsies, a wholesome diet was recommended, as

A Water Gnome by Hanuš Schwaiger (1854–1912) painted in 1886

well as the avoidance of alcohol and of becoming cold.

Brought by the Gods

According to Greek myth, fall begins at the equinox, the date when the goddess Persephone returns to the underworld for her winter sojourn. Her story began when, as daughter to Demeter the goddess of fertility, she was picking flowers in a field when she was abducted by the god Hades and taken to the underworld to be his wife. Here he not only changed her name to Persephone but also forced her to eat pomegranate seeds as a symbol of their union's consummation.

In despair at her daughter's disappearance, Demeter searched high and low, eventually learning the truth when she visited the sun god Helios, who told her of Hades' actions. In her fury she put a curse on the earth, making it barren of vegetation. To return the earth to fertility, Zeus sent Hermes to the underworld to investigate. Attempting to compromise, Zeus declared that Persephone could emerge from the underworld each spring to live with her mother but return to the underworld each fall. As a token of her agreement, Demeter promised to make the earth green again each year, but to go into mourning every time her daughter disappeared to the underworld.

Monumental Symbols

At hundreds of ancient sites around the world, builders of old deliberately aligned their constructions in order to create special effects at the autumn equinox. The Great Pyramid of was not only a magnificent burial chamber but is also incredibly accurately aligned relative to the heavens. The centres of its four sides—each slightly concave—are uniquely indented with an extraordinary degree of precision,

forming the world's only eight-sided pyramid. However this phenomenon is visible only at dawn and sunset on the autumn and spring equinoxes and only from the air.

Nearby, adjacent to the Sphynx stands the Temple of the Sun. At the equinoxes it is possible to trace the

. . . Demeter promised to make the earth green again each year, but to go into mourning every time her daughter disappeared to the underworld.

path of a beam of light from the setting sun through the east-west axis of the temple, along the right side of the Sphynx, then through a chamber in which once stood a statue of Osiris. The beam would have illuminated this sanctuary, linking, so scholars believe, the ascent and descent of Osiris, god of the afterlife, with the pyramid.

Mexico has two highly significant monuments, regularly visited by people who believe that being present at the equinox will endow them with a special charge of energy. At the autumn and spring equinoxes Chichén Itzá is even more spectacular than at the summer solstice. As the equinoctial sun sets, the play of light and shadow over its stones creates the effect of a diamond-backed snake slinking its way down its stepped construction. At Teotihuacán, the country's Aztec capital, the four sides of the Pyramid of the sun are aligned to follow the sun's path across the sky and at the equinox, faces the exact point on the horizon where the sun sets.

At the Old Spout Run in Clarke County, Virginia, archeologists who published their findings in 2012 unearthed a 12,000-year-old site with significance to the seasons. Not only do the three concentric rings of the

Paleo-Indian construction align with the equinoctial sun but the site also contains a pair of footprint-shaped rock engravings or petroglyphs. 'When stood on during the equinox' reported local archeologist Jack Hranicky, 'the sun causes a halo effect over a person standing on the prints.'

Europe has similar monuments. Between 4000 and 3000 BC a series of chambered cairns was built at Loughcrew in Ireland, among them Cairn T, complete with an inner chamber in which is an equinox stone. As the sun rises on September 21 (and also on the morning of the spring equinox), it illuminates the stone with a beam of light.

Festival of the Archangel

'And there was war in heaven: Michael and his angels fought against the dragon; and the dragon fought and his angels. And prevailed nor; neither was their place found any more in heaven.' So the Bible's Book of Revelation describes the victory of St. Michael, whose victory is celebrated on September 29 the feast of St. Michael and All Angels. In the old British farming year, Michaelmas was one of the quarter days, on which rents were paid, and traditionally the date on which annual rent reviews were made and agreed for the year ahead. It was also a key day for the hiring of labour.

Goose was the celebration fare for Michaelmas, its symbolism summed up in the saying: 'Eat goose on Michaelmas and you will not want for money for a year.' The English novelist Jane Austen (1775–1817), writing in 1813, was certainly aware of the superstition, hoping that having dined on goose on Michaelmas Day it would 'secure of good sale of my second edition.' To keep their landlords sweet, English farmers would add to their rent a 'goose fit for the Lord's dinner.'

To bring good luck grain would be liberally scattered for the geese, chickens, ducks—and wild birds.

In Scotland on the Isle of Skye a special large cake known as a *struan* incorporating flour from all the different grains grown on each farm is still baked on Michaelmas eve, and eaten as an accompaniment to lamb. After the meal it was customary in times past for any left over food to be given to the poor, ahead of street processions, sports, and horse races. Each evening gifts would be exchanged and dancing enjoyed by all.

Amongst country folk it was always maintained that you should never pick and eat blackberries from the hedge-rows after Michaelmas because this was the date on which Satan was banished from heaven and cursed the brambles as he fell into them. Alternatively it is said that he dragged his tail over them, waved his club over them, or made them totally unpalatable by spitting or even urinating on them.

Spirts, Saints, and Souls

Hallowe'en, October 31, which is the eve of All Hallows of All Souls Day, has long had the reputation as the date when the forces of evil are most abundant. On this night, it is said that the gates of the underworld open to admit the sun, allowing ghost, demons, and other evil spirits to escape to do their worst. As darkness falls, witches are reputed to ride their broomsticks and in 1596, witches put on trial in Aberdeen, Scotland, confessed to dancing with demons at midnight on Hallowe'en around the city's market cross. To stem the powers of evil, bon-fires were lit, although in England this ceremony was subsequently transferred to Guy Fawkes day, November 5.

Even today, witches gather at Hallowe'en to create magic circles, drawn on the ground in a clockwise

motion using chalk, charcoal, or made with the point of a wand or sword. Within two complete circles, made entire to prevent evil spirits from entering, the inner one measuring 8 feet in diameter, the outer one a foot wider, objects including bowls of water and crucifixes are placed to act as

> *Indoors, girls would cover their mirrors with a cloth, hoping when these veils were pulled off at midnight, to see the faces of their husbands to be.*

additional barriers against any evil spirits. Finally a witch or sorcerer enters the centre of the circle where ritual magic is performed and demons raised in a safe setting. Spectators located beyond the outer circle, burn incense and candles whilst chanting words of encouragement.

Trick or treat at Hallowe'en originated from a desire to placate the evil of witches and from the custom of putting out food for the dead on this night to prevent their spirits from re-entering the homes they once inhab-ited. The Hallowe'en pumpkin, lit from within by a candle derives from the belief that their brilliance will scare away demons, devils, or other malign beings who might be on the prowl.

Hallowe'en is a night of divination or fortune telling, often with romance in mind. Both girls and boys would throw nuts into the fire—if the nuts burned quietly then love would last, but not if the nuts jumped apart. Out in the fields, boys would pull up cab-bage or kale stalks and, from the size of the roots and the amount of soil clinging to them, predict the tallness and richness of their future wives. Indoors, girls would cover their mir-rors with a cloth, hoping when these veils were pulled off at midnight, to see the faces of their husbands to be.

The departed faithful remain the focus of attention on November 1, All Saint's Day, which in Ireland and Scotland was a festival of the dead on which it was customary to offer sacrifices of food and ale to a sea god. Next day, November 2, All Souls' Day, is the time to remember the departed and children would knock on doors begging for 'soul-cakes,' which householders would make and pile on the table in the same fashion as the shewbread described in the Bible as being placed in the tabernacle by the Levites.

All Kinds of Weather

Fall can bring weather of all kinds—with luck an Indian summer, an expression coined in North America to describe hot weather beyond the end of September. A late spell of fine weather is known as 'St. Luke's Summer' from his feast day that falls on October 18. In his play *Henry IV* Shakespeare tells his audience to 'expect St. Martin's summer, halcyon days,' referring to the period of calm weather that usually descends on Europe around St. Martin's Day or Martinmas—November 11.

The name halcyon is linked through mythology with the life of the king-fisher. In Greek legend, Halcyone was known as the daughter of Aeolus, god of the wind, and the wife of Ceyx. On a journey to consult the oracle at Delphi, Ceyx was drowned, and Hal-cyone so grief stricken that she jumped into the sea to be with her beloved. However the gods took pity on the pair and changed them into kingfish-ers. Zeus declared that in their honour the winds should not blow for seven days before, and seven days after December 21, the winter solstice.

Fall is also a time for predicting weather. It is said that if the leaves of the trees and vines do not fall before St. Martin's Day, a cold winter may be expected. Conversely, if Martinmas is fair, dry, and cold, the cold in winter will not last long. A cold November was thought to presage a mild, wet winter, as in the saying: 'If the ice in November will bear a duck, there'll be nothing after but sludge and muck.'

Aside from the harvest of grain, acorns, and mast—the fruits of the oak and beech trees respectively—were a necessity to the diet for our prehistoric ancestors and their food animals, a fact reflected in the old saying 'A good October and a good blast, so blow the hog acorn and mast.' In North America, acorns were eaten by both white settlers and Native Americans. For the Hupa of California they were so important that a 'first fruit' ceremony was held during which they were ground into a mush and cooked on a ceremonial fire. Prayers were offered to Yinukatsisdai, the god of vegetation, asking that the crop would not be stolen and eaten by rodents.

RUTH BINNEY

FURTHER READING: B. Blackburn and L. Holford Strevens. The Oxford Companion to the Year. *(New York, NY: Oxford University Press, 2003); R. Binney.* Wise Words and Country Ways: Weather Lore. *(Newton Abbot, UK: David and Charles, 2010); D. Pickering* Cassell's. Dictionary of Witchcraft. *(London, UK: Cassell, 2006).*

Fertility

The world of magic and religion is often bewildering due to the variety of beliefs and practices that a 150 years of scholarship has accumulated. It is drawn from every age of mankind, and from every corner of the world. Much of it is extremely remote either in distance or time, and therefore difficult to interpret. And yet because of the common bond that links us with bygone races, an attempt at understanding should be made.

'Fertility' is an exceedingly common word in religious history. By it we mean firstly, the principle of reproduction and growth, as it is manifested in man, in animals, and in the plant world; and secondly, by implication, the belief that reproduction and growth can be controlled by magical or religious means.

Man has always had a passionate concern with fertility: it has been a consistent feature of almost every type of human society, and particularly, agricultural society. Consequently, scholars have often seized upon the ideas of, and the rituals connected with fertility, as a key with which to attempt to decipher the mysteries of primitive religion and magic.

Ripeness is All

The obsession itself is not difficult to account for. Man's knowledge of the biological and physiological processes controlling fertility is of very recent date, and human life expectancy only a century or so ago was assured only on condition of frequent reproduction, for as long as the female of the human species remained capable of bearing children. Death was perhaps a calamity; but not so great a calamity as barrenness. Human life depended, too, upon the fertility of the fields that man tilled, the fruit that he gathered, the animals that he ate, milked, or hunted. It is only in the technological societies of the past century that man has become to some extent liberated from a life-and-death struggle for existence, in which the need to reproduce his kind, and to see his crops growing and his animals bearing young, has been paramount. At almost any other point in history before the twentieth century, failure of fertility, whether of man, animal, or field, has meant simply and starkly, death. Small wonder, then, that the idea of fertility has loomed so large in his thinking and feeling.

Man's constant attempts to promote fertility are equally easy to explain, at least on one level. We know that in the past, the world has not as a rule been particularly amenable to man's efforts to control it. Despite this, the human animal has obstinately refused to give in. We must not fall into the trap of supposing that archaic man's attitude to the world in which he lived was one of dull resignation. Where archaic and primitive man differs from modern man is that whereas modern man strives to master certain fields of knowledge and influence, and acts accordingly, archaic man was convinced that ultimate power was never in his own hands. There were sources of power, but these lay without exception in the spirit world—the unseen, super-

Halcyone, by Herbert James Draper (1863–1920) shows Halcyone seeking her husband

natural world of gods, spirits, demons, and ghosts. What man had to do was to establish contact and rapport with the unseen world, with a view to channeling and applying its power. For power was a property of spirit; and thus the spirit world had to be approached, and if possible controlled, if man was to have a share in its blessings. Equally, since that power could (and frequently did) work in ways inimical to man, it had to be propitiated and kept friendly, lest it should simply sweep him, his children, his cattle and his crops away.

Fertility was entirely subject to the power and control of the spirit world, whose greatest gift was the gift of life. When life came into being, it was because the spirits had made it so; when life ebbed and disappeared, or was withheld, this too was the work of spirits. In this most vital area of human experience, there was no effect without its spiritual cause. If a woman conceived, it was not because she had intercourse with her husband, but because the spirits had put a child into her womb. If the corn sprouted in due season, it was because the Sky Father had impregnated the earth Mother and caused her to bring forth. If a child died, it was not through disease or malnutrition, but because an evil spirit had stolen the child's soul.

To archaic man then, the world appeared to be governed by its own immutable laws: not the biological laws we think we know so well, but the laws of universal cause and effect, of giving and withholding, of correspondence and adjustment. And fertility was completely subject to this pattern.

Rhythm of the Seasons

The first characteristic of the pattern of fertility, as man has experienced it for the greater part of history, is its cyclical character. In the temperate zones the rhythm of the seasons, on which so much depended, was utterly reliable and could without difficulty be regarded as a divine ordinance, as in the ancient Hebrew tradition: 'While the earth remains, seedtime and harvest, cold and heat, summer and winter, day and night, shall not

> *If a woman conceived, it was not because she had intercourse with her husband, but because the spirits had put a child into her womb.*

cease' (Genesis chapter 8).

In parts of the world where the seasons were less well defined, other patterns took their place—patterns dominated by the alternation of wet and dry periods, by the phases of the moon, and the like. To the seasons corresponded the stages in the growth of the crops, and the mating habits of animals. Crops, animals, and humans had their appropriate gestation periods. The menstrual cycle of women was seen to correspond with the phases of the moon. All this adds up to a conception of time, not as an ordinary linear progression from point A to point B, but as an infinitely repeated series of cycles, in which growth succeeds birth, maturity succeeds growth, and death succeeds maturity. However, even death was not the end, for spring came to drive out winter, and the annual miracle of the rebirth of the crops served to remind man that life was always latent in death.

It is easy thus to characterize the fertility cycle as a series of 'natural' phenomena; but archaic man did not think of it in that way. The power of life was not an impersonal entity, which merely needed to be left to its own devices. Accordingly we may say that its second characteristic was its personal, 'hierarchical' nature. Personal not necessarily because it was regarded altogether in human terms, but because it was able to be approached by humans, with whom it had some features in common, and could be, in some cases, communicated with.

Hierarchical because it was thought of as a graded hierarchy of spiritual beings, from the mighty gods of the sky to minor, and in many cases malevolent, demons and ghosts. Whether the various deities and spirits that went to make up the supernatural chain of beings were intrinsically benevolent or malevolent is an open question. Many could be either or both, according to their moods and to the extent to which they had been acknowledged and propitiated. Perhaps it would be safe to say that any of them *could* be dangerous, especially if slighted or ignored.

Art and Magic

The third characteristic of the fertility pattern, depended on the first two. The various cycles of fertility were thought to depend for their continuance upon the activity of the supernatural powers: the great cycles upon the great powers; the lesser cycles on lesser powers. In other words fertility, at whatever level, is always caused; it never just happens. Once the dependent Nature of fertility in the thought of the greater part of mankind is recognized, it becomes clear firstly, that should the supernaturals choose for any reason to withhold the gift of life, this is a sufficient explanation for famine, failure in hunting, miscarriage, and barrenness. Secondly, that the nucleus of primitive and archaic religion and magic alike concerns man's attempts to reconcile and appropriate the power, or life-force, that the supernaturals wield. Therefore man does what he can to ensure that the gods and spirits remain

The Ainu people of Japan sacrifice a bear as part of a fertility ritual

friendly. This may involve playing off one against another—a greater power against a lesser, or a benevolent spirit against a malevolent.

An example of this attempt to control Nature is the celebrated cave art of southwestern France and the Pyrenees. It has been supposed by some authorities that their main purpose was magical: to ensure a supply of game animals, and success in hunting them. It has also been noted that the more dangerous the animal, the more often it occurs in the paintings, and the more seldom its bones appear in prehistoric kitchen refuse heaps. Scenes in which a bison, for example, is shown transfixed by spears or arrows, as well as recording an actual successful event may well have been intended to ensure repeated success. To this extent the purpose of the paintings appears entirely magical. But the underlying attitude, which saw the prey that a hunter hoped to catch as controlled by forces outside man's control, verges upon the religious; it presupposes the existence of a supernatural world, and the need for man to take that world

into consideration.

The various hunting tribes of the northern hemisphere (the United States, Europe, and Asia) appear to exhibit a similar mixture of motives. Native American tribes, for instance, combine magical rituals, designed to ensure the increase of the species, with a firm belief in the 'Owner of the Animals,' who owns and rules the particular species in the same way as the Supreme Being rules over the universe and the world of men. The bear, which was always held in especial reverence, was hunted; but the killing was done with apologies and with as little blood as possible, and after death honour was paid to the skull. Doubtless the motive was in this case one of sharing in the great power of the bear; but in the case of the Ainu of Sakhalin Island in Japan, when a bear was killed, it was despatched with ceremony and sent home to its Owner, to tell of the good treatment it had received and to ask that more game be released. Should the Owner be offended, on the other hand, bear cubs would not be born and the bear could not be hunted.

Festivals to Ensure Fertility

In agriculture, the great fertility cycle is that of the seasons of the year, and in agricultural communities, two major events—the sowing of the seed and the harvest—were frequently the occasion for particular celebrations or festivals. Lesser festivals, though with virtually the same significance, took place at midsummer and midwinter. Traces of all these festivals survive to this day in the West, sometimes changed out of all recognition, sometimes—as in the case of the Scandinavian *Jul* (Yuletide or Christmas)—retaining enough of the original symbolism to demonstrate its origins. In the same way, the widespread 'first-fruits' and harvest rites practiced by Native Americans (in common with peoples all over the world) find a modern reflection in the United States' festival of Thanksgiving.

In all such cases, the objective was the continuation of the seasonal pattern, and the ensuring of a good and fertile year. The High Gods of the sky were the protectors of the cosmic order and the great givers of fertility, and so the festivals were centered, explicitly or implicitly, around the mighty deeds of these gods. Another feature that must be borne in mind is that the annual renewal of fertility was in very many cases seen as a repetition of an original act of creation, in which order triumphed for the first time over chaos, fertility over barrenness; accordingly, the festival itself was a magico-religious renewal of creation.

In the Babylonian *Akitu* (New Year) festival, the great epic of creation was recited, celebrating the victory of the god Marduk over the dragon of chaos. In addition there was a pattern of ritual, to which the myth served as a type of libretto. Centering on the figure of the king as the representative of the High God, this took the form of a symbolical dramatic confrontation between the god and the powers of chaos: chaos wins a temporary victory, law and order is forgotten for a time, the king is divested of his symbols of office; but then order is restored, rejoicing breaks out, the king is enthroned anew, and celebrates a 'sacred marriage' with a chosen priestess. New Year festivals of this type ensured the fertility of the land for another cycle. Since the power of fertility was in the hands of the High God, who stood at (or near) the head of the pantheon, only the king, as the head of the human hierarchy, could take it upon himself to approach the god and appropriate this power on behalf of his people.

The sacred marriage could be repeated on all levels of the hierarchy. Here, as elsewhere, we are confronted with an elaborate correspondence of man with the cosmos. The intercourse of the king and the priestess might be believed to increase the fertility of the fields. References are scattered through the literature of popular religion and folklore to this practice. In the *Odyssey* (800 BC) there is mention of the occasion' . . . when fair-tressed Demeter, yielding to her passion, lay in love

with Iasion in the thrice-ploughed fallow land . . .' Intercourse on the field forms the climax of many recorded fertility rituals, and the 'May King' and 'May Queen' of European folklore may be supposed to have symbolically fertilized the fields for another season.

This correspondence of function

Cihuacoatl, an Aztec fertility goddess

extends to the person of the woman and the 'person' of the earth. In mother goddess symbolism, the earth is regarded as a woman; conversely, the woman may be regarded as a ploughed field and the male organ as the plough. Regard for the sacredness of the 'body' of the earth has, however, been known

A shrine to a tribal goddess of fertility at the hot springs at Taptapani, Berhampur, Orissa, India

to give rise to a refusal to cultivate it. A North American chief is recorded as having said: 'You ask me to plough the ground! Shall I take a knife and tear my mother's bosom? Then when I die she will not take me to her bosom to rest. You ask me to dig for stone! Shall I dig under her skin for bones? Then when I die, I cannot enter her body to be borne again. You ask me to cut grass and make hay and sell it, and be rich like white men! But how dare I cut off my mother's hair?'

The Water of Life

Fertility as resulting from the interaction of male and female is a principle that animates virtually the whole of primitive and archaic religion. There is reason to suppose that many High Gods were at one time thought of as being androgynous, that is both male and female, but in historical times, one or other principle generally becomes dominant, usually, in the case of the gods of the sky, the male. The High God was the god of the sky and atmosphere, and as such controlled the phenomena of the weather, particularly the sun and the rain. Examples of this might be drawn from very many sources—the Greek Zeus, the Roman Jupiter, the Finnish Jumala and Ilmarinen, the Babylonian Marduk, and the Israelite Yahweh. As it says in the Old Testament: 'He covers the heavens with clouds, he prepares rain for the earth, he makes grass grow upon the hills' (Psalms 147).

The idea of the High God as sole dispenser of fertility accounts for only a small part of early beliefs. Lesser gods, ghosts, and demons have their own proper areas of influence, too. In a surprisingly large number of instances, the fertility of man is thought to rest with ghosts. One African tribe, the Nyakyusa, believe that the departed spirits control semen and seeds, and are always present at intercourse. Another tribe, the Lele, believe that human fertility is controlled by spirits residing in the deepest and dampest parts of the forest. Water has always been regarded as a major factor in fertility and amphibian or scaly animals are thought to be close to spirits and especially 'powerful' in this regard. The connection between fertility and rivers, streams, and wells is obvious.

In Derbyshire, England, the custom of 'well-dressing,' is still carried out at more than a dozen villages, during which wells are decorated with flowers and various rites performed. The origins of this custom are no longer remembered, but its significance is evidently propitiatory: each well had its own guardian, who had to be honoured, lest he should cause the well to dry up. The custom is now Christianized, and takes place on Ascension Day, immediately following the three Rogation Days—days on which God's blessing is asked for the crops.

In India, there is a sacred grove, near Tiruttani, in Tamilnad, containing seven pools, or *yonis* (this is also the word for the female organ). Round the pools there are trees, in many of which votive offerings are hung by women wanting children. Offerings are similarly made in the precincts of many Hindu temples, usually under a pair of trees—male and female.

The Potent Gods

The symbolism and mythology of fertility in the cosmos corresponds to the interaction of male and female that is so large a part of human experience. In the cosmos, as in human experience, the generative power of the father is met and accepted by the receptive fecundity of the mother. A common overall pattern is therefore that of the Sky Father and the Earth Mother, repeated, with infinite variations, through the world of religions.

In the ancient Vedic religion of India there is the primordial pair Dyaus Pitar and Prithivi Matar, and in Hinduism Shiva and Shakti, Kali or Durga, Vishnu and Sarasvati, Krishna and Radha; in Egypt (where the pattern is to some extent reversed, the sky being regarded as the goddess Nut, sometimes symbolized as a cow) Osiris and Isis; in Mesopotamia Anu and Ishtar, Marduk and Sarpanitu; in Greece Zeus and Hera; in Scandinavia Frey and Freya. Not all these pairs can simply be identified with sky and earth, but rather with generation and fecundity as universal principles. Either may be dominant; the cult of the bull in the Semitic area and in the Minoan-Mycenean religion of Crete and Greece witnesses to the domi-

Venus of Laussel

nance of the male, while cow-worship in, for example, Hinduism points in the opposite direction. The 'mother goddess' figure in particular is capable of many varieties of expression, and may bear many names, as her attributes (the chief of which is that of the 'vessel') are taken over by local goddesses, belonging to the lower orders of the hierarchy.

Human male and female meet in the act of sexual intercourse; and the overall symbolism of fertility gods and goddesses is very frequently derived directly from that act. The great male gods were often represented with an erect phallus (ithyphallic), and mother goddesses either as pregnant, or with exaggerated breasts and labia. Ithy-

phallic figures are found in Paleolithic cave paintings and in the Bronze Age rock carvings of Scandinavia, as well as in the paintings and sculpture of many preliterate peoples.

Evidence of phallic cults is found in the civilizations of antiquity: in Greece connected with Hermes, Demeter, and Dionysus; in Rome, at the festival of Liberalia; in Egypt, Osiris was a phallic god, and the mysteries of Isis contained phallic elements. Farther north, in the greatest of the pre-Christian Scandinavian temples, that at Old Uppsala, in Sweden, it was recorded by the German writer Adam of Bremen that down to the eleventh century the image of the fertility god Frey was ithyphallic. In early India, one of the best known of the seals discovered at the Indus Valley site of Mohenjo-Daro (c. 2500 BC) represents a three-faced, horned deity, sitting in a yogic position and surrounded by animals; this figure, which has been identified with the later Shiva, is likewise ithyphallic. In later Hinduism, the phallus (*lingam*) is the symbol of Shiva, and although many Hindus would today contest the origin of the symbol, the evidence of erotic sculptures leaves the matter in little doubt.

Mother goddess symbolism is of many kinds, ranging from great crudity to great sophistication. Among the earliest attempts made by man to represent the symbol of maternity in plastic form are the so-called 'Venuses,' rudimentary female figures shaped during the Upper Paleolithic period out of bone, ivory, or stone. While their sexual characteristics are greatly exaggerated, their faces are seldom more than hinted at. The use to which they were put must remain a matter of conjecture, but it seems at least likely that they were fertility charms, the possession of which was believed to bring about the condition they represent, that is, pregnancy.

A somewhat more sophisticated—at the same time more realistic—expression of the principle of fecundity is the figure of the mother and child. Images of this kind are found in ancient Egypt, and an unbroken line may be drawn from these to modern figures of the Virgin and Child in Christian churches. Of course, the symbol has undergone many modifications in response to theological and other pressures, but its significance is still not far removed from that which it originally possessed—the divine principle of fecundity and motherhood nourishing the 'son of man' from her own body.

Cycle of Birth and Death

In the past it has frequently been believed that children are indeed born from the divine Earth, from caves and ravines, springs and wells; and as man is born of the sacred soil, so he must one day return to that same soil from which he once emerged, perhaps to be reborn—the image on which the Greek mysteries depended—perhaps not.

The fact that the divine Earth gives birth to man, beast and plant, and also receives the lifeless corpse in burial and decomposition—in other words, that the idea of fertility has as its corollary the idea of destruction—has been responsible for many grim images. Today we are apt to fall back upon abstract notions of the passage of time, such as 'Time, like an ever-rolling stream bears all its sons away,' but the myth-maker was once less easily satisfied. Particularly in those religions in which the female principle was dominant, in which the body was buried—returned to the womb of the earth—rather than being cremated, the same images that represented fertility also represented death and destruction. So it is that mythology tells how the great mother goddesses descend into the realm of departed spirits—the Mesopotamian Ishtar into the shadowy realm of dust and death, Kore (Persephone) into the House of Hades—symbolizing the annual death of vegetation and the fate awaiting all men. They emerge, however; and in the Greek mysteries, of which the rite of Eleusis may be taken as typical, the initiate may assure himself of immortality by assimilation to the cosmic fertility pattern they represent. Demeter, goddess of Eleusis, presides over birth and death alike, and offers to her devotees the gift of life— eternal life.

Elsewhere there is hope of reincarnation. The most striking of these ambivalent images is perhaps that of the Hindu goddess Kali, who is undoubtedly a mother goddess but equally a goddess who devours even her consort, Shiva the destroyer. Her tongue protruding, her body wound round with snakes or with ropes of human skulls, her fangs dripping blood, she dances in triumph on the prostrate body of Shiva.

An ancient Hindu marriage ritual contains the words, spoken by the bridegroom: 'I am the sky, you are the earth.' To comprehend the place of fertility in the world of religion and magic one must understand the vast correspondence between the microcosm that is man and the macrocosm, which is the universe in which man lives. Both depend for their life and their continuation on the power of the spirit world, and what is done in one reflects in unimaginable ways on the other.

ERIC J. SHARPE

FURTHER READING: M. Eliade. Patterns in Comparative Religion. *(New York, NY: New American Library, 1974);* The Sacred and the Profane. *(San Diego, CA: Harcourt, Brace & World, 1968); J. G. Frazer.* The Golden Bough. *(London, UK: St. Martin's Press, 1980); A. E. Jensen.* Myth and Cult Among Primitive Peoples. *(Chicago, IL: Univiversity of Chicago Press, 1973); E. Neumann.* The Great Mother. *(Princeton, NJ: Princeton University Press, 1972).*

First

The offering of the first-born is the theme of one of the most dramatic stories in the book of Genesis (chapter 22.1–19). It concerns Abraham, the patriarch of the Hebrew people. In its present form it is clearly intended to demonstrate his faith in Yahweh, the god of Israel. However, the story was based upon a primitive custom, and in its original form it was doubtless an aetiological myth—a myth designed to explain the cause of something.

The original theme is stated in the opening verses. Yahweh is represented as commanding Abraham: 'Take your son, your only son Isaac, whom you love, and go to the land of Moriah, and offer him there as a burned offering upon one of the mountains of which I shall tell you.' Abraham is obedient to the command, and the narrative describes the journey and the preparations for the sacrifice. Having built an altar and laid his son, bound, thereon, 'Abraham put forth his hand, and took the knife to slay his son.' At this fatal moment, the angel of Yahweh intervenes and Isaac is saved. Then, instead of his son, Abraham sacrifices a ram 'caught in a thicket by his horns.' The episode ends with Yahweh again addressing Abraham: 'By myself I have sworn . . . because you have done this, and have not withheld your son, your only son, I will indeed bless you, and I will multiply your descendants as the stars of heaven and as the sand which is on the seashore.' Thus the story shows how Yahweh, having tested the faith of Abraham, promised that his descendants would henceforth become a great nation.

But behind this edifying tale of Abraham's faith there is clearly another purpose, that of explaining how an ancient custom of sacrificing first-born sons to Yahweh was superseded by the offering of an animal victim. There is an abundance of evidence in the Hebrew scriptures that such a custom was once observed by the ancient Israelites. For instance, in the ritual law set forth in the book of Exodus, Yahweh is depicted as commanding Moses: 'Consecrate to me all the first-born; whatever is the first to open the womb among the people of Israel, both of man and of beast, is mine . . . Every firstling of an ass you shall redeem with a lamb, or if you will not redeem it you shall break its neck. Every first-

born of a man among your sons you shall redeem' (chapter 13). The reason assigned for this savage practice is that it commemorates Israel's exodus from Egypt, when Yahweh 'slew all the first-born in the land of Egypt, both the first-born of man and the first-born of cattle.' However, this historicized explanation is typical of many others given in the Bible to account for ritual customs of which the origin was unknown in later times.

The ritual killing of the first-born is found elsewhere among primitive peoples. It seems in origin to have been a

> *The passage of the seasons, the displacement of the old by the new, were once believed to be disturbing processes.*

propitiatory rite addressed to supernatural powers to ensure their benign attitude toward later offspring. There could be some variation of motive: for example, the first-born son could be made a sacrifice for the well-being of a city or offered as a vicarious sacrifice made by a father for his sin. 'Shall I give my first-born for my transgression, the fruit of my body for the sin of my soul?' asks the prophet Micah.

Babies Buried in Jars
The many skeletons of infants buried in jars that have been found on Canaanite sites attest to the practice of infant sacrifice among the ancient inhabitants of Canaan. In a revealing passage, describing the reforms of King Josiah at Jerusalem, it is recorded: 'He defiled Topheth, which is in the valley of the sons of Hinnom, that no one might burn his son or his daughter as an offering to Molech' (2 Kings 23.10). It is now generally accepted that the word 'Molech' was not the

name of a god but a technical term for child sacrifice, indicating that the Israelites were once accustomed to burn their children as sacrifices, probably to Yahweh.

The same custom was practiced by other Semitic peoples, for instance the Phoenicians and Carthaginians; the calcined bones of children, sacrificed to Tanit and Baal-Hammon, have been found at Carthage. Other forms of the sacrifice of the first-born among non-Semitic peoples are recorded by J. G. Frazer in *The Golden Bough* (1890).

Every departure from the familiar in the life of mankind is in effect a step into the dark, a journey into the dangerous unknown. In primitive societies that are dominated by superstition, each new occurrence is generally regarded as potentially harmful unless its impact can be countered by rites specially devised to placate the gods. The passage of the seasons, the displacement of the old by the new, were once believed to be disturbing processes. The first action undertaken and the first object received, even the emergence of the new crop in the fields or the birth of a child, could be a source of danger to the community unless made safe by magical rites.

From time immemorial it has been the custom among many of the world's people to consume the first fruits of the harvest in a ceremonial feast, or dedicate it wholly or in part to the tribal deity, as a method of offsetting the jealousy of the gods or the envious dead, or the spirit of the crop itself. Fishermen in many countries nail the first fish of the season to the ship's mast and believe that it is possible to determine from its sex the prospects of

Opposite page:
A depiction of the sacrificing of Issac

the forthcoming fishing season. If the fish is female the hauls are expected to be good, but if it is male, poor. Closely allied to this custom is the importance attached to the first coin received by a merchant in his day's takings. Handsel money, as it is called, must be first spat upon and then kept separately in the pocket to ensure a good day's trading. Theatrical people believe it possible to determine the fate of a new production from the age of the purchaser of the first ticket. If he or she is old the production will have a long run; if young, the future of the show is bleak.

Stepping Into Danger

The belief that the future of a building had to be insured against evil and misfortune on completion, before it was safe to use, lies at the root of many foundation rites, including the sacrifice of young children. The old terror of human sacrifice in turn probably reinforced the superstition that it is dangerous to be the first to enter a new house. Some form of protection is afforded, however, by taking the initial step with the right foot. The new bride is also shielded from baleful influences when she enters her home for the first time by being carried over the threshold. However, in the United States this custom may spring from the superstition that the first one of the newly-weds to step over the threshold will be the first to die.

Primary actions of any kind have all the force of magic behind them, a very well known example being the 'crossing the line' ceremony with its mock ordeal and its attendant galaxy of sea gods. The significance of first actions permeates our superstitions. The seamstress who puts the first stitch in a bridal dress will be married within the year. In love magic, if nine peas are found in the first pod opened by an unmarried girl and one of these is placed on the lintel of the outer door, the first single man who crosses the

threshold afterward will be the one she will marry.

The newly born child was believed to be extremely vulnerable to the influence of witchcraft in its first few days of life, and its first and therefore magically potent gifts often included salt, which was thought to provide protection against the forces of evil. There was a time when even the first kiss received by a baby from any individual other than its mother was thought to transmit to the child the characteristics of the person who gave it; great care had to be exercised in warding off undesirable people.

Even greater dangers might face the dead, for the soul of the first person to be laid to rest in a new cemetery was assumed to become automatically the property of the Devil. Until very recently it was the custom in parts of eastern England for children to dance seven times round the

oldest (or first) gravestone in a cemetery and at the conclusion to place their ears close to the ground and listen for the sound of 'the Devil rattling his chains.'

The New Year

The sense of wonder tinged with alarm at the transition from one phase of time into the next provides the motive force for those magical ceremonies that are still observed by the adult community. At the first sight of the new moon many people continue to turn over their money, reciting at the same time the ritual words 'white rabbits' as a charm to encourage good fortune during the next four weeks. With the emergence of the New Year the church bells acclaim the presence of a renewed first moment in time in which all enter a state of ritual rebirth. In the United States, the custom in most towns and cities of greeting the New Year's arrival

Members of the Pennsport String Band perform during the Annual New Year's Day Mummer's Parade in Philadelphia, Pennsylvania

with a prolonged torrent of noise, far greater than mere bell-ringing, resembles primitive noise-making to frighten off devils. Perhaps in this way the New Year noise clears the air of the previous year's evil, allowing for a fresh start.

In a practice that extends from east to west, the household prepares to usher in the New Year in symbolic form. In the British Isles the New Year will be represented by the first male person to cross the threshold after midnight, known as either First Foot or Lucky Bird. He must be tall and dark haired, and also bear token gifts representing the basic needs of the household for the year: money, coal, and a piece of bread. It is important that there should be nothing ill-omened about his appearance and those with crossed eyes or with eyebrows that meet across the brow are rigorously excluded, since these are signs of the Evil Eye, the first glance of which is doubly lethal. US belief, where the 'first footing' custom still holds, finds other ill omens if the first visitor is a widower or red-headed.

FURTHER READING: For sacrifice of the first-born, see: D. Harden. The Phoenicians. *(London, UK: Thames & Hudson, 1962); J. Hastings, ed.* Dictionary of the Bible. *(New York, NY: Scribner, 1963). For 'first' generally, see: M. Eliade.* Myths, Dreams and Mysteries. *(London, UK: Fontana, 1968); C. Hole.* English Folklore. *(New York, NY: Scribner, 1940).*

Food and Drink

Since the deepest needs of man's nature are reflected in religion, myth, magic, and superstition, it is hardly surprising that beliefs, ceremonies, and prohibitions relating to food and drink should be found in all of them.

The idea expressed in the saying 'Man is what he eats' is basic in many primitive societies: men are thought to acquire the characteristics of the animals (or human beings, or gods) that they consume. Indigenous people in Ecuador eat birds, monkeys, and game rather than the flesh of heavier animals because they believe that such a diet will make them more agile. Some East African tribesmen used to eat the hearts of lions in order to acquire the courage of lions and avoided hares' hearts lest they should become as timid as hares. In different parts of the world, however, the attributes of the same animal may be variously assessed—in Borneo, for instance, the young warriors avoided venison because the deer was thought of as an animal that is easily scared; but Native Americans in the north preferred to emphasize the deer's speed and sagacity. In *The Golden Bough*, Sir James Frazer records that a man in Seoul 'bought and ate a whole tiger to make himself brave and fierce.'

So much for the mythical virtues derived from eating animals, of which many more instances could be given. But the same principle has been widely extended to the eating of human flesh—most often the heart and liver of a conquered victim. Sometimes when a particularly gallant enemy was killed in battle, parts of his body were cut off and burned to ashes: the ashes were mixed into a kind of paste, and this was preserved until it was time for the tribal initiation rites, when it was solemnly distributed to the youths who were being initiated into full membership. In 1824, when Sir Charles McCarthy was killed by the Ashantis, the chiefs devoured his heart and his bones were kept as national fetishes. Even today cannibalism is sometimes practiced ceremonially, either to inherit the dead man's virtues or with the purpose of ensuring future food supplies. One person is responsible for this vital task—the king or chief of the tribe or a specially

A witchety grub

hallowed rainmaker. If there is a drought, and consequently a poor harvest, the unsuccessful rainmaker is likely to be killed; parts of his body are eaten ritually, the rest scattered over the fields in the hope that these may be thus fertilized. Until fairly recently a rain-making priest in the mountains of Ethiopia would be stoned to death if the harvest failed—his nearest relatives had to cast the first stones at him.

The Witchety Grub

Imitative sympathetic magic is involved also in attempts to maintain the supply of food. Where fish is a main article of diet, a model of a fish may be thrown into the water and prayers chanted; or a wizard will mime the movements of a swimming fish. As recently as the late nineteenth century, in the Scottish Highlands, when boys went fishing without success, they would make as if to throw one of their party overboard and haul him in like a fish: it is recorded that the charade sometimes worked.

The most famous example of imitative magic is probably that formerly found among the Asunta, in the barren

The *pan de muerto* (Spanish for bread of the dead) is baked in Mexico during the weeks leading up to the Day of the Dead

lands of Central Australia, where the tribes are divided into totem clans, a totem usually being an edible animal. Some of the tribesmen eat an insect called the witchety grub; so there is a clan whose totem is this grub. In order to ensure the increase of this insect for the use of the community, the men would sit inside a structure of branches shaped roughly like its chrysalis; they then shuffled out, squatting, and sang of the grub's emergence from the chrysalis. Comparable pantomimes were intended to safeguard the supply of emus and white cockatoos.

A more macabre method of ensuring a good crop was used by the Lange tribe in Uganda at a festival held every five years. On this occasion there would be a raid on a neighbouring tribe, the Kumam; a tribesman and his dog were killed and their genital organs cut off. The scrotum of the man and that of the dog were stuffed with millet seed, a rain dance was performed, and the millet shared. The men took this specially treated millet home and mixed it with the ordinary seed before sowing. The results were said to be excellent. Such practices, horrifying as they seem today—not least to many Ugandans—were truly a part of religion, in its magical aspect; magic seeking to provide, at whatever cost in human suffering, for the most basic human requirements.

Give Us Our Daily Bread

Every civilization has celebrated with special observances the seasons of sowing and harvest, and in these observances may always be traced vestiges of the same reliance on supernatural aid. Ancient Romans and Greeks, Jews, and the various branches of the Christian Church—all have had their harvest festivals. In England, although the old festival of Lammas on August 1 was marked by the offering to God of a loaf made from the new wheat (the word 'Lammas' is a corruption of loaf-mass), the Harvest Festival as it is now observed in the Church of England is a reintroduction from around the 1840s. With its piles of fruit it is a function almost entirely pagan in feeling, with a thin top-dressing of orthodox Anglicanism. Equally pagan, but no less religious in origin, is the custom, still observed in Essex, England, and elsewhere, of weaving ornate 'corn dollies' from the last sheaf of wheat cut on the last day of harvest. It was once believed that the spirit of the wheat dwelled in them and that they must be kept safely until the next spring to ensure continuity. One large-scale farmer is reported annually to invite the rector of his parish to bless his crops, paying him £50 for doing so, and charging this as a necessary expense against income-tax—with a note to the Inspector of Taxes: 'I defy you to assert publicly that this does not improve the property.'

Among Christians, as among believers in other faiths, certain important occasions in life are observed not only by religious ceremonies but also by secular feasts; christenings, weddings, and funerals are marked by the serving of special food and drink. In everyday life, believers are admonished to show thankfulness for their food: the prayer most frequently recited by Christians of every allegiance is the Lord's Prayer—a central petition in which is 'Give us this day our daily bread.' This constant reiteration of Christian concern for material goods and needs has parallels in other religions also—even among those great religions of the East that repudiate the flesh and bodily desire and aspire to pure spirituality. Some worshippers of Krishna, for instance, make an offering at his shrine—a plate full of food—before starting a meal. They believe that then the food they are eating has been blessed (and even, mysteriously, consumed) by Krishna, and that meditating on him while they eat will increase their resources of spiritual energy.

The anthropologist Bronislaw Malinowski (1884–1942) held that the Trobriand Islanders did not understand the association between food and the maintenance of bodily strength: they ate because they wanted to, out of greed, or because it was the custom.

Dangerous Food

At least as important as the positive aspects of sympathetic magic in the feeding habits of human beings are the negative aspects—the thou-shalt-nots of myth and magic that can conveniently be summed up in the word taboo. Positive magic means doing something to produce a desired result: negative magic means avoiding a bad result by not doing something.

Even taboo, however, is not wholly a negative concept. It embraces two meanings that may seem to be opposite. A taboo person or object is untouchable, either because, being a tribal chief, a totem animal, or god, he or it is too potent and sacred to be touched by lesser persons, or because, like a pregnant woman (in many cultures) or the caste of untouchables in India, the person or thing is considered too unclean to be touched. In the first case, the profane contact will bring a terrible retribution on the toucher: he has been guilty of presumption, since in the words of Sigmund Freud (1856–1939) 'to touch is the beginning of every act of posses-

'. . . to touch is the beginning of every act of possession, of every attempt to make use of a person or thing.'

sion, of every attempt to make use of a person or thing.' Even an accidental offender may be so overwhelmed by guilt that he will not recover from his shame. The case is recorded of a healthy young Maori who happened to see the remains of a meal by the roadside and ate it without knowing that the food had been that of a high-ranking chief. As soon as he was told this, 'he was seized by the most extraordinary convulsions and cramp.' He died at sundown.

In the second case—taboo meaning unclean—the infection is equally transmitted by touch. The person who touches a taboo object or eats taboo food becomes taboo himself, and, if he survives, has to undergo lengthy penances and purifications. The common factor between these two concepts is that, whether the person or thing is too holy or too unclean to touch, to touch him or it is dangerous. According to Wilhelm Wundt (1832–1920), the distinction between the two meanings did not exist in the earliest stages of taboo: there was simply a demonic power within the person or object that punished the toucher by bewitching him.

The most obvious example of food taboo that is still widely observed is, perhaps, the dietary system of Orthodox Jewry. This is based on the Mosaic law as originally recorded in certain texts in the books of Genesis, Exodus, Leviticus, and Deuteronomy. The prohibition: 'You shall not boil a kid in its mother's milk,' occurs first in Exodus 23.19. Like all these Jewish dietary rules, this has been interpreted and elaborated by Rabbinical scholars: it is still taken to mean, in practice, that milk may not be drunk, or butter eaten or used in cooking, at a meal at which meat is eaten; and strictly *kosher* restaurants would refuse to serve a glass of milk if it were ordered at such a meal. More specific detail about permitted and forbidden foods is given in Leviticus, chapter 11 and Deuteronomy, chapter 14. The orthodox are allowed to eat beasts that are cloven-hoofed and cud-chewing, such as the ox, sheep, and goat, but not to eat beasts that are cloven-hoofed but not cud-chewing—the swine— or cud-chewing but not cloven-hoofed— the camel, coney, and hare. Finny and scaled fish may be eaten, but not shellfish. Eagle, raven, owl, and many other

Ingredients for charoset, a sweet paste that is eaten at the Jewish Passover

birds are forbidden, but 'clean fowls' are permitted. Winged insects that 'go upon all fours' are forbidden, except for 'those which have legs above their feet with which to leap on the earth'; the locust and the cricket are allowed.

Kosher (that is 'fit' or 'proper') meat is not only the flesh of one of the permitted categories of animals: it must have been killed by approved methods, which involve draining all the blood from the body. No animal that has died naturally may be eaten. Indeed—a clear parallel with the taboo customs of other cultures—anyone who merely touches or carries the carcase of such an animal 'shall wash his clothes and be unclean until the even.'

These dietary laws were instituted, according to Jewish authorities, 'for reasons of hygiene and the avoidance of idolatry.' Many non-Jews also regard them as sensible safeguards in a hot climate. This is so; but there is clearly no hygienic need for their continued observance in cool climates, and with modern refrigeration. This survival is valued by Orthodox Jews as a symbol and reminder of the earliest traditions of their race and of their special calling as Yahweh's chosen people. Non-Jewish anthropologists would see it rather (examining it objectively and without any trace of antisemitism), as an example of the tenacious hold on the human

consciousness and practice of primeval taboos even when they have long ceased to have practical relevance.

Eve's Dinner Party

But I will haste and from each bough
  and brake,
Each Plant and juiciest Gourd will pluck
  such choice
To entertain our Angel guest, as he
Beholding shall confess that here on Earth
God hath dispensed his bounties as
  in Heav'n.
So saying, with dispatchful looks in haste
She turns, on hospitable thoughts intent
What choice to choose for delicacy best,
What order, so contriv'd as not to mix
Tastes, not well joined . . . fruit of all kinds,
  in coat,
Rough or smooth rin'd, or bearded husk,
  or shell
She gathers, Tribute large, and on
  the board
Heaps with unsparing hand; for drink
  the Grape
She crushes, inoffensive must,
  and meathes
From many a berry, and from sweet
  kernels pressed
She tempers dulcet creams . . .
     A while discourse they hold;
No fear lest Dinner cool; when thus began
Our Author. Heav'nly stranger, please
  to taste
These bounties which our Nourisher,
  from whom
All perfect good unmeasured out,
  descends,
To us for food and for delight hath caus'd
The Earth to yield . . .
     So down they sat,
And to their viands fell, nor seemingly
The Angel, nor in mist, the common gloss
Of Theologians, but with keen dispatch
Of real hunger, and concoctive heat
To transubstantiate; what redounds,
  transpires
Through Spirits with ease; nor wonder;
  if by fire
Of sooty coal th' Empiric Alchimist
Can turn, or holds it possible to turn
Metals of drossiest Ore to perfect Gold
As from the Mine. Meanwhile at Table Eve
Ministered naked, and their flowing cups
With pleasant liquors crowned . . .
         John Milton
         Paradise Lost

Sir James Frazer, analyzing the Jewish taboo on the pig, remarks that (in pre-Christian centuries) 'the attitude of the Jews to the pig was ambiguous.' He goes on to say: 'The Greeks could not decide whether the Jews worshipped swine or abominated them. On the one hand they might not eat swine; but on the other hand they might not kill them. And if the former rule speaks for the uncleanness, the latter speaks still more strongly for the sanctity of the animal . . . we must conclude that, originally at least, the pig was revered rather than abhorred by the Israelites. We are confirmed in this opinion by observing that, down to the time of Isaiah, some of the Jews used to meet secretly in gardens and eat the flesh of swine and mice as a religious rite . . . And in general it may perhaps be said that all so-called unclean animals were originally sacred; the reason for not eating them was that they were divine.'

Forbidden Flesh

There are striking similarities between the dietary laws of Judaism and those of another great religion—Islam. The Koran forbids 'only that which dieth of itself, and blood, and swine's flesh.' The traditions and sayings of Mohammed supplement these injunctions: animals are unlawful food unless slaughtered by a method similar to that of the Jews, also if slaughtered by an idolater or an apostate from Islam.

Food can become unclean for a Moslem by contact with the unclean. It is recorded that one extremely strict Moslem was away from home and his wife was busy, when their baby began to cry: to quieten him, a young woman who was visiting gave her breast to the baby. The father came in, snatched the baby from her, and held it upside down to drain out any of her milk, for fear it might be tainted if her observance of the dietary laws were less scrupulous than his own.

In general, however, the strictest observance of such taboos in Islam and Judaism, as in other religions, is nowadays tempered in practice. Wine is forbidden in the Koran, but many indulge, at least in private, in a glass of wine or beer. A Moslem prominent in public life will not do this in a public place; and few of these are so fortunate as a former Aga Khan—hereditary spiritual leader of the Ismaili community—who was able to drink as much champagne as he liked, since by miraculous dispensation it turned to water as it passed his lips. Even a comparatively lax Moslem, however, while sharing a bottle of wine at dinner, will scrutinize most carefully any stew or soup set before him, to satisfy himself that it contains no fragment of flesh of the forbidden pig.

Whether Frazer's theory of the origin of the dietary taboos of Judaism and Islam applies to the domestic animals that are kept as pets in many countries, especially in Europe and the United States, is a matter for speculation. Cats, which were venerated in ancient Egypt, receive almost comparable attention from their owners in these Western countries, and dogs probably receive even more. These are

modern versions of totemism: both animals are taboo as food, and so are eaten only at times of extreme necessity, as during the siege of Paris in 1870 or the siege of Madrid in 1936.

Eating the God

Certain attitudes, it seems, are common to both 'savage' and 'civilized' man, although in the more advanced societies a refined and often impressive symbolic ceremonial replaces the crude brutalities of primitive ritual. The devout Christian invokes Christ as the 'Lamb of God' and shares in a sacred meal; and this meal, however elevated the thoughts and emotions of those partaking of it, has something in common with the primitive tribal practices of which Frazer writes in the section of the Golden Bough entitled 'Eating the God.'

Indeed Catholics insist that the central action of the Mass—the sacrament of Christ's body and blood—is not merely a 'spiritual' or memorial rite, and that the consecration by a priest of the elements of bread and wine brings about such a change in them that Christ himself is really present on the altar. So, after the consecration of the bread and the

Bread and wine at the Lord's table

wine, those who approach the altar or pass before it bow the knee in homage to the divine presence; and when they share in the Communion—consuming token portions of the consecrated elements—they will thereby be strengthened and purified. No Catholic will agree with the scepticism of the Roman orator Cicero, who sneered at the sacraments of the corn god and the wine god. 'When we call corn Ceres and wine Bacchus, we use a common figure of speech; but do you imagine that anybody is so insane as to believe that the thing he feeds on is a god?'

Cicero anticipated the unbelief of modern humanism; but the age-long instinctive consensus of mankind is against him. When the Christian missionaries arrived in Mexico and in India, they found that the ancient local religions had their rites of transubstantiation: in Mexico, the pagan priests turned bread into the true body of their god; in India the Brahmins taught that the sacrificial rice-cakes were changed by the priests into actual human flesh.

But why is there this almost universal belief in the sacramental principle that real values can be conveyed through material instruments and, in particular, that this principle reaches its highest expression in a meal at which a divine entity—a totem animal, a god or a substitute for a god—is solemnly eaten by the worshippers?

There could be many explanations of the phenomenon. Freud followed Charles Darwin (1809–1892) in thinking that the first society—like that of the higher apes—was a 'primal horde' led by a violent chief or father, jealously possessing all the women and eventually killed by the strongest of the younger males. Later came the totemic clan, in which 'the totem animal is really a substitute for the father'; the totem animal was taboo—but on special occasions its killing and eating strengthened the clan's kinship with it.

TOM DRIBERG

Harvest

It is difficult for us to realize nowadays, with tins and frozen foods available throughout the year, and imported tropical fruits on our tables in the middle of winter, the anxiety that our ancestors felt as they waited for the annual harvest. When man first progressed from the stage of gathering wild foodstuffs to cultivation of the soil, the procession of the seasons became increasingly important. In an agricultural economy his very life depended on the success or failure of the crops, and enormous efforts were made to ensure a fruitful harvest.

The Jews still celebrate Succoth—the Feast of Booths or Tabernacles—as they have done since the time of the command in Deuteronomy (chapter 16), 'You shall keep the feast of booths seven days, when you make your ingathering from your threshing floor and your wine press; you shall rejoice in your feast.' Citron, palm, myrtle, and willow (the 'four kinds') are carried in procession during the synagogue service, and families build a booth before the festival begins. As a rule it is set up in the garden if there is one, or if not, on a flat roof. The top of the booth is covered with green boughs, arranged so that the starlight can shine through. This reminds the Jews of the time of the Exodus, when they were nomads. Inside are decorations taken from the season's produce—apples, grapes, pomegranates, and brightly coloured corn.

The Harvest Supper

Churchgoers today send vegetables, fruit, and flowers to the Harvest Festival service, a popular occasion followed by the traditional Harvest Supper. Best known as Harvest Home, it had many dialect names, like Kern, Mell, and Horkey Supper.

On the evening of the day when the last load had been brought in, the farmer and his wife would traditionally provide a good meal for the reapers. As a rule it was served in the barn, which had been specially decorated with garlands and branches. In Lincolnshire, England, the Old Sow often put in an appearance, two men disguised with sacking and wearing a head stuffed with furze, which they used for pricking the others.

Frumenty sometimes used to be served, a milk pudding made from wheat boiled in milk with raisins and currants, and flavoured with spices and sugar. More often there would be a round of beef, followed by plum pudding and served with plenty of beer.

Harvest suppers continued to be of great importance and spread throughout the New World. During the autumn of 1621, settlers and Native Americans in Plymouth Colony gathered to give thanks for the harvest after their first difficult year in the New World. This was the United States' first Thanksgiving. The exact date of this first celebration has never been established (it has even been said that it was in February). But in 1864, President Lincoln set aside the last Thursday in November as the appointed day as a way to honour the heritage of the first settlers. (Canadians hold Thanksgiving earlier, in October.)

Today Thanksgiving Day is an important family occasion, with a traditional meal that includes roast turkey, corn on the cob, and pumpkin pie, in honour of the Pilgrims' typical fare. The day is also rich in special leisure activities, among them important football games. Interestingly, the ancient Mayans held an annual harvest celebration each autumn, which also featured turkey on the festive menu and ritual ball games. And many forest Indians of the American South, such as the Natchez, celebrated the harvest with a feast of specially grown corn

The Harvest Festival by Agost Elek Canzi (1808–66)

and their own forms of ball games.

The English ancestors of the Pilgrims traditionally brought in their harvest with great style. The last load, decorated with branches and garlands, was taken, triumphantly through the village. Handbells were rung, everyone cheered and shouted, and children who helped were presented with slices of plum cake. At some stage people hiding in the bushes threw buckets of water over the cart; the custom was rooted in imitative magic, designed to ensure rain for next year's crop.

Seated on top of the load, and probably drenched to the skin, were the Lord of the Harvest and his Lady. Before the coming of mechanization farmers were obliged to engage extra hands to assist with the harvest. The

men appointed one of their number to negotiate with the farmer and take the lead in the scything: he was called Lord of the Harvest. The second reaper, a man dressed as a woman who replaced the Lord in his absence, was known as the Harvest Lady. If anyone swore or told a lie in front of the Lord of the Harvest, he was obliged to pay a fine. In Cambridgeshire, England, each new workman was 'shoed' by the Lord of the Harvest, who tapped the soles of his shoes in return for a shilling.

Mechanized farming eliminated the Lord and Lady of the Harvest. Gone too are the elaborate rituals surrounding the cutting of the last sheaf, in which it was supposed that the power of the harvest resided. In some countries a few stalks of wheat

were left standing in the field because people were afraid of exhausting the strength of the crop. They were said to be an offering for Odin's horses, or those who dwell under the earth. However, cutting the last sheaf was a more usual ceremony. This could be a great honour, but it also seems to have been regarded as a disagreeable duty. In England the men sometimes used to throw their sickles at it in turn, as if they were anxious that the responsibility should be shared. Behind this custom lay the old belief that the spirit of the wheat had taken refuge in the last sheaf.

Crying the Mare

Sometimes the last sheaf was carried to the farmhouse but often it was

A depiction of the first Thanksgiving

dumped on a neighbour's land to get rid of it, in case it brought bad luck. Around Herefordshire and Shropshire in England the final handful of wheat was grasped and tied together. The men flung their sickles toward it and whoever was successful cried: 'I have her!' A brief ritual exchange followed: 'What have you?' 'A mare, a mare, a mare!'

This was called Crying the Mare. An old Devonshire custom known as Crying the Neck suggests, on the contrary, that the final sheaf was thought to bring good luck. While the reapers were finishing, an old harvester went round, selecting the best ears he could find. These were gathered into a bundle, known as the neck, which he plaited and arranged. When the work of harvesting was done, everyone formed a circle and the man who had made the neck stood in the centre, holding it firmly with both hands. He stooped, lowering the neck down to

the ground, and all the men took off their hats; they too bent low, hats in hand. Then slowly standing upright, they raised their hats above their heads, and the man with the neck held it high in the air. Everyone cried 'the neck,' and the whole ceremony was repeated three times over. There was a great deal of cheering and, during the melee that followed, someone seized the neck and ran with it to the farmhouse. A maid was waiting, ready at the door with a bucket of water. If the man could get past her, or enter the house by any other route, he was allowed to kiss her. If he failed she soaked him with water.

Harvest competitions of this kind used to be very popular. In Scotland and the north of England, groups of three or four men each took a ridge of grain and raced to see who would finish reaping first. But there used to be a day when 'kemping' as this was called, and indeed all harvesting, was

forbidden. As John Brand, the Newcastle antiquary, tells us: 'There is one day in harvest on which the vulgar abstain from work, because of an ancient and foolish tradition, that if they do their work the ridges will bleed.'

A version of this strange belief turns up in the Shetlands. Swinaness, on the Island of Unst, was traditionally thought too sacred for cultivation because, so it was said, the sea kings had fought many furious battles there. One man ignored the prohibition and planted some wheat seeds but when harvesting time came, to his horror the ears dripped, not dew, but salty tears and the stalks were filled with blood.

This suggests that there was thought to be some connection between the harvest and the realm of the dead —'those who dwell underneath the earth.' In Germany peasants used to break the first straws of hay brought into the barns, saying, 'This is food for the dead.' Many peoples throughout the world hold annual festivals honouring the departed. The time of year chosen varies according to the region but there is a tendency to associate it with harvest.

In Arabia the last sheaf is ceremonially interred in a miniature grave, specially prepared with a stone placed at the head and another at the foot. The owner of the land, announcing that the Old Man is dead, prays that Allah will send 'the wheat of the dead.'

If the harvest fields are associated with the realm of the dead, there are probably more ways in which they are linked to fertility and new life. In some countries people used to speak as if a child had been separated from its mother by the stroke of the sickle. A Pole who reaped the last handful of corn was told: 'You have cut the navel string.' In Prussia the last sheaf was called the Bastard: a boy was concealed inside, and the woman who bound it cried out as if in labour. An old woman acted as midwife until the 'birth' took place, and the boy inside the sheaf then squalled like a baby. The sheaf was swaddled with sacking and carried into the barn.

The Baby Rice Soul

In early Egypt fertility of the crops was closely associated with human fecundity. Min, god of vegetation and sexual reproduction, is always represented with phallus erect and a flail raised in his right hand. He was honoured as Lord of the Harvest, and temple carvings show him receiving a ceremonial offering of the first sheaf. Indonesians perform a ritual marriage at the time of the rice harvest. Two sheaves are fastened together in a bundle: this is called the bridal pair. One sheaf contains a special rice, the bridegroom. The other, which contains rice of the ordinary variety, represents the bride. A magician lays them together on a bed of leaves, so that their union may increase the next yield of rice.

Elaborate rituals surround the 'birth' of the Baby Rice Soul at harvest time in Malaya. Rubbish and unpleasant smelling herbs are burned in advance to drive away evil spirits, and a magician is employed to choose seven stalks of rice, which are cut and swaddled like an infant. The Rice Baby is carried to the farmer's house, and all the protocol surrounding a human birth is carefully observed. On each of the three days following, only one small basket of rice is allowed to be gathered. The reaper works in silence, taking care that his shadow never falls across the plants. But the real work of harvesting cannot begin until the seventh day after the birth of the Baby Rice Soul. Whatever is gathered then must be donated toward a feast held to honour the spirits of dead magicians.

Dolls Made of Wheat

The power that was thought to exist in the crops was in fact often personified, not necessarily as a baby. Sometimes it took animal form—a wolf, pig, goat, hare, or cock—perhaps because small creatures often took refuge in the final sheaf when the rest of the field had been scythed. In England the last sheaf was used to make an effigy that was dressed in women's clothes and carried on the Horkey Cart to the Harvest Supper, where it sat on a special chair. This puppet had many regional names: kern baby, mell doll, harvest queen and, in Kent, the ivy doll. The Yorkshire mell sheaf was made from different varieties of corn, plaited together and decorated. It was placed in the middle of the room for people to dance round. Sometimes the kern baby was hung up in the farmhouse and kept through the following year to bring good luck and protection against witchcraft. A Lancashire farmer is said to have cursed anyone damaging his puppet before the coming harvest.

In 1899 an Old Lincolnshire woman remarked that one of these dolls—made of barley straw and stuck up on a sheaf facing the gate—would ward off thunder and lightning: 'Prayers be good enough as far as they goes, but the Almighty mun be strange and throng with so much corn to look after, and in these here bad times we musn't forget old Providence. Happen it's best to keep in with both parties.'

Rick decorating used to be quite popular in England. A wheat dolly or

Indonesian farmers belonging to the indigenous Sundanese tribe parading with freshly harvested fruits during annual harvest ceremony locally known as 'Seren Taun'

An East Anglian Corn Dolly used as part of harvest rituals to bring good luck

from her marriage, she went secretly to the harvest fields on a Friday night. Taking a straw from the stooks for every child desired, wheat for a boy and oat for a girl, she plaited them into a garter, murmuring a charm referring to the straw on which the Christ Child lay in the manger. The garter had to be worn until the following Monday morning. If it stayed in place the omen was good, but if it broke or slipped the spell would not succeed. It was also very important that the girl's fiancé should know nothing about this. Only a virgin could use the charm: a girl who was not would cause harm to all her children.

In southern Europe, August 15, the Feast of the Assumption of the Virgin Mary, is sometimes called the Feast of Our Lady in Harvest. In Italy it replaced the festival of the goddess Diana on August 13: farther north, where the harvest comes later, the crop is dedicated to the Virgin Mary on September 8, the Feast of her Nativity.

A young virgin features in the central role of a once popular Polish custom. *Wienjec*, the harvest wreath or crown, was made from the final sheaf and prettily decorated with a variety of flowers, nuts, and apples and perhaps even a gingerbread cake. It was blessed in church, usually on the Feast of the Assumption when herbs were also blessed, and worn by the chief girl harvester. It was essential that she should be chaste for if she were not, it was supposed that the fertility of the land would be destroyed and the harvest would be a poor one. The girl was expected to walk in procession to the farmhouse door, where she was received by the farmer who drenched her with water—a rain charm again.

This custom of throwing water on the last sheaf, or else on the person who brings it, is widespread. In the north of the Greek island of Euboea, when the corn sheaves had been stacked, the farmer's wife brought out

rather a 'corn dolly,' (as wheat is often referred to as corn by the British) was worked into the corner of the stack to bring good luck. Some stacks in West of Somerset still carry a little stook at each end of the ridge, and a peaked projection on some cottages in that area is called the dolly by very old people. A few farmers leave the last stook in the field to stand till it falls apart, or it may be hung in the barn.

But if the farmer is questioned about this custom, he usually replies that it is intended for the birds; the meaning has been forgotten.

Harvest knots—twists of straw in attractive shapes—are still made in parts of Ireland. Girls wear them in their hair and men fasten them to their coats. At one time they were exchanged as tokens of love. In England, if an engaged girl wished to bear children

a pitcher of water and offered it to the men for washing their hands. Each sprinkled water on the corn and on the threshing floor. The farmer's wife then held the pitcher at an angle and ran as fast as she could around the stack without spilling a drop. When this had been done she made a wish that the stack would last as long as the circle she had just made.

Human Flesh to Aid Crops

Rituals of this kind are harmless by any standards. Not so some of the customs of the past: 'The seven of them perished together. They were put to death in the first days of harvest, at the beginning of barley harvest' (2 Samuel, Chapter 21). This ambiguous remark, referring to the killing of seven men in time of famine, dates back to biblical days. However, English bystanders at the burning of Bishops Latimer and Ridley on October 16, 1555, are said to have remarked that the executions might have saved the crops, had they been performed at the proper time.

The Khonds, a tribe of Bengal, offered a sacrifice to assist the harvest until the middle of the nineteenth century. The victim, often the descendant of other victims, was called the *Meriah*. About two weeks before the sacrifice was due to be offered, his hair was cut off, and he was taken in procession to a virgin forest and anointed with melted butter. When the moment arrived he was drugged and crushed to death, or roasted over a fire, and cut into little pieces. Representatives from many villages arrived for the occasion. Each of them was given a small portion of flesh, which was taken home and ceremonially buried in the fields. What remained, chiefly the bones and head, was buried and the ashes scattered over the farmland so that the harvest would be successful.

In Tibet, to the north, the chief purpose of the Harvest Festival was to propitiate the *Zhidah*—local spirits of the mountains—so that they would send enough sun and rain to assist the crops and hold back any frost or hail. The *Yonnehcham*, Dance of the Sacrificers, was performed specially in their honour. This took place around the middle of September. For 100 days before, the priests stayed indoors to avoid accidentally stepping on any of the many worms and summer insects about at that time of year. They were forbidden to quarrel amongst themselves and anything borrowed had to be returned. It was also very important that the sky should not look upon a corpse, so anyone who chanced to die during the festival was temporarily buried in a stable. Since there was always the risk of light from moon or stars, even night burial was ruled out. Harvest was a gay occasion and large crowds came to see the dancing. They pitched tents and cooked on outdoor stoves: some popular favourites were noodles, meat balls, steamed wheat bread, and green peaches.

Evidently the Zhidah were among those spirits well disposed toward mankind. Probably the forces appealed to by ringing church bells in England were imagined to be less benign. The ostensible purpose of this custom was to ensure the safety of the gathered crop. In Cheshire bells were rung three times over oats and twice over wheat.

'Burning the Witch,' a Yorkshire custom, perhaps also derives originally from some ritual disposing of a malevolent influence. At harvest time peas were left to dry in small piles, known locally as 'reaps.' On the last day, when the remaining corn had been cut, some of these piles were pushed together and burned in the straw. Boys and girls ran about, blacking each other's faces with charred straw. Everyone enjoyed the peas and there was dancing and Cream Pot Supper—cream and currant cakes flavoured with caraway.

In Shetland the menu for the *Foy* was not dissimilar. This traditional party, held at the skipper's house, is interesting since it was, in effect, a Harvest Home of the sea. It was held at the beginning of August, when the summer white fishing season closed. Crew members and their wives had high tea and plenty to drink. A favourite toast was: 'Lord! Open the mouth of the gray fish, and hold thy hand about the corn . . .'

VENETIA NEWALL

FURTHER READING: M. Eliade. Patterns in Comparative Religion. *(New York, NY: New American Library); E. Estyn Evans.* Irish Folk Ways. *(London, UK: Routledge & Kegan, 1966); Sir James G. Frazer.* The Golden Bough. *(London, UK: St. Martin's Press, 1980); E. O. James.* Seasonal Feasts and Festivals. *(New York, NY: Barnes & Noble, 1961).*

Harvest Booths

Boughs of fruit-trees, branches of palm-trees, of leaf-trees and of Arabah-trees from the river beds were taken, and from them and their foliage, booths were constructed in which the congregation of Israel dwelt during the Feast of Tabernacles. The later texts alleged that this was done to commemorate the deliverance from Egypt, but this was clearly a reinterpretation of an earlier agricultural practice, the purpose of which was to promote fertility at the end of harvest, and to secure the much-needed rain at a critical moment marked by the Rosh hashshanah (New Year's Day) on the first of Tishri, when the autumnal rites began.

No doubt in their Canaanite form they included feasting and erotic dancing such as obtained outside the vineyards at these seasons, referred to in the book of Judges, when ecstatic revels not very different from those engaged in by the Maenads of Dionysus in Thrace and Phrygia, were held in joyous abandon for the bounty received, and to secure a fresh outpouring of vital energy in the crops and in mankind in the forthcoming season.

E. O. James
Seasonal Feasts and Festivals

Hearth

The evocative terms hearth and home conjure up visions of domesticity and peace, for the hearth is the traditional centre of family life, symbolizing warmth, security, and companionship; a place for dreaming where it becomes possible, by peering into the embers, to find physical and mental renewal, and to discover by signs and portents, the secrets of the future. In another sense the glowing hearth is the symbol of the domestic sun, the Promethean fire stolen from the heavens to become the caged servant of the human race, a feeble yet significant substitute for the parent sun.

The hearth consists of a clay or stone slab placed at the centre of a cave or hut to supply a foundation for the domestic fire, and in this form it continued relatively unchanged from prehistoric to Norman times. In the Middle Ages it was moved to the wall, and later still, in the sixteenth century, the grate was introduced. From surviving traditions and relics of ancient customs it appears that a communal fire was maintained in former times within each village or township, providing the basic 'stock' from which the community drew its individual requirements. This fire was religiously maintained by specially appointed fire-tenders and delivered to each household by runners. The fire-tender's role was vital to the community for should the communal fire ever be allowed to go out, social life might be threatened, while symbolically such an omission represented the destruction of the community's collective spirit or soul. This attitude prevailed long after the act of fire-making had become general; and was maintained as a magical rite sanctified by time and by usage. Within the home itself the fire symbolized the soul of the family and it was traditional that when a son broke away from the family unit to set up a separate establishment he took a portion of the ancestral fire with him, thus keeping alive from age to age the sense of domestic continuity. The lighting of this first fire in the new home has come down to us in modern times as 'house warming.'

In pre-Christian times the bride, upon entering her house for the first time, would be ceremonially taken to the hearth and presented with a pair of tongs as a symbol of her new authority. In the East it was the younger son who became the hereditary tender of the domestic hearth. In Irish peasant life the importance of preserving the domestic fire as an unbroken link between past and present was a restatement of the same theme. The turf fire was tended continuously through the year as a symbol of family continuity, and is responsible for the expression, 'When the turf fire goes out the soul goes out of the people of the house.'

Grandma's Hearthstone (1890) by John Haberle (1856-1933)

Altar of the Domestic Gods

Side by side with the domestic and public fire rites there developed a cult of sacred fire that provided a focal point for the religious instincts of the community. Indeed, the Latin word *focus*, from which our word is derived, conveys the meaning of fireplace, home, and altar. The sacred fires of the Greeks were under the jurisdiction of Hestia, the fire goddess, protectress of household, family, and city, who symbolized not only the home but the earth's centre and later even the earth itself. Among the Romans the cult of Vesta with its sacred fire-tenders, the Vestal Virgins, probably represented a survival of an earlier practice in which the daughters of a chieftain or king were allocated the task of keeping alight the tribal fires. For the Romans the hearth constituted the core of family life and the altar of the domestic gods, the Penates, and of Vesta.

Relics of hearth worship continued to persist in European folk customs until very late and took many curious forms. As an act of propitiation to the spirit of fire the Estonian bride flung a handful of coins into the hearth, while her Bohemian sister threw bread crumbs instead; such a custom had no place in the British Isles, where the burning of bread was considered a crime against man and God. However, there is evidence in Britain of sacrifice to the hearth gods from the discovery of the bones of animals buried beneath the floors of cottages, and coins and in some cases mummified animals and birds bricked up in chimney breasts.

In European folklore the fire spirit is generally represented by the grotesque bearded dwarf or house fairy of about the size of a young child, who often dwells by the hearth and makes his entries and exits by the chimney, and is known variously as Kobold, Nis, Brownie, or Billy. The Irish peasant housewife had as her last duty at night to 'smoor' the fire, that is to ensure that a glowing turf was left burning in the centre of the ashes 'or otherwise the fairies would be displeased.'

There is a distinct possibility that at some period in the past the worship of the fire spirit became fused with ancestor worship. This is suggested by the fact that the Russian household spirit is named Domovik, meaning 'Father of the Family;' when the Russian peasant removed to a new house he would take with him an ember from his old hearth which he would place on the new hearth saying: 'Welcome, grandfather, to the new home.'

On special ceremonial occasions such as sacred anniversaries it was once the custom in Europe to light a new fire by friction. This special fire was known in the British Isles as 'need fire,' and it was essential at this time for the fires in every household to be extinguished or the spark would not come. Once ignited, brands from the need fire were carried to each household, sometimes by runners, and the domestic fires were then rekindled from the 'new life-giving flame.' It was essential for the need fire to be carefully tended and never extinguished until the next kindling of need fire, if the luck of the household was to be preserved.

An analogous principle lies behind the custom of igniting the Yule-log at Christmas. This log, which was in reality a combustible fire-back, was borne into the house on Christmas Eve with a great deal of ceremony and sometimes with a girl enthroned upon it. It was essential that it should be kindled from a portion of last year's Yule-log that had been preserved for that particular purpose. The Yule kindling was a domestic symbol of family regeneration and a time of fertility.

It was customary in the west of England to burn an ashen faggot, in an identical ceremony. In Ireland, a carved tree stump sometimes called 'Cailleach Nollich' (The Old Woman

Statue of Vestal Virgin in the courtyard of the Roman Forum

of Christmas) was burned to ashes in the heart of a peat fire in the belief that it would 'keep off the Angel of Death' for the ensuing year.

At Burghead in Scotland a very ancient fire rite called Burning the Clavie is still observed at the New Year. A large tar or herring barrel is ignited with burning peat, and the pieces then distributed to the various houses to bring luck. Finally the Clavie becomes the nucleus of a huge bonfire of split casks on the site of a Roman altar called Doorie. The villagers scramble for portions of the burning barrel from which they kindle their own domestic New Year fires, while the embers are placed in the chimneys as a defence against witches.

In Lancashire the hearth fire was religiously kept burning throughout the night of New Year's Eve, but not a single ember or lighted candle would be passed to another householder, however desperate his need, as this would transfer the good luck from the house.

Fortune in the Fire

The original connection between the sun and its domestic counterpart is very possibly responsible for the well-known superstition that sunlight has the power to extinguish the domestic fire. There is a suggestion here of a reluctance on the part of the greater luminary to countenance the presumption of the lesser one. In this respect it is interesting to note that the blazing sun was the symbol selected by the founders of the sun Fire Office. An imagined connection between the sun's rays and the glance of the human eye is no doubt responsible for the US superstition that anyone who looks into a fire while it is being kindled will hinder its combustion.

Inseparable from the cult of the hearth is the lore of the chimney that appears as a frequent motif in folk beliefs. The chimney sweep, if seen in his working clothes, brings the luck of the hearth spirits to the bride who meets him on her wedding day, but only if he is walking toward her; and a 'sweep's sixpence,' a blackened silver coin brings good fortune to its finder. On the other hand, witches and devils, those implacable enemies of domesticity, were said to preside over smoky chimneys, by means of which they entered and left the home and from which vantage point they constantly sought to extinguish the fire in the hearth. It was for this reason that the poker was frequently placed against the top bars of the grate, ostensibly to make the fire draw, but in reality to form a cross and frustrate their designs. It was perhaps only poetic justice

that the last case of witch-burning in the British Isles, that of Bridget Cleary at Clonmel, Ireland, in 1894, was carried out by members of her family upon the domestic hearth.

Our ancestors used to see signs and portents, as they sat by the hearth, and innumerable were the inferences drawn as to the vicissitudes of fate from the behaviour of the fire. A hollow oblong cinder that spurted from the coals represented a coffin and was therefore an omen of death, while an oval cinder symbolized a cradle; most welcome of all, a round cinder indicated a money box. One might even receive advance information of a visitor, for if the fire suddenly blazed up or a flake of soot became suspended on the bars it meant that a stranger was about to enter one's life. Should the coals burn brightly after being poked, it was an indication from the oracle of the hearth that the absent lover, husband or wife, was in good health for the spark of life still burned. To dream of seeing a spark fall on another's arm or breast signified that a dead child would soon lie there.

Before the days of the barometer, fire served mankind as an infallible weather prophet, for in Wellsford's *Nature's Secrets* (1658), we learn that 'When our common fires do burn with a dull flame they presage foul weather. If the fire do make a buzzing noise it is a sign of tempests near at hand. If the ashes on the hearth do clodden together of themselves it is a sign of rain.' Ashes provided an ever potent oracle for these were in effect the seed of fire, a manifestation of the elemental spirits of the hearth. For a flame to spurt without warning from the ashes was a symbol of good fortune. In the Isle of Man the ashes were carefully examined for signs and if a shape like a footprint were discovered pointing toward the door, it was thought to signify a death in the family, but if pointing inward a new arrival, a birth.

The Vestal Virgins

Whatever happened to other people's fires, there was one which must always have been carefully tended in a little early community, and that was the domestic fire of the chief or king. So long as that burned, there was a supply of fire for the whole people, and there is some reason for saying that it was in a sense an embodiment of the communal life . . . So it is not to be wondered at that there was a public Vesta in Rome, and that her fire was tended by virgins, the successors of the king's daughters . . . There were six of these women in historical times, originally, it is said, four. They were chosen, while still little girls, from families of patrician origin, that is to say descended from original or early settlers of Rome, and they served for thirty years (originally it had been but five), during which time they must not marry. If one of them was found unchaste, she was not executed, for she was too holy to kill, but put into an underground chamber in the Field of Ill-Luck (*Campus sceleratus*), and there left to die of hunger and lack of air, or be miraculously rescued, if Vesta chose thus to vindicate her innocence. It was an ordeal, not an execution. Her lover, if known, was beaten to death.

H. J. Rose
Ancient Roman Religion

From camp fire to house fire, the domestic hearth has continued to provide a point of contact between man and man. In the course of ages rigid rituals grew up around this most sacred of the symbols. The master of the house sat at the right of the hearth of the home and the mistress on the left. The custom was universal among the Gaels of Ireland and the Highlands; the Mongols also allocated the right hand side to the men, and the left to their womenfolk.

ERIC MAPLE

FURTHER READING: E. Estyn Evans. Irish Folk Ways. (London, UK: Routledge & Kegan, 1957); E. Estyn Evans and L. Wright. Keep the Home Fires Burning.

(London, UK: Routledge &
Kegan Paul, 1964).

Herbal Medicine

Between 1957 and 1961, a team from Columbia University excavated a cave at Shanidar, now in Iraq. Amongst the remains of a Neanderthal male who died some 60,000 years ago they discovered traces of medicinal herbs still valued by herbalist today, including the marsh mallow used to soothe sore throats and intestinal troubles, and the grape hyacinth administered to encourage better urination.

This evidence lends factual evidence to the conjecture that humans have been using plants to remedy their ills throughout their evolution. First to record the herbal powers of plants were the Chinese. The *Pen Tsao*, dating to around 3000 BC contains more than 260 medicinal herbs, including ephedra, which remains an effective treatment for asthma. Both the ancient Greeks and Romans compiled herbals with now proven scientific credentials, but some herbs were credited with special properties, notably vervain 'the divine weed' able, so the Romans believed, to avert sorcery and the power of witches and evil spirits as well as curing everything from the bite of a rabid dog to the plague, and cinquefoil (dubbed from its leaf form, 'the five fingers of Mary').

Incantations chanted as a plant was picked also boosted the healing powers of herbs. When picking vervain it was customary in sixteenth-century England to intone this verse:

*Hallowed be thou, Vervain, as thou
growest on the ground,
For in the mount of Calvary there
thou wast first found.
Thou healest our Saviour Jesus
Christ, and stanched his bleeding
wound;
In the name of the Father, the Son,
and the Holy Ghost, I take thee
from the ground.*

The science of herbs became yet farther invested with magical properties during the Dark Ages, when astrology and superstition became

'The Lord hath created medicines out of the Earth; and he that is wise will not abhor them.'

central to herb lore. In Europe 'herb-wives' played a central role at this time, undergoing elaborate rituals to make their treatments efficacious. Plants would, for instance, be gathered at night when Mother Earth was unable to witness them being stolen from her. Equally, plants would be deemed most effective if gathered on days of great significance such as Midsummer Eve or Ascension Day.

Similar practices existed across the globe. Native American medicine men and women were revered throughout history for their ability to effect herbal cures, very often with the added bonus of driving out evil or the malign influence of witches at the same time. Even the look of a herb was significant; the mandrake, on account of its human-like form—and its reputation for screeching when cut—was a popular cure all across the globe. Colour mattered, too so yellow plants such as the dandelion and cowslip were favoured for treating jaundice, whilst red plants such as the foxglove—which in time yielded to medicine the drug digitalin—were popular for curing conditions of the heart and blood.

The Magic of Herbs

In his herbal of 1653, the English herbalist Nicolas Culpeper (1616–1654) created his herbal treatments with regard to the Doctrine of Signatures, the philosophy of herbal medicine first propounded by the ancient Greeks, including Dioscorides and Galen. This states that herbs best suited to treat different parts of the body are those that most resemble each organ or body part— peony root for gout, the blue flowers of chicory for failing sight and sore eyes.

Astrology also played a large part in Culpeper's herbal treatments. He decreed that every disease was caused by a governing planet, which needed to be identified, and by a law of opposites. In his own words: '. . . You may oppose diseases by Herbs of the planet, opposite to the planet that causes them: as diseases of Jupiter by herbs of Mercury, and the contrary; diseases of the Luminaries by the

Mandrake plants often have branches in their roots that represent the human figure.

herbs of Saturn, and the contrary; diseases of Mars by herbs of Venus, and the contrary.'

The ancient traditions of herbal medicine continue to this day, our links to the past persisting in drugs such as aspirin, which in its 'natural form' was ingested by country folk centuries ago when they chewed the bark of the willow trees to quell pain and the symptoms of fever. For as the Bible says in Ecclesiasticus (38.4): 'The Lord hath created medicines out of the earth; and he that is wise will not abhor them.'

RUTH BINNEY

FURTHER READING: Culpeper's Complete Herbal, *facsimile edition (Hertfordshire, UK: Wordsworth Editions Ltd, 1995); Gabrielle Hatfield.* Hatfield's Herbal of All Sorts. *(London, UK: Allen Lane, 2007); Geoffrey Grigson.* A Herbal of All Sorts. *(London, UK: Phoenix House, 1959).*

Hobby-Horse

A person who 'rides his hobby-horse' is one who dwells obsessively on his own special interest. However, the original hobby-horse was a man who appeared at certain seasons in the guise of a horse, sometimes in the company of dancers and other characters.

A primitive form of hobby-horse is made from a pole on which is fixed a horse's head, sometimes made of wood but often a real horse skull. This is known as the skull-and-pole type of hobby-horse. The skull is cleaned of flesh by burying it for several months; it is sometimes painted and the bottoms of glass bottles are inserted in the eye sockets. The man carrying the pole is shrouded in a sheet so that the horse seems to be rearing.

The hobby-horse is mentioned again and again in early ecclesiastical and civic prohibitions as appearing at house doors during the Saturnalia and the Calends of January. The skull-and-pole type was frequently accompanied by a stag and a calf made in the same way. The Bishop of Barcelona speaks of a stag-maker in AD 370; this is the earliest mention of the custom. He was followed by St. Augustine (AD 354-430) who forbade the 'filthy practice of dressing up like a horse or a stag.' Through the centuries these pagan animal masks continued to be forbidden.

The Tourney Horse

Some time before the sixteenth century, when the hobby-horse started to take part in masques and entertainments, he began to appear in the form of a man riding a horse—the tourney horse. It is in this form that he is now usually to be seen at his seasonal outings, although the more primitive skull-and-pole type has by no means died out. This heavy tourney type of horse required all sorts of adjuncts—a sword for the man, a pair of false legs in stirrups or dangling free, and many trappings and decorations.

Great Britain keeps alive some remarkable hobbies, notably the Padstow Old Hoss, which comes out regularly on May Day and attracts crowds of local Cornish folk and visitors from much farther afield.

In Bohemia hobby-horses are so large that three men hide beneath the cloth, while another rides.

He is made of a round frame about five feet wide covered with black tarpaulin, with a smallish horse-head in front and a tail at the back; the effect is more like a round dining-table than a horse. The man wearing the frame has a tall pointed cap, and a strange painted facemask with whiskers and a red tongue hanging from the mouth; that is, the figure riding the horse is a horse as well. Another character, the Teaser, dances backward directing the Hoss with his curious padded sceptre. Both Teaser and Hoss dance beautifully a series of small rapid steps. The Hoss pursues and catches women and girls under his 'cloak' (his round body) and this is considered a powerful fertility action.

The Minehead Horse, another hobby of the tourney type, is still larger, but oblong. The man wears a tall pointed cap and a metal mask. The horse body has lost its head, but boasts a long rope tail used to tie up some onlookers. They can be swung off their feet and 'booted,' that is, beaten ten times with a boot carried for the purpose, while the blows are counted aloud.

The Cheshire horses appear at All Souls (November 2) after the Soulers have given their mummers' play. The hobby-horse, sometimes called Dicky Tatton or Old Ball, then appears with his Driver or Jockey and is sold. He then shakes himself to bits at the feet of his new owner.

Glass-Eyed Mari Lwyd

The best known skull-and-pole type of hobby-horse, with glass bottle bottoms for eyes and a pair of old gloves for ears, is the Mari Lwyd, the famous horse of South Wales. He is beautifully decked out with ribbon and horse-bells, and appears at midwinter, rearing and plunging in the dark street, while the party accompanying him holds a singing contest with the inhabitants of whichever house they visit. Each side improvizes a verse. If the householders give out first they must admit the horse and give refreshments all round. If the Mari Lwyd gang is at a loss first, they have to retire and try their luck at another door. Once admitted, the horse teases and nudges the girls and, neighing, pretends to bite them.

The Mari Lwyd is accompanied by a Sergeant, a Merryman who is the fiddler, and a couple now called Punch and Judy who may be recognized as the figures known throughout Europe as the Fool and Old Woman. The latter. is a man dressed as a woman, carrying a broom. These characters often blacken their faces for a disguise.

This type of Mari Lwyd is known in Glamorganshire and Carmarthenshire and is still being made. Another, very rare, type was made from a square of canvas stuffed with straw, sewn up to form a head and snout; it could be made to move about on a pitchfork stuck into the stuffing.

The Great White Horse of Kerry in Ireland was a skull-and-pole creature 8 feet high, the man carrying it being covered with the usual white sheet. He came out at midsummer, chased the women and jumped the mid-summer fires. This was a rite in honour of the sun and to promote increase of every useful kind.

Continental Horses

In France the hobby is called *le cheval-jupon*. The most celebrated dancer is the Zamalzain in the Soule province of the French Basque country, who is accompanied by a whole company of dancers, singers, and musicians. On the Spanish side of the Pyrenees are other Basque hobbyhorses. There is another at Lanz in Navarre, connected with a giant; at Pamplona there is a Zaldiko-Maldiko (horse-mule) that lashes out with a fool's bladder; also in Navarre two stuffed hobbies, heavy, and difficult to manipulate, are brought out at a local feast. There are many hobbies, 'cavallets' and 'wild mules' in Spain

Poland's Lajkonik is represented as a bearded man with a tourney horse

and Portugal that take part in processions, but processing seems to have detracted from their more ancient ritual character.

Belgium has hobbies of all shapes and sizes. Few of these carry out ritual acts, but they frequently accompany processions. A hobby-horse represent-

ing Cheval Bayard, a giant horse of legend, carries the four sons of Aymon on his back high above the crowds in various festival processions.

In Switzerland, hobbies recite carnival verses outside houses, loudly whinnying to the girls. The Schimmel, the white horse of Upper Murthal in the Austrian Alps, follows a troop of carnival runners calling in high falsetto voices, whose leader cracks a long Alpine whip. When these bringers-in of spring have run off to their next place of call, the Schimmel appears and is put up for sale, as amongst the Souler-Mummers in Cheshire villages. If anyone is foolish enough to buy him, the white horse shakes himself to pieces at his new owner's feet.

On the Slovenian side of the Alps lives Rusa, an inoffensive hobby though his head and neck are covered with porcupine quills. Sometimes he is accompanied by terrifying human maskers of strongly Alpine influence. Like nearly all hobby-horses, Rusa is a seasonal horse—he helps to bring in the spring and must be paid for his services.

In Bohemia hobby-horses are so large that three men hide beneath the cloth, while another rides. In the same region, and around Brno in Moravia, a horse-head carved in wood is carried on a stick at the head of wedding processions. The general name for these heads is the Klibna, said to mean Mare; they tend to be comic rather than frightening. Sometimes accompanied by goat-maskers, they come out during carnival; occasionally they appear on St. Nicholas's Day (December 6). They too bring in the spring and fertilize farm stock, not forgetting the women and girls who, screaming, join in the kitchen skirmishes with annual zest.

Poland too owns hobbies round about Kracow; one celebrated one which appears in early summer on Corpus Christi Day in a suburb of that town is said to commemorate a victory over a Tartar invasion. The horse rider is supposed to be dressed as a Tartar. The hobby rushes through the streets and lies down for a few minutes on the steps of the bishop's palace; this may signify a momentary death.

Village Comedy

The hobby-horse is known far beyond Europe, providing an important link in Indo-European tradition. In southern India at Madura, a village comedy is enacted in which a woman—really a man dressed as a woman—is robbed as she sleeps, even to the pillow beneath her head. Two hobby-horses appear, one takes the woman as his own and refuses to let anyone come near her. These horses go to weddings, as in many European regions.

Sometimes musicians give chase to the horse, who at last allows himself to be caught and dances with his captors. Near Mysore, the horse prances on stilts, and halfway through the performance sheds his outer garment and appears as a woman. Yet another hobby makes his own horse's head on the spot, cut out of an araca palm; attendants of the local deity sit on the ground and the horse prances round them, finally falling into a trance. Here the horse ritual has been combined with the local religion.

Beautifully plaited rushes form the hobbies of Sarawak, and the ritual animal-masker is a well-known figure in China.

VIOLET ALFORD

Hogmanay

Name for New Year's Eve in Scotland and parts of the north of England; the departure of the old year and birth of the new is celebrated with much feasting and drinking; children go from door to door singing songs and asking for cakes, small gifts, and coins; also the occasion for the custom of First Footing.

House

The earliest house was probably erected to shelter the helpless infant from the cold and was designed as an imitation of the lairs and burrows of wild animals. Almost certainly the most primitive forms of architecture were based on Nature, whether in the form of tree branches thatched to provide protection against rain and sun or the chieftain's grave, which was so often a mound that was the replica of the green hills of the countryside.

In the cold North, the prehistoric cave was man's first home, usually selected because it faced in a westerly direction to avoid the biting east wind of winter. The cave entrance must have been of immense physical and psychological import from the beginning for it provided not only the means of egress and ingress but was also the way of entry for the elemental powers of Nature—light, wind, rain, and sun. Within the cave there could be security, warmth, and relaxation while outside lurked the dangers of untamed Nature, often in the demonic shapes with which mankind peopled the realms of darkness. It is perhaps understandable that the recesses of the cave should have been dedicated to religious rites and that cave art provided perhaps our earliest experience of abstract form.

With the development of more sophisticated types of habitation—firstly the stone house on the hillside and later the log hut in the valley—the house must have become ever more important socially, for the more widely one's awareness of the world develops, the more intense are the terrors it excites, and it is only within four walls that man can be completely insulated emotionally against the enervating and destructive power of fear. At a later stage still came the hall, a single-storied, unpartitioned room with the hearth at its centre, the entrance or threshold of which provided a barrier separating the known from the unknown.

In symbolism a house is expressed

as an enclosed space and also as a receptacle that, like the chest and the womb, is female in character. As a secret enclosure it also symbolizes the repository of all wisdom. There are mystics who have seen in a house, with its storeys, doors, and windows, a psychic projection of the human body with its various layers and apertures. It is certain that the sophisticated symbolists of our present age have endowed the house with qualities that would have been inconceivable before the development of psychoanalysis, as for example in the interpretation of dreams in which it is said to represent the different layers of the psyche.

As a further extension of the same theme, the exterior of the house is said to symbolize the human personality, the roof representing the mind and the subconscious being relegated to the basement. The kitchen becomes 'the laboratory of psychic transmutation,' echoing Paracelsus's definition of the belly as 'the grand laboratory.'

> *There are many who . . . believe that it is unlucky to enter a new house for the first time by the back door, which is in effect an unconsecrated aperture . . .*

While such philosophical speculations would have been beyond the comprehension of the ancestral house owner, it is evident that certain abstract qualities were never far from his mind when he erected his home, since the process of building continued to be associated with elaborate magicoreligious rites until compara-tively modern times. The selection, orientation, and layout of the site was determined by augury, for any false alignment in relation to the sun could cast a blight upon the future.

Psychic Household Insurance

The foundations of house-holds in old-world Europe were customarily 'laid in blood,' the sacrificial rite devised to neutralize the en-mity of the earth deity and to ensure the stability of the structure in accordance with primitive architectural theory. As a relic of this old practice, the superstition is still common in the north of England that the building or rebuilding of a house or the cutting of a new doorway results in the death of one member of the family. Another reminder of the custom of burying

Antique English doll's house

The bark facade of ceremonial house is painted with protective spirits in Maprik, Australian New Guinea

The belief still prevails in many parts of Europe that a newly completed house should be placed under the protection of a lucky tree or bush, and as an additional insurance against the attacks of hostile spirits the houseleek, a plant dedicated to Thor, is sometimes grown upon roofs. As another insurance with the household deities, human and animal skulls were used as magical amulets, and were sometimes embedded in walls, those of the horse being particularly favoured in northern Europe.

The main defence of the house against intruders of all kinds consisted of the wall, which has been described as a 'restrictive force that kept out prying eyes and enemies.' Infinite care had to be observed in its construction. In Ireland it is still considered dangerous to build part of a gravestone into a new wall as this 'builds death into the house.'

The window or 'wind eye,' originally a mere hole in the wall protected by branches or a curtain and exposed to the wind, in symbolism represents the idea of penetration; if situated at the summit of a tower it becomes the symbol of consciousness. In addition, the window opens the inner darkness to the holy power of light. It is said that some primitive communities worshipped the first ray of the sun when it reached the window. In Ireland a cup of milk is placed on the sill as refreshment for the wandering family ghosts who chance to pass that way at Christmas time. The entry of an alien spirit by way of the window could be prevented by suspending a witch ball, a multicoloured glass sphere, near the opening, where it distracted the eye of the approaching witch and was thought to absorb the first impact of her venom.

The threshold of the house has always been an important centre of household rites as it is essentially a barrier against the enemy without,

human victims alive beneath a cornerstone is provided by the superstition that corner houses are unlucky places in which to live.

Originally it would have been necessary for any new building to be consecrated by a priest before it could be occupied, to provide ritual protection against demons and ghosts. In the Celebes, in Indonesia, the most elaborate ceremonies were carried out even in modern times to protect those

who entered their new homes from the psychic dangers within, and in many lands including Persia (now Iran) and China offerings were always made to the protective spirits before entering a house. A comparable superstitious practice is still observed by those of Anglo-Saxon stock in northern Europe and the United States who carry bread and salt into a new house to ensure the prosperity of the occupants.

whether human or elemental. In mysticism the doorway, the place of 'comings and goings,' represents the free will, while its archway has long been the site of purificatory rites and ritual healing. Specially devised ceremonies, often involving sacrifice, were performed at the threshold of the house to propitiate the household or guardian spirits and to protect the family from evil. There are many who even today believe that it is unlucky to enter a new house for the first time by the back door, which is in effect an unconsecrated aperture, or to leave a house by a different door from the one at which one came in.

In biblical times the threshold or gateway was the scene of mystical ceremonies as in Exodus (chapter 12) where we read that the blood of a lamb, sprinkled on the lintels and doorposts of the Israelites' houses, protected them when God killed the first-born of Egypt. After the erection of the principal entrance to an Indian building the woodwork is even today ritually anointed with the oil of the sandaltree. The sacrosanct character of the house imposed many prohibitions upon those who entered it, including the need to avoid any contact between the foot and the threshold; in the Orient, for instance, visitors remove their shoes. The sanctity of the doorway is farther emphasized by the inscriptions that traditionally appear above it. These may vary from the sacred to the profane, and in the Far East are often obscene. In parts of North Africa the genitalia of animals are set above barn doorways as a warning to the passing demon. An interesting feature of some English houses is the stone carving of a woman's head that can often be seen placed above the doorway. The grotesquely designed door knockers on English cottages also served to warn off devils, as did the horseshoes that were nailed to the doorways of barns.

To certain gods and goddesses have been allocated the task of supervising the threshold of the house, and altars were erected near the entrances in their honour. The Roman Janus, god 'of the beginning of things,' is perhaps the best known deity of gates and doors and his name is related to our modern 'janitor.'

The symbolism of the door key pervades mythology and religion, for whether it is expressed as the key of heaven or as the key to wisdom, it is the symbol of entrance to the mysteries. For this reason priests and priestesses of the ancient religions carried keys as evidence that they were participants in the rites of the gods. Even today, the key is of great symbolic importance, and to welcome an honoured guest by handing him the keys of the city is in effect to offer him open house.

The keyhole represents a chink in the household's armour, an aperture by which devils may enter and it must therefore be rendered secure; however, if the key is left in the lock, the home is safe. People once believed that stopping the keyhole was important during childbirth to prevent fairies from stealing the baby, and that this action barred the evil spirit known as the nightmare from entering the house.

In the past, certain special actions performed with a strict eye to magic were involved in entering or leaving a house, some of which remain part of contemporary folklore. The new bride is still carried over the threshold when she enters her home for the first time, while stumbling at the threshold must be avoided if one is embarking upon a journey. Until recently it was customary in Devon, England, to scrub the bride's footprints from the front doorstep of her parental home after her departure as a sign that she had left her old house and had chosen another.

Ladder to the Gods

The various rooms of a house are said to be symbols of individuality; a closed room without windows is an obvious symbol of virginity. The stairway, leading upward and downward to unite the various floors, symbolizes the principle of ascension, graduation, and communication between different levels of the personality. This however is little more than a reiteration of the old folk theme that steps and ladders provide a mode of ascension to the land of the gods. For this reason it is considered unlucky to pass someone on the stairs, since he could well be a god in human shape who would resent the presence of a mortal on his sacred territory. There is a pleasant domestic rite still observed in many places in which a baby is carried to the top of the stairs on its first journey, in the belief that it should 'go up in the world before it comes down.' Superstitious flat-dwellers have been known to resort to a step-ladder for the same purpose, so tenacious is this old tradition in our midst.

The furnishings of the rooms are included in the magical framework;

Gilded bronze doorknocker

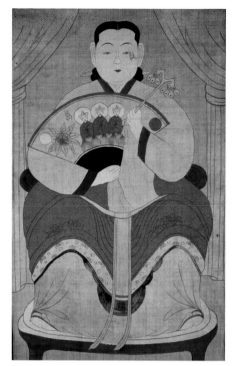

Daesin manura, the female shamanist deity that governs a house and kitchen

the house again if he should stand his chair against the wall before leaving the house. A falling picture is an omen that a member of the household will die, especially if it is his portrait, while three knocks on the window, or the presence of crows encircling the roof, is advance intimation to the householder that he would be wise to keep his life insurance up to date.

Death in the Home

Although a house may be protected by magical and religious rites from the assaults of external spirit forces it is, paradoxically, the abode of domestic elementals who have one common feature in that they are capricious, troublesome, hard to please, and even spiteful. The household spirit is known as the boggart, brownie, fairy, goblin, or kobold, according to nationality. The kobold was a common feature of English domestic life and as long ago as the twelfth century a house-kobold caused a considerable stir at the Suffolk home of Sir Osborn de Bradwelle by discussing learnedly in Latin 'on Scriptural subjects.'

A Danish kobold advanced farther in this field, ultimately becoming clerk to an archbishop. Promotion from domestic spirit to the higher ecclesiastical ranks was rare, however, and in the main the kobold was restricted to passing the time by playing tricks upon the household; hiding farm equipment and consuming considerable quantities of food. Today the last relics of kobold lore have been reduced to a vague belief in lucky and unlucky houses having happy or unhappy atmospheres.

Innumerable are the magical rites associated with the interior of the house, which were once employed as protection against evil. People with some unusual feature such as red hair, cross-eyes, or whose eyebrows met across the nose, were never permitted to cross the threshold as they were either bad luck bringers, witches, or involuntary possessors of the Evil Eye. A witch who entered the house immediately acquired power over its occupants; she could be kept from the threshold, however, by secreting a pair of scissors or a knife beneath the doormat, for like all enemies of good she was unable to step over cold iron.

It is in matters connected with death that the magic of the house is most apparent. When one of the family is due to pass over, according to tradition, the family ghosts discreetly return and await the reunion. If the dying are not to suffer a 'hard death' the deathbed must be in alignment with the floorboards and never across them. An older superstition held that if pigeons' feathers were used to stuff the mattress the death agonies might be prolonged indefinitely. Immediately after death all the mirrors in the room were covered lest the soul in its departure (which had previously been facilitated by the opening of every door and window in the house) should snatch at a mourner's reflection and bear it away to keep it company in the afterlife.

The old belief that a house might

a change in the clock's rhythm being a death omen, especially if it should strike thirteen. Sleeping has its magic rites, for the bed should face east-west in alignment with the sun, or otherwise the sleeper will suffer from nightmares. New shoes must not be placed on the table as this brings death upon the household, a superstition doubtless arising from the old custom of placing a new pair of shoes on the feet of a corpse. In East Anglia it is considered a sign that a visitor will never enter

in some mysterious manner become 'impregnated' by death has often taken strange forms. For example, the Kamchadales of northeast Asia abandoned the cabins in which members of the tribe had died. There are many who fear to live in a house of death believing this to be an open invitation for the spirit of death to embrace the living. In some primitive communities this morbid terror has been responsible for houses being burned down as a purificatory rite, following a death.

It seems that none of the elaborate precautions undertaken to guard the threshold from evil spirits provides adequate protection against the return of the family ghost. At one time a room would be shut up after a death, often for years on end; the eighteenth century essayist Addison refers to a house as being 'three quarters locked up as haunted.' There appears to be some connection between the common European belief that an empty house is an abode of ghosts and the old tradition that after a dwelling has been empty for some time it becomes occupied by devils. In the author's own collection of ghost stories from the North of England is a terrifying legend of a house 'haunted by a pair of eyes.' These had apparently entered the building while it was empty, and finally drove the new tenant insane.

When the family dead choose to return to their old homes they show all the old traits they once possessed as living humans, being either quiet, philosophical and good-tempered, or petulant and vengeful. Sometimes the contest between the dead and the living for the possession of the house becomes so disturbing that an exorcist has to be called. In Pliny's day houses were 'hallowed' against evil spirits with brimstone. Once the spirit is expelled the house will often remain free of unwelcome intruders of this kind for a considerable time.

Exorcism constitutes possibly the last surviving magicoreligious ceremony associated with the house. It appears that there are certain wanton household spirits who do not submit as readily as ghosts to the commands of the exorcist. These are the poltergeists whose activities are closely bound up with the family. The poltergeist has much in common

Taksin Memorial Spirit House, Tak, Thailand

with the old kobold, of whom it is doubtless a direct descendant, being capricious, troublesome, and occasionally violent, hurling stones and wrenching bed clothes off people who are sleeping, and occasionally setting a house alight. In the Isle of Man immediately before the World War II reports of a household elemental in the shape of a talking mongoose created a national sensation. There are few houses as adequately secured against hostile presences from both inside and outside the threshold as Bettiscombe Manor in England, which is protected by a human skull that prevents evil spirits or ghosts from troubling the tenants.

In dream lore a house is a symbol of security, and to dream of standing outside one indicates a forthcoming change of plans, while to enter the house means a fresh start in life. A house in course of erection symbolizes happiness to come but if it is being pulled down it portends an unhappy love affair. Folktales contain a wealth of lore reflecting the importance of the house in childhood fantasies. This is as it should be for the house began as a sanctuary for the helpless child, only developing into a psychic shrine with the passage of the years.

The garden is in effect part of the precinct, an extension of the house itself; it has been described as a place 'where Nature is subdued, ordered, selected and enclosed.' It is here that protective plants and trees were grown for the purpose of providing a first magical barrier against approaching evil. The mountain ash protected the home against witchcraft and the bay withstood the assaults not only of witches but also of devils and storms. The plants purslane, pennyroyal and pimpernel were defenders of the house against devils and misfortune generally.

Certain garden flowers have long been associated with sickness or death and for this reason are rigorously kept from the house. The white lilac is among the most notorious of these flowers, but even the purple and red varieties are said to bring disaster. The lily, perhaps because of its close association with funerals, is considered a death omen, while the white flower

The acorn . . . the seed of the oak that is the sacred tree of the thunder god, affords protection to both house and home against storms and lightning . . .

of the hawthorn is almost universally excluded from the house since it brings with it tragedy. The glorious daffodil, beloved of the poets, has a more dubious reputation in terms of bad luck and for this reason is banned from the house in some parts of the North of England.

The acorn, on the other hand, the seed of the oak that is the sacred tree of the thunder god, affords protection to both house and home against storms and lightning; it is for this reason that the bobbins on window blind cords are traditionally acorn shaped. A more positive device for keeping misfortune at bay is to cultivate the visit of bees to the house, since they are not only great luck-bringers but firm friends of domestic harmony. At one time it was the rule to 'tell the bees' of every change in the household or otherwise the whole hive might take umbrage and fly away. The common house spider is also a luck-bringer to any home. 'If you wish to live and thrive, let a spider run alive' is a useful maxim for the superstitious home-lover.

ERIC MAPLE

FURTHER READING:
Dorothy Donnelly. The Golden Well. *(London, UK: Sheed & Ward, 1950).*

Hunting Magic

In contemporary Western societies hunting magic persists in the attenuated form of sporting hunters' and fishermen's use of good luck charms and other common superstitious practices. But for other cultures who often depend heavily on hunting and fishing for their sustenance, magic may assume great cultural importance.

Hunting (and fishing) magic in such societies may reflect profound cultural concepts of the essential qualities that distinguish men from animals, and of the complex and delicate relationship between human society and the natural world. Less obviously, the beliefs and practices of hunting magic may indirectly reveal much about the tensions and problems of the societies in which they are found. This is because dependence on such inherently uncertain sources of food poses special problems for simple cultures whose fragile yet rigid social structures are threatened in a variety of ways by fluctuations in the luck of the hunters.

Magic is a means of establishing a personal relationship with an otherwise indeterminately related, unknowable, and uncontrollable object or situation, which makes possible effective knowledge or control of that situation. It works by symbolically projecting onto such relationships and situations the orderly, predictable, or controllable, yet potent properties of familiar social or natural phenomena. The magical act of symbolic projection thus necessarily relies upon a systematic and logically coherent

Fremont Indian hunter rock engraving found in Nine Mile Canyon, Utah

set of ideas about the relations between the magician, the object of his magic, and the symbolic properties of the substances used in his magic. Magic may take the form of positive action directed toward the achievement of a goal; but magical beliefs may be equally important in a passive or negative sense, as explanations for the occurrence of unfortunate or unusual events, or as rules for the avoidance of certain contacts or associations that would have the effect of frustrating the achievement of a purpose, or bringing about actively harmful consequences.

The natural world, and above all the animate beings, the animals that inhabit it, constitute the domain of uncontrollable, unpredictable, and unknowable events. They form a mysterious realm beyond the ken or control of the laws of human society. The magic of hunting cannot be understood unless it is realized that the hunt is frequently defined in cultural terms as a kind of rite of passage, a venture out of the safe and secure domain of human society into the ritually perilous, alien world of natural beings.

The structure of the hunt itself resembles that of an initiation ritual. The hunter must first prepare and separate himself from society, then encounter and subdue his prey, which requires him to enter into a relationship with an inhabitant of the asocial, natural world, and finally he must return again to human society. The return is often a ritually complex operation, for in many cultures the hunter cannot become fully reintegrated into the society of men without taking the necessary measures to purify himself of his relationship with his prey, which is magically dangerous because of its asocial, inhuman, and hostile qualities, and to protect others from its effects. In some societies, this is achieved simply through the social distribution of the meat; in others, by rites of purification for the hunter; in still others by ritual treatment of the corpse of the victim. The prey itself undergoes its own rite of passage, a transition from its wholly 'natural'

existence, through the stage of contact and slaughter by the hunter to its complete integration into the human cultural world as cooked food.

Lord of the Animals

Magical rites and beliefs may surround every phase of both hunter's and victim's passage between human society and Nature. The hunter's weapons and auxiliary animals (usually dogs or horses) are also frequent objects of magical treatment. There is, of course, enormous variation from culture to culture as to which aspects of these complex phenomena become the objects of magic, what are the explicit and implicit goals of the magical practices, what constitutes the objective content of the magical rites and beliefs themselves, and what basic ideas underlie them.

In some cultures, all hunters share knowledge of the important magical techniques; in others, each man may have his own techniques, either learned from others or discovered by himself. In still others, only specialists, shamans, or priests possess the requisite knowledge or are able to perform the necessary rituals or provide the requisite medicines or charms. In certain societies, the ritual of hunting magic is performed by an entire band or community, in others by lone individuals. The techniques employed vary widely: they include the use of spells, amulets, charms, shrines, and medicines; offerings or sacrifices to the animals themselves, to the divine guardians of the animals, or to the familiars or gods of the hunters.

Certain cultures concentrate on producing clairvoyant visions and telepathic or dream communication with the animals, to learn their location or secure their cooperation with the hunter. Others stress the establishment of a special relationship between an individual hunter and a particular species of animal, which may consist in an ability to understand its language, a particular skill in tracking or killing it, or occasionally a compact with that species under the terms of which its members allow themselves to be killed and taken by that hunter. A frequently employed technique is the application of medicines or charms to the weapons and body of the hunter or his dogs. The making and manipulation of representations of the quarry, whether in dance, song, or in art, seems also to have been a common device of hunting magic since Paleolithic times.

Much of the magic associated with hunting is directed at the quarry itself, with varying purposes, such as to cause it to multiply as a species, to locate it, and perhaps to induce it to come to the hunter, to pacify it or neutralize its strength if it is dangerous. Hunting magic may also be practiced to deceive the animal with respect to the hunter's presence or real intentions toward it, to kill it, to make it lighter so that it can be the more easily carried home, to placate or compensate it for being killed and eaten, to forestall the vengeance of the dead animal's spirit or supernatural patrons or protectors, or to counteract the potentially dangerous effects of contact with its physical substance (it is widely believed that the hair, meat, and blood of wild animals has a dangerous 'potency').

Another array of magical practices is concerned with preparing the hunter (through fasting, sexual continence, performance of rites, and so on) for the hunt, in ways calculated to sharpen his powers of tracking and finding the game, his strength, skill, and endurance in all phases of the hunt, or perhaps to protect him from attack by his quarry or other wild beasts. Still other techniques are employed for making the hunter invisible or otherwise imperceptible to his quarry, for protecting him from the supernatural danger that may result from his having killed, and purifying him after the kill so that he may be reincorporated into human society.

The concept of the man-animal relationship underlying the practice of hunting magic is often extremely sophisticated and complex, and also varies widely from culture to culture. Many peoples base their beliefs and behaviour toward wild animals on a tacit, or occasionally explicit, assumption of reciprocity and equilibrium between the wild species and themselves. This is frequently expressed by beliefs that animals at one time possessed culture and language, and bestowed their gifts upon man, thereby losing them for themselves.

In some societies, it is thought to be man's responsibility to perform the rituals necessary to insure the renewal and fertility of the animal species: in this way man, through the ritual increase of game species, counterbalances the reduction caused by hunting. There are widespread beliefs in the necessity to apologize to, or otherwise placate, the game animal for taking it, often associated with beliefs in supernatural 'parents' or protectors of animal species who must be placated by the hunter.

In many cases animals are directly linked to notions about human death. Among the Desana of the Colombia-Brazil border, according to Gerardo Reichel-Dolmatoff (1912–1994), it is believed that the souls of the dead who have led sinful lives are captured by the 'Lord of the Animals' and taken by him to the caves in the mountains that the Desana believe are the 'wombs of the animals,' to be reincarnated in animal form. To kill an animal is therefore to kill a man; animals and men share a common kinship of souls, and, as the Desana put it, of blood. A hunter must propitiate the Lord of the Animals, or distract his attention by inducing him to remain slumbering in one of his caverns if he is to succeed.

It is tempting to conjecture that the great painted caves of Paleolithic Europe, which are often chambers buried deep in the cliffs or mountains far from the sites of human habitation, and which seem to have been used solely for ceremonial purposes, may have served as 'wombs' of the animal species found painted so vividly on their walls, somewhat along the lines of the Desana conception. Effigies of animals modeled in clay and pierced by spear-thrusts have been found in the caves, lending some support to the conjecture that hunting rituals may have been practiced in the caves, but we shall probably never know with certainty what beliefs and rituals were celebrated by the Stone Age hunters in their subterranean sanctuaries.

A more extreme example of the belief in the relation of game animals, hunting, and human death is reported by Edward Schieffelin (1847–1897) from certain New Guinea tribes, who believe in a dual universe. In this system, every human soul has, as a 'double,' an animal soul in the 'parallel' world. The souls of the animals of this world are, in the same way, the doubles of the people of the other world. To kill the animal double causes the death of the human counterpart in the complementary world. Human deaths are thus explained as the results of hunting by the men of the other world, and hunts are occasionally organized by the tribes in question to retaliate against the men of the other world for causing deaths by their hunting.

Such beliefs, reflect a fundamental belief in the interdependence of human and animal life, expressed in the concept that both form parts of a delicately balanced equilibrium which men only upset at their peril. Hunting magic often serves as the vehicle of these ideas, sometimes by imposing significant restrictions on the behaviour of the hunter (such as sexual abstinence) as preconditions of success, or sometimes by more overtly

emphasizing the contractual nature of the hunting relationship between man and animal, for instance by requiring reciprocal rites or gestures by the hunter toward the quarry animal.

It would be misleading, however, to interpret such beliefs as being

> *To kill an animal is therefore to kill a man; animals and men share a common kinship of souls, and, as the Desana put it, of blood.*

based solely upon an objective grasp of the principles of the balance between human society and the animal populations of its surrounding territory. In some societies, the concept that is formed of the balance between man and Nature is often tightly bound up with the character of the social relations between man in his role as hunter and his fellow men.

Hunter's 'Luck'

The Brazilian anthropologist Roberto Da Matta (1936–), for example, has shown in a brilliant analysis of the magical beliefs about 'bad luck' in hunting and fishing held by the population of a small Brazilian town on the Amazon, how these beliefs tend to maintain the inflexible social structure of the community. The lowest strata of the town's population, the hunters and fishermen, have no means of raising their status in society other than through some 'lucky' contact or event originating outside the social structure of the community itself. This might take the form of help from a distant relative, a generous employer from the big city, or persistent luck in hunting and fishing. This would provide an opportunity for the successful hunter to expand his network of social relations and raise his social standing by distributing presents of meat to those he might wish to put under an obligation.

Xingu Indians in the Amzon, Brazil, bringing back a kill

The hierarchical social structure of the town is, however, too rigid to tolerate such mobility: it depends on maintaining the amount of hunting at a fairly rigidly fixed level, as well as on strictly regulating the distribution of the proceeds of the hunt. The magical beliefs and taboos surrounding the distribution of meat by the hunter are so defined that any man who hunts with unusual frequency and success would be almost sure to violate one, thus bringing 'bad luck' in hunting upon himself. This system of taboos tends to constrain hunters to limit their activities, at the cost of losing their 'luck.' It also tends to inhibit their losing their place in the social structure of the community.

There is a separate system of beliefs in the same town that animal species, watercourses, and other natural resources have 'mothers' who permit modest utilization of the resources under their protection but punish overexploitation beyond the normal subsistence needs of an individual and his immediate family. This set of beliefs, counterparts of which are found in many primitive and peasant societies, obviously has the same social effect as the system of taboos surrounding the distribution of game.

The main point of Da Matta's analysis is that societies with simple but rigid social organizations, like most primitive and rural, or peasant communities, may attempt to restrict their relations with the natural world (above all, hunting) within narrowly prescribed limits of quantity and quality, in order to protect their inflexible social structures from the repercussions that would result from uncontrolled individual variation in hunting productivity.

Those that do not attempt to regulate hunting production frequently surround the distribution of the meat with taboos tending to ensure equitable sharing, in this way minimizing the danger of conflicts arising from discriminatory distribution and inequalities in hunting luck and skill among individual hunters. For a rigidly structured simple society, natural equilibrium (including the equitable distribution of natural produce) is

> *Hunters enjoy great prestige, . . . because they are considered . . . to be quint-essentially masculine, tough, and . . . above the law of ordinary men.*

the prerequisite of social equilibrium. Magical beliefs, as Da Matta shows, may fulfil a vital function as regulating mechanisms of this double equilibrium, by establishing direct connections between the hunter's behaviour and relationships within society, on the one hand, and his fortunes as a hunter, on the other.

The hunting magic of the Ndembu of Zambia, although radically different in form and content from that of the Brazilian people analysed by Da Matta, reveals the same intimate link between the social relations of the hunter and his success as a huntsman. The Ndembu are a simple society of shifting cultivators. Game has become increasingly scarce in their territory, but enjoys a degree of prestige as food that is out of all proportion to its actual quantitative importance as a component of the Ndembu diet. Hunting has become a specialized activity pursued as a vocation by a small number of men, who characteristically scorn to have normal families and settled lives in conformity with the accepted life style of the agricultural villages.

Hunters enjoy great prestige, in large part because they are considered, by the nature of their professions, to be quintessentially masculine, tough, and to some extent above the law of

ordinary men. These very qualities, however, make them to some extent a threat to the fabric of conventional social relations. They are, for example, likely to boast of their numerous adulterous affairs. The stereotype of the Ndembu hunter reflects the culturally significant properties of hunting as an economic activity: it is a difficult craft demanding considerable skill, physical endurance, and luck, pursued in isolation from settled communities, prestigious but peripheral to the central social and economic life of the people.

Among the Ndembu the craft of the hunter is bound up with two (very similar) cult associations, which exist for the purpose of performing rituals to 'cure' bad luck in hunting. The Ndembu conceive of huntsmanship as analogous in certain respects to a physical substance, that can be lost or spilled and replenished by magical means: the rites of the Ndembu hunting cults are aimed at restoring and increasing the powers of huntsmanship, while attacking the agency responsible for their loss. This is invariably conceived to be the shade of a recently deceased ancestor who was himself a hunter, and who has become displeased because the unlucky hunter has failed to honour one of a wide variety of social or ritual obligations to his kinsmen, to other hunters, or to the ancestral hunter's shade itself. The hunting rituals simultaneously propitiate the ancestral shade and initiate the novice hunter into the cult of hunters, which doubles as a kind of professional association. Great emphasis is placed on the solidarity of initiated hunters.

However, the presence or assistance of the novice's kinsmen, and the reaffirmation of his social bonds with them is as important for the performance of the rites as the support of his prospective colleagues of the hunter's cult. The magical rites of the hunting cults, which focus upon the erection of a shrine to the shade of the hunter-ancestor who is causing the affliction, serve to confront and reconcile two sets of relations and qualities that are to a large extent opposed and contradictory in normal life. On the one hand, they emphasize the distinctness of the calling of the hunter and the very qualities that serve to set him apart from, and to some extent in conflict with, conventional society; on the other hand, they stress the integration of the hunter into conventional society through the ritual reaffirmation of his ordinary kinship obligations, which form the basis of the Ndembu community.

The hunting ritual of the Ndembu, an African tribe, and the magical beliefs of the backwoodsmen of modern Brazil illustrate a common point: the underlying purpose of hunting magic is frequently as much to integrate the hunter safely into human society as to promote the success of his ventures into the animal world.

TERENCE TURNER

FURTHER READING: Victor W. Turner. The Forest of Symbols. (Ithaca, New York, NY: Cornell University Press, 1968); J. G. Frazer. The Golden Bough. (London, UK: St. Martin's Press, 1980).

Hadza huntsman, from Tanzania, plucking feathers from a hunted bird

Initiation

In every initiation ceremony there is some idea of a new birth as part of the process of assuming full status in the group. 'Except a man be born again' is the Christian phrasing for a process that in many ceremonies involves acting out a return to a symbolic womb. Part of the ritual of the Kunapipi, an Australian aboriginal group, involves the initiates being brought into the sacred ground 'to enter the Mother; they go into her uterus, the ring place, as happened in the beginning.' In acting out the ritual they are covered over with bark and hung from a pole. 'They are,' as Mircea Eliade shows, 'in the womb, and they will emerge reborn— "their spirit comes out new."'

The theme of rebirth is paralleled by the equally important recurring theme of death. Both are closely linked structurally in the whole process of initiation. The new life cannot start until the old has been disposed of. Ritual death to the old life, the former sinful, corrupt condition, is expressed in the elaborate mythology surrounding most puberty rites. In the Congo on the Loango coast boys between ten and twelve years old have a ritual death in the village when they are given a potion to make them unconscious as a prelude. Now 'dead,' they are taken into the jungle, circumcized, buried in the fetish house, and painted white, a sign that they are ghosts of their former existence.

Rebirth may be expressed by the infantile behaviour of the initiates when they return. They may appear helpless, like babies. The stay in the bush serves the important function of signifying the death of the previous relationship between a son and his mother. Initiation ceremonies serve several functions in relation to the social structure and they also emphasize the deeper belief system. The newly initiated have a special status because they have learned the mysteries, survived the ordeals, having escaped the belly of whale or serpent or whatever other experience may be central to the creation myth of the group.

Initiation into secret societies, shamanic, or other groups of priests, witches or warriors, follows a similar pattern but with a more elaborate and distinctive indoctrination of the individual. In these ceremonies the demonstration of some magical, divine, or shamanic power by the

> *The hero becomes seized with power, he becomes heated, baptized with fire.*

initiate is looked for as a sign that he has attained the appropriate characteristics of a god, animal, or spirit. A transcendent existence, and the powers that go with it, replace the mere human condition. In most hero legends the young warrior characteristically undergoes an experience of a sacred, mystical kind that gives him superhuman powers or magical elements that he can use in his ordeal. The tasks that are set to those who hope to win the hand of the beautiful princess in the classical fairy tales depend on more than normal attributes in the performer. The hero becomes seized with power, he becomes heated, baptized with fire. Mircea Eliade (1907–1986) describes how in Germanic secret societies, the young man became a berserker in a frenzy of fury: 'He became "heated" to an extreme degree, flooded by a mysterious, nonhuman, and irresistible force.' The initiation of the Kwakiutl Indian warrior in British Columbia involves a similar frenzy of possession and heating and the same

Cuchulainn and the Brown Bull, by Karl Beutel (2003) depicts the heroic young warrior of Irish legend. The image is based on the tale of Ireland's warrior champion and the great bull of Ulster.

thing is recorded in the Irish hero legends of Cuchulainn or the Greek and Indo-European initiations of cultural hero figures.

Rebirth through Pain

Trials of strength and endurance, as tests of fitness to share the sacred membership with the ancestors or folk heroes, are common to all initiations. Formal learning and preparation for the new status in the 'initiation school' is only part of the experience that is bound up with a complex of fear, awe, and dread in face of the mysteries. The adult must be brave in the face of danger and must be steadfast in the face of pain. Consequently the novice is subjected to the fearful noise of the Melanesian bull-roarer—a wooden instrument that makes a booming sound—or to the beating with stinging nettles, and the dropping of hornets on to their backs which the Naudi adolescents in East Africa experience.

The common experience of fear and pain provides an important social bond between the novices who have survived the experience. They are incorporated into a group distinguished sharply from outsiders who have not shared in the ordeal. By having passed through the sacred experience they have attained a new status prescribed by tradition. Their circumcision, the decoration of their skin by cuts, their ordeals in the initiation school, their skill as warriors, show that they are boys no longer but men ready to take a full part in the life of the community.

One Melanesian experience described by R. M. Berndt includes a progressive series of nose bleedings caused by slivers of bamboo that are covered with salt and then twirled in the nostrils. The tongue is also cut and the penis rubbed with rough, abrasive leaves. By the time he is eighteen or twenty years old the young man is introduced to penis bleeding caused by progressively larger objects pushed into

Glove made of palm leaves, used for initiation rituals of the Sataré-Mawé people, Brazil

the urethra and twirled. Some of the puberty rites for girls include similar insertions into the vagina to cause bleeding. These rites demonstrate strength (if a man's penis is strong his arrows will be also) while blood has importance both as a symbolic representation of menstruation and of the religious and magical qualities associated with sexual elements.

Masculinity Trials and Secret Societies

The ritual rapes of Kikuyu warrior bands following circumcision have attracted a certain amount of notoriety, particularly when English women living in the Kenyan highlands were the victims. The explanation for the ceremonial rape lies in the need of the young men to purify themselves after the initiation rites. This could be achieved by passing on the 'contagion' to a woman through intercourse before they could return to the group to claim a wife of their own. Often a band of young men wandered the countryside far away from their homes until they found a woman who was of married status and a stranger to them.

Initiates of American young male groups are often involved in acts of 'dares.' Apart from tests of skill and daring, initiates in organized groups, such as fraternities, are often subjected to debasing ceremonies of an equivalent kind. Initiates of one fraternity must wear an iron ball and chain

padlocked to their ankles for a week, others must wear women's or children's clothing or have their hair cut in a special way. Another quite common practice involved an initiate being taken to a deserted spot often at a considerable distance and there left without clothing or money (or with a minimum of each) to see if he could get back.

Similar, less formal initiation rites are conducted in most social groupings to emphasize the common and shared trials through which members have passed and on which their solidarity is based. A typical newspaper report (*Daily Telegraph*), from the 1970s, describes the bullying of a sixteen-year-old garage hand on his first day at work. After a certain amount of general ragging of the 'new boy' he was tied up and petrol was sprinkled round him and set alight. In this case he was badly burned but it was noted in the court hearing that he had submitted willingly—recognizing that this kind of initiation ritual was a condition of his acceptance by his workmates.

Tests of endurance, strength, ridicule, and fear are used in the more elaborate initiation 'schools' as a means of emphasizing and disciplining the novice as he learns the cultic knowledge and mysteries of the group. An important feature of many initiation ceremonies, especially in the secret preparation period or 'school,' involves the use of figurines symbolizing traditional magical or religious characters, ancestors, or elements in the total knowledge and moral structure of the society. These figurines are often carefully guarded by the members of a particular group and are not allowed to be seen by those who have not been initiated. They have spiritual significance and consequently are carefully guarded from enemies. The special rituals appropriate to each are similarly reserved for fear that the sacred objects might be angered or polluted by those who had no right to see them, or did not know 'how to behave' in their presence. The sacraments are similarly reserved in the Christian Church for those who have become full members.

Lessons in Sex

Initiation figurines are either kept as part of a store of sacred objects or are fashioned anew for each group of novices. Examples from East Africa include instructive, cautionary and punitive figures. They are all associated with songs, proverbs, or riddles that the novice must learn. One example of a simple and obvious kind is the model of a hare used by the Sambaa as part of the rites for boys. The teaching that is depicted is that it is foolish to be quarrelsome and the associated words state that the hare is cleverer than most animals but he is never anxious to start a fight. A large majority of the figurines are used to convey lessons about sexual behaviour or morality and here again proverbs are taught to the initiates to define correct behaviour. A good example of such a riddle is shown in the female figurine used by the Zigua with a riddle that runs: 'There is only one person who laughs when she should mourn and who rejoices in her loss,' to which the answer is 'A girl on her wedding night.' As well as being used in puberty ceremonies, these figurines are used in the entry rites to secret societies and associations. Clay or wooden figures are handled ritually and associated with a fixed form

of words sung or recited. Again the objects depict familiar social roles, or common objects as well as highly stylized art with a very complex symbolism. The figures and the form of words are treated as sacred and are kept secret from those who are not initiated.

The initiation schools and the lengthy process of disciplined teaching of the lessons associated with the puberty rituals in tribal societies have inevitably been affected by social change. Often lack of time and the constraints of formal education or occupation have meant that both the ceremonies and the training period of the initiation must be curtailed. Where figurines are used the number may be limited or the verses only will be learned. These effects of social change only serve to emphasize the important and complex function served by the initiation of adolescents in tribal society. They ensured that each individual was fully educated in the central belief system, moral codes, and normative standards of the society, and was intellectually as well as emotionally prepared for adulthood.

One particular set of initiation ceremonies involves the installation of new incumbents into various offices. Kings, chiefs, presidents, and professors are all expected to observe formal ritual procedures and take part in ceremonies connected with their assumption of the prerogatives of office. Coronation ceremonies are an elaborate example of the combination of rituals designed to acknowledge formally and acclaim publicly and anoint the one chosen for the office. Part of the ceremony usually involves admission to a ritually appointed place or locus of office. The professor has no actual 'chair' but a bishop has a cathedral throne and knights of orders of chivalry are ceremonially led to their stalls in the chapel of their orders. Similarly with a mayor or president, the office holder is sanctified with the symbolic

elements of authority: orb and sceptre, crown and sword, seal or gavel. These objects signify that the incumbent has been properly chosen, indoctrinated, and acquainted with the mysteries that surround the office. The laying on of hands, the anointment, represents the conferring of divine or magical power which alone sets the initiated incumbent of office 'apart.' Where the succession to office is hereditary, or where the successor is selected in childhood (as in the case of the Dalai Lama before the Chinese invasion of Tibet), the whole process of growing up forms an overall initiation which points toward the eventual attainment of office.

Humiliation and Abuse

Much of the ritual surrounding the initiation of new holders of office shares the characteristics that have been noted in the rites surrounding puberty. The symbolic death of the old and rebirth to the new condition and status is represented in the divesting of original clothing, and the profane objects of life. The new ruler, as in the coronation ceremony of the British monarch, assumes a new royal robe as well as other symbols of office: orb or sceptre, crown, and sword.

Some of the ceremonies are dignified and formal, enshrined with pomp and circumstance, but it is significant that even the most solemn occasions also have a festive and irreverent side in which 'the gods are mocked.'

The chancellors of Scottish universities, elected by the students, however honoured and dignified, endure a bombardment of flour, missiles, and abuse as part of their inaugural ceremony, and it is customary for the professors at some US universities to be subjected to similar horseplay. These examples show clearly the conflicting and complementary elements of debasement and honouring that characterize the initiation process. Just as we

Initiation ceremony in a Viennese Masonic Lodge, during the reign of Joseph II

have seen with puberty rites, the candidate must be 'cut down to size' and divested of his former status before he can assume the new. The experience of the army recruit is no different once he joins up. The admonition 'Get your hair cut—you're in the Army now' demonstrates the removal of the civilian status and the assumption of the new status of 'soldier' with uniform, dress, style, regulations, and equipment just as clearly.

Modern examples of initiation rituals abound and demonstrate many of the features already noted. In some cases the ceremonies are merely vestigial remnants of earlier, more elaborate and public rituals, involving the whole community. Infant baptism 'casts out the devil'

and 'makes new' and the baptismal water is an indication of the washing away of sin. Adult initiations in some churches often involve baptisms by total immersion and 'speaking in tongues,' spiritual trance and 'possession' in the new member. The transcendental religious or magical recognition of the new member both fortifies the faith of the group and signifies that the initiation procedure was correctly performed.

The organization of fraternities and sororities probably has been most fully elaborated in the Western world in bodies such as the Masonic Order, Guilds, Knights, and more recently formed bodies, most of which claim ancient lineage such as the Orange Lodges, the Lions, Elks, and many

others. Freemasonry is defined in the ritual of symbolism associated with great religious orders and categories of progressive initiations in ancient Egyptian, Hindu, and Buddhist traditions. Similarities have been pointed out between the Eighteenth Degree of the Freemasons, 'Knight of the Pelican and Eagle and Sovereign Prince Rose Croix of Heredom' to which any Master Mason of one year's standing is eligible, and the initiation rites of the Australian Bora aborigines. The symbolic teaching of this degree describes the passage of man through the valley of the shadow of death, accompanied by the Masonic virtues of Faith, Hope, and Charity and his final acceptance into the abode of light, life, and immortality.

A Jewish boy reading the Torah during his Bar Mitzvah

Symbolic Social Statement

Just as in the initiation ceremonies of secret societies, in simpler societies membership represents a distinct and far-reaching social statement about the individual. Being adult or being a Mason or being a Baptist or being a witch represent far more than the mere labels. They are involved statements about the whole society and the place and significance of different groups within the society; statements that have significance in all those aspects of the social structure in which particular kinds of belonging can be a means of articulating social relations. The questions of whom you may marry, where you can live, or whom may you work with when belonging to the Roman Catholic Church or the Loyal Orange Order become the

prime defining characteristics of life in Northern Ireland; or being a Jew or an Arab define sharply the possible relationships in a situation of conflict in the Middle East. Where 'belonging' in this sense is open to the individual the significance of the transition from

The emerging initiate is reborn in a symbolic and spiritual way. The return announces that the mystery of rebirth has been accomplished.

one condition to another is very apparent. Those who have succeeded in the world of espionage are acutely conscious of the dimensions and social significance of the new roles they have chosen to adopt. But even in these

rather mundane examples, the questions are not simply social in the sense of setting out rules of behaviour. They are symbolic, as all social statements are inevitably symbolic, because they are statements about man, the world, the cosmos, and the possibilities of human existence, as well as statements about life and death. It is precisely in those areas where the maintenance of distinct boundaries is most important to the people in a particular society that one finds a particular emphasis on their maintenance and on the proper observation of the boundary-crossing rituals of initiation.

In some societies age distinctions may be pivotal, in most societies sex differences, and in many societies differences of race or ethnic origin or language may serve to demarcate structurally the bounds of social relationships. In many societies the division between male and female is sharply observed in territorial definitions of space in the settlement or living quarters. Male and female areas for eating, washing, and defecation are reserved and this latter distinction can be seen also in contemporary Western societies. A good example is the division by sex of public lavatories and the recognition that for very small children the rigid differences generally observed are considered unimportant. The point of importance is that these particular divisions are pivotal for the world view of these particular societies. It is not surprising that one finds fraternities of men or sororities of woman's groups of one kind or another that as distinct sex groups serve the important function of emphasizing and symbolizing these distinctions that their own initiation into the particular group both recognizes and supports.

In her interesting book *Purity and Danger* Mary Douglas (1921–2007) shows how important is the act of separation between sacred things, places, and persons from the profane or polluting world. All religious groups, cults, and societies develop a conscious boundary between those who have membership and those who do not. Fear of malevolent or benevolent spirits or beings often characterizes the concern with which it is felt necessary to observe the proper 'passage' ceremonies that connect these two states. Quite apart from the examples of initiation that we have already discussed, birth and death are surrounded by similar ritual observations designed to placate various forces that may have an influence on the destiny of the child or the dead person. Even in tribal societies no necessary claim will be made for these rites as essential and empirical measures that

will bring the desired result. However, man is not only a practical being and even in contemporary societies initiation ceremonies convey the mixture of beliefs at a variety of levels—mystical, magical, metaphysical, and religious, as well as scientific—which can coexist without difficulty in the same individual and group.

Initiation rituals surrounding death are often elaborate, both at the level of preparation and in the way in which the dead are treated. There are numerous examples in the rites of burial of the placing of money in the hand or mouth to secure the passage of the dead across the Styx that illustrate that the characteristics of initiation are found here as well. Burial in the foetal position also symbolizes the recognition of rebirth following death.

Death and rebirth characterize the features of all initiation rites. This is illustrated in boys' puberty initiation schools and it is found equally in the often less developed puberty rites for girls. Girls' ceremonies tend to involve a less intentional process than those of boys that represent a more deliberate introduction to a world of spirit and culture. For girls, as Eliade points out 'initiation involves a series of revelations concerning the secret meaning of a phenomenon that is apparently natural—the visible sign of their sexual maturity.'

This does not preclude considerable emphasis being given to some female puberty rites in certain societies. The Dyaks exemplify this in the separation and isolation of girls for a whole year in a white cabin, dressed in white and only eating white foods. This separation—the wilderness experience—recognizes the fact that during this period the initiate is 'nothing,' neither man nor woman, asexual. Together with other separations—Christ's forty days in the wilderness—it is a condition of the attainment of spirituality. The emerging initiate is reborn in a

symbolic and spiritual way. The return announces that the mystery of rebirth has been accomplished. Eliade gives the example of the Kavirondo Bantu to illustrate a characteristic imagery found also in Brahmanic initiation in India and the recognition of the double character of birth in the egg from which the chick emerges. It is said of the Kavirondo initiates when they complete their ritual: 'The white chick is now creeping out of the egg, we are like newly fired pots.'

Journeys through the Dark

The soul (at the point of death) has the same experience as those who are being initiated into great mysteries . . . At first one wanders and wearily hurries to and fro, and journeys with suspicion through the dark as one uninitiated: then come all the terrors before the final initiation, shuddering, trembling, sweating, amazement: then one is struck with a marvelous light, one is received into pure regions and meadows, with voices and dances and the majesty of holy sounds and shapes: among these he who has fulfilled initiation wanders free, and released and bearing his crown joins in the divine communion, and consorts with pure and holy men, beholding those who live here uninitiated, an uncleansed horde, trodden under foot of him and huddled together in mud and fog, abiding their miseries through fear of death and mistrust of the blessings there.

Attributed to Plutarch
(trans. George E. Mylonas)
Initiation into the mysteries of Isis:
. . . I will record as much as I may lawfully record for the uninitiated, but only on condition that you believe it. I approached the very gates of death and set one foot on Proserpine's threshold, yet was permitted to return, rapt through all the elements. At midnight I saw the sun shining as if it were noon: I entered the presence of the gods of the underworld and the gods of the upper-world, stood near and worshipped them. Well, now you have heard what happened but I fear you are still none the wiser.

Apuleius *The Golden Ass*
(trans. Robert Graves)

One final example will serve to illustrate something of the elaborate character of initiation mythology. An ascetic period of isolation is characteristic of many Native American initiations. The novice leaves the community in order to obtain those dreams and visions that will identify for him a particular spirit with which he will then continue to be associated. He will fast and exhaust himself until the spirit appears to him, usually in animal form. Once he has achieved this personal sacred experience he can return to the tribe, having died to be reborn with his guiding spirit.

The Dancing Societies of the Kwakiutl Indians studied by F. Boas show a more elaborate version of the same isolating and sacralizing experience. The ritual commences with the initiate falling into a trance to signify his death to the profane world. He is then carried off to be initiated by the spirits. He may be taken to a cave or to a special hut in which the spirit lives. An extreme example is that of the Cannibal Society where as part of the initiation the candidate is served by a woman while he is secluded in the forest. He is identified with the god and demonstrates this by swallowing strips of a corpse that she prepares for him. His cannibalism is a reversal of the horror of the Kwakiutl for human flesh. To overcome this revulsion he must indeed be divine and the similar acts of frenzy in which he engages on his return serve also to demonstrate this possession by the god.

In the final ceremony he acts like a beast of prey attacking all he can reach, biting their arms. He is almost impossible to restrain but finally is subdued after the woman who served him in the wilderness dances naked before

him with a corpse in her arms. His frenzy is finally subdued by repeated immersions in salt water and his new personality and identity is achieved.

J. A. JACKSON

FURTHER READING: M. Eliade. Rites and Symbols of Initiation. *(Gloucester, MA: Peter Smith); J. Henderson.* Thresholds of Initiation. *(Middletown, CT: Wesleyan University Press, 1967); G. Herdt, ed.* Rituals of Manhood. *(Berkeley, CA: University of California Press, 1982); A. van Gennep.* Rites of Passage. *(Chicago, IL: University of Chicago Press).*

Left

Traditionally the side of evil; probably because the left hand is normally the weaker; black magic is 'the left-hand path' and to move deliberately to the left in magic is to appeal to evil influences; the Latin word *sinister* meant both 'left' and 'evil:' in palmistry the left hand represents what you are born with, the right what you make of yourself.

Light

On the night of September 21, 1823, at his house in Palmyra, New York, Joseph Smith, then a boy of 17, was deep in prayer. 'While I was thus in the act of calling upon God, I discovered a light appearing in my room, which continued to increase until the room was lighter than at noonday, when immediately a personage appeared at my bedside, standing in the air . . . Not only was his robe exceedingly white, but his whole person was glorious beyond description, and his countenance truly like lightning. The room was exceedingly light, but not so very bright as immediately around his person. When I first looked

upon him I was afraid; but the fear soon left me.' This radiant personage was the angel Moroni, who told Joseph Smith where to find the buried golden plates of the Book of Mormon.

In religion, legend, and symbolism light is primarily connected with good and with creative power. Gods and saints are said to radiate light; 'illumination' is a term frequently used for the revelation or discovery of the divine, not merely talking symbolically but, as in the case of Joseph Smith, as a description of an experience, an encounter with light.

Among the first experiences of a baby must presumably be the sensation of coming out of darkness into light, and all our lives one of the fixed characteristics of our environment is the alternation of light and darkness, on which we pattern the basic rhythm of our lives. In daylight we are active, at night we turn off our conscious energies and go to sleep. Light lets us see, darkness walls us in and makes us blind, groping, and afraid. The light and heat of the sun bring Nature to life in the spring, the winter comes in with darkness and cold.

As a result, light has come to mean good, activity, creativity, spiritual vision, while darkness means evil, fear and doubt, inactivity, sterility, and spiritual blindness. What is done in the light of day is open and innocent, but what is done in the dark is secret, furtive, harmful, or shameful. The crowing of the cock at the first glimmer of dawn puts to flight the evil beings which infest the night.

However, nothing, in symbolism or in reality, is as simple as this clear cut antithesis. The darkness of love-making, of dreams, of the womb or the depths of the mind, has its own powerful fruitfulness. Light can be the life-creating radiance of the sun but also the scorching and destroying flame that withers the desert (which, conversely again, may be a symbol of revelation and the presence of God in the wilderness of asceticism). Ghosts emit a faint and ghastly radiance, the luminescence of putrefaction. The flickering will-o'-the-wisp leads the unwary traveler astray. Satan puts on the guise of an angel of light.

Let There Be Light

People generally seem to feel that darkness precedes light. Darkness is somehow older, more primitive, more fundamental, and light penetrates a darkness that was there before it. 'From nonbeing lead me to being,' says the *Bradaranyaka Upanishad*, 'from darkness lead me to the light, from death lead me to immortality.' For the Jews and Arabs, the Germanic peoples, the Celts, and many others, each day begins in the evening—the night comes first and the light afterward.

Similarly at the very beginning of things: 'at first,' according to a creation hymn in the *Rig Veda*, there was only darkness wrapped in darkness.' In Hesiod's *Theogony*, 'Out of Void came Darkness and black Night, and out of Night came Light and Day, her children.' In Genesis, in the beginning there was darkness and God said: 'Let there be light.' It was only after making light that God went on to fashion his other creations.

Some people have maintained the opposite tradition, that light existed first and darkness came later. One explanation of why this happened is that the Creator grew weary of endless light and created darkness for relief.

Others say that light and darkness have coexisted from the beginning. In China the two great opposites of

Yang and Yin correspond to light and darkness respectively.

According to a Scandinavian myth, there was a great abyss of emptiness, charged with magic power. To the south of it was a realm of blazing heat and to the north a realm of freezing darkness. It was the meeting in the abyss of ice from the north and sparks from the south which made life, so that creation resulted from mingling of opposites, of light with dark and heat with cold. But when the *Prose Edda* comes to deal with day and night, night existed first and was the mother of day.

The Armour of Light

In the Bible, light is connected with God and goodness. 'There are many who say, O that we might see some good! Lift up the light of thy counte-

Exterior of Carthage Jail by C. C. A. Christensen, depicting the death of Joseph Smith, Jr. By some accounts Smith was shot several times after he fell from the window, but a beam of sunlight from parting clouds prevented a mobster from decapitating Smith's body.

nance upon us, O Lord!' (Psalm 4). When God becomes king over the whole Earth, there will be perpetual light and warmth: 'there shall be neither cold nor night, for at evening time there shall be light' (Zechariah, chapter 14). But God manifests himself not only in light and lightning but also in smoke and darkness. When the Israelites were in the wilderness and camped below Mount Sinai, there was a thick cloud on the mountain and a violent thunderstorm with flashes of lightning. 'And Mount Sinai was wrapped in smoke, because the Lord descended on it in fire and the smoke of it went up like the smoke of a kiln, and the whole mountain quaked greatly . . . And the people stood afar off, while Moses drew near to the thick darkness where God was' (Exodus, chapters 19, 20). Again, in the vision of God's glory in Ezekiel (chapter 1), 'a stormy wind came out of the north, and a great cloud with brightness round about it, and fire flashing forth continually . . .'

In other passages, to be in a state of sin, to be far from God, is to be in darkness, and in the New Testament, Christ is 'the true light that enlightens every man' (John 1.9), which echoes a famous verse in Isaiah (9.2): The people that walked in darkness have seen a great light.' Jesus said: 'I am the light of the world; he who follows me will not walk in darkness, but will have the light of life' (John, chapter 8). For God sent the Son into the world,' says St. John (chapter 3), 'not to condemn the world, but that the world might be saved through him . . . And this is the judgment, that the light has come into the world, and men loved darkness rather than light because their deeds were evil.'

A Light to Lighten the Gentiles
The missionary work that took Christianity outside Judaism was seen as the bringing of light to the Gentiles.

During the Hindu festival Diwali, lamps are lit to signify the triumph of light over darkness

Warning the faithful to be ready for Christ's imminent return to the earth, St. Paul says, 'Let us then cast off the works of darkness and put on the armour of light' (Romans 13.12). Light of Light became one of the titles of Christ, and the Devil, by contrast, was regarded as chief of the powers of darkness.

The same general imagery of light as good and darkness as evil appears from the start with Islam in the Koran. 'Allah is the light of the heavens and the earth,' but the doings of unbelievers are like 'darkness on a bottomless ocean spread with clashing billows and overcast with clouds; darkness upon darkness . . . Indeed the man from whom Allah withholds his light shall find no light at all' (sura 24).

In Zoroastrianism, with its rival gods of good and evil, the contrast of light and darkness is sharply drawn. The good god Ohrmazd lives in eternal light. 'That light is the space and place of Ohrmazd . . . omniscience and goodness are his totality.' His opponent Ahriman is the master of darkness, 'the will to smite is his all, and darkness is his place.' In the end, when Ahriman has been defeated, 'all Ohrmazd's creation will be reunited with him in the eternal light and in

unceasing joy forever and ever.'

In ancient Greek religion there is a contrast—though no real distinction between good and evil—between the Olympian gods who lived in a 'comprehensible and businesslike atmosphere of daylight,' and the chthonian powers who lived underground, shrouded in mystery and approached by night. Behind this is the contrast between the worship of sky gods who live in the light of day, and the worship of the Great Mother whose roots are deep in the darkness of the earth.

The Divine Spark
The Manicheans, who were Zoroastrian heretics, taught that there were two eternal and uncreated entities, God and Matter, which could also be called Light and Darkness. Through a series of mythological events, the powers of darkness were able to seize some particles of the divine light, which meant that they had captured part of the essence of God. To keep these ill-gotten spoils, they fashioned Adam and Eve, in whom they imprisoned the captive light. Adam and Eve were ignorant of the nature of the light within them, until they were redeemed by a heavenly messenger, himself sometimes called 'Jesus the brilliant light.'

The theme of the divine spark, the gleam of heavenly light imprisoned in man and matter, also appears in the Gnostic systems of the southern and eastern Mediterranean and has had a profound influence on mysticism and occultism in the West. It is a way of expressing the belief that in a man's innermost being there is an element of the divine. The discovery and liberation of this inner potential godhead, the true self, is a basic theme of European magical practice.

A magician is usually very ready to think of himself as a potential god, but for a mystic the problem is to avoid putting man on a level with God while claiming that there is a divine element in human nature. In the fourteenth century, for instance, Meister Eckhart (1260–1328) said that there is a spark of divine light in man but emphasized that his soul is a mere receptacle of God's light. A German Protestant mystic of the sixteenth century, Hans Denck, said: 'No man can see or know himself, unless he sees and knows, by the Life and Light that is in him, God, the eternally true Light and Life . . . He must find God in himself, and himself in God.' And again, 'The Kingdom of God is in you [a reference to Luke 17.21] and he who searches for it outside himself will never find it; God, the all-highest, is in the deepest abyss with us, and is waiting for us to return to him.'

In the seventeenth century, the doctrine of the 'inner light,' the divine light within each human being, was central to the teaching of George Fox, founder of the Quakers, and his first followers were sometimes known as 'Children of Light.' In the eighteenth century William Law (1686–1761) took up the same theme: 'Consider the treasure thou hast within thee: the Saviour of the world, the eternal Word of God lies hid in thee, as a spark of the divine Nature.'

The Splendid Lights

In the Cabala, the process through which the hidden God makes himself known is described in terms shot through with the imagery of light. It begins with a concentration of divine energy in a 'luminous point' or a point 'dark with luminosity.' The sefiroth, which are aspects of God and stages in the process of divine self-revelation, are called 'splendid lights' in the *Zohar*, and God is 'an absolute light but in himself concealed and incomprehen-

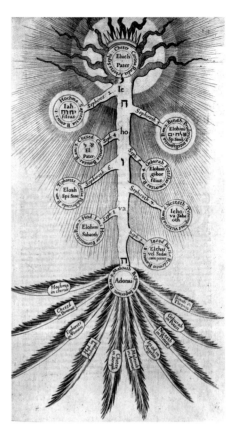

Cabalists believe the Tree of Life to represent how the Universe came into being.

sible,' comprehended only through the 'luminous emanations' of the sefiroth. The Zohar also contains the doctrine of the divine spark, the vital element in man that can eventually find reunion with God from whom it came. According to the Lurianic Cabala the light of the godhead retracted itself, to create a vacuum into which God infused his light. But the vessels containing the light shattered and some of the divine sparks fell into chaos.

In the early Church baptism, the initiation into Christianity, was described as 'illumination' and it was the custom for candidates at the baptism service to carry torches. Perhaps this symbolism was borrowed from the mystery religions, for at the climax of the Eleusinian Mysteries there was a sudden blaze of torches.

The Encounter with Light

The illumination is sometimes not a metaphor but an experience. When the apostles received the gift of the

Holy Spirit on the day of Pentecost, 'a sound came from heaven like the rush of the mighty wind, and it filled all the house where they were sitting. And there appeared to them tongues as of fire, distributed and resting on each one of them' (Acts, chapter 2). St. Paul was converted on the road to Damascus, when 'a light from heaven flashed about him' and he heard the voice of Jesus (Acts, chapter 9).

The sight of light playing on the surface of a dish stimulated in Jacob Boehme a mystical experience which he called a 'spiritual triumph' and which could only be compared with 'that where life is born in the midst of death.' Ghazali, the great Mohammedan mystic, was saved from skepticism by 'a light that God threw into my breast.' In the Indian tradition, among the experiences of the adept who successfully awakens the *kundalini* is 'a vision of light, which passes from a bright glow to a heaven full of brilliant dots, like stars,' eventually followed by a 'suffusion of shining whiteness that is . . . an awareness of the supreme Radiance itself.

Mircea Eliade (1907–1986) says that 'for Indian thought, the Light mystically perceived denotes transcendence of this world, of profane and conditioned existence, and the attainment of another existential plane— that of pure being, of the divine, of supreme knowledge and absolute freedom. It is a certain sign of the revelation of ultimate reality—devoid of all attributes. This is why it is experienced as a dazzling white Light . . .'

In the *Mahabharata*, the god Vishnu reveals himself in a flash of lightning as bright as the light of a thousand suns. In the *Bhagavad Gita*, when the god Krishna shows himself in his true form, he is compared to the radiance of a thousand suns shining at once. 'I see the splendour of an infinite beauty which illuminates the whole universe. It is thee with thy crown and scepter and circle. How difficult thou art to see! But I see thee; as fire, as the sun, blinding, incomprehensible.'

Light of Battle

That divine beings radiate light is accepted in all the major religions. There is a Buddhist legend that a crowd of gods went to visit Buddha, meditating in a cave. The cave was filled with brilliant light; some said this was the radiance of the gods but others said it came from the ecstasy of the Buddha himself. In Japan, Amida is 'Lord of Boundless Light,' his head encircled by a halo more glorious than the sun at noon. Mohammed's face shone with its own light.

The face of Jesus shone like the sun and his garments became as white as light when he was transfigured on the mountain and the voice of God pronounced, 'This is my beloved Son' (Matthew, chapter 17). In Christian art the Father, Son, Virgin Mary, and the saints have radiant haloes and the Holy Spirit emits rays of light.

Sanctity emanates light and in legends so do beauty and blood-lust. There are Indian folk stories of a prince who marries a woman so lovely that she lights up the bridal chamber on the wedding night. In the *Iliad* (book 18), when Achilles went out in

Jesus Christ is depicted as having a halo of light around his head

A mask probably representing a shamans spirit flight, with the face in the centre representing the shamans soul

fury against the Trojans, the goddess Athene 'shed a golden mist around his head and caused his body to emit a blaze of light.' When the great Irish hero Cu Chulainn was roused in battle, the warrior's light rose from his forehead as long and as thick as a whetstone. We talk of the 'light of battle' being in someone's eye. Similarly, the 'heat of battle' is a familiar figure of speech and when Cu Chulainn's terrifying battle frenzy was upon him, the heat he radiated was so intense that he boiled and burst two vats of water.

The radiating light of sacredness is also the light of spiritual vision. Eliade quotes Inuit shamans who say that you cannot become a shaman without

going through the 'illumination' or 'lightning.' The shaman suddenly feels in his head and body a mysterious light, 'an inexplicable searchlight, a luminous fire.' This light enables him to see in the dark, not only literally but in the sense that he becomes clairvoyant. He also has the sensation of rising.

This rising sensation is one of the marks of being in what Western occultists call the astral body or 'body of light.' The astral plane is said to include but extend beyond the physical plane of our everyday world, and the astral light transmits the rays of human willpower, thought and imagination. In Jungian terms, it is the medium of the archetypes, the basic ideas of the

collective unconscious. In the astral plane thought, fancy, and emotion have the same reality as a solid object on the physical plane, and the astral light is like a great reservoir of occult power. Every human thought makes an impact on the astral light, it is said, and in it the seer can read the history of the past in the Akashic Record or Cosmic Memory.

RICHARD CAVENDISH

FURTHER READING: T. Brill. Light: Its Interaction With Art and Antiquities. *(New York, NY: Plenum, 1980); Mircea Eliade.* The Two and the One. *(Chicago, IL: University of Chicago Press, 1979); Israel Regardie.*

The Tree of Life. *(York Beach, ME: Weiser, 1969).*

Marriage and Betrothal

When marriages were arranged for practical reasons, rather than for love, child brides were usual. St. Elizabeth of Hungary, betrothed at the age of four to an eleven-year-old bridegroom in 1211, was carried to his home in a silver cradle, and Mary Villiers, a ward of Charles I, was already widowed by the time she was nine years old; soon after her husband's death she was seen climbing trees in her black dress, pretending to be a bird.

Since the purpose of such marriages was to ensure the union of prominent families, children were sometimes betrothed soon after birth. Although betrothal, the binding promise of marriage, has little significance for us today, it was at one time an occasion for considerable ceremony. In Greek Macedonia, for example, it was conducted with prayers and exchange of rings, in the presence of a matchmaker, the priest, family, and friends. The bride offered her married relatives the traditional formal refreshments—jam, coffee, alcohol—and presented the groom's parents and the matchmaker with socks she had knitted herself. They thanked her with the customary greeting: 'Mayest thou enjoy the kerchief in good health.' During Cheese Week, which immediately preceded Lent, the young man sent his betrothed sweet cakes, and on the eve of Easter she received gifts of a coloured candle and Easter eggs.

The nomadic Vlachs, a people scattered through the Balkans, arranged for a group of friends and relations, acting on behalf of the groom, to call at the home of the bride. There they found a low table covered with fine cloth and laid with three soup plates.

Two of these contained sweets. The third, which was empty, had to be filled with gold, sometimes made into a necklace. It is still a common Balkan custom for a woman to wear her betrothal gift in this fashion. When the groom's party returned, they threw flour over him, wishing him a long life with the words: 'May you grow white like this flour.' Meanwhile, the same custom was performed for the bride, by her family.

In seventeenth century Holland the betrothed couple was required to sit together on a bed and kiss each other in the presence of both families; the ceremony was ratified by exchange of rings. These were very big, sometimes engraved with suitable pictures, and sometimes, like the English gemmel ring, formed of two parallel circles. The halves, separated between the partners at the betrothal, were joined together as a wedding ring for the marriage ceremony. To pledge fidelity, the couple would cut themselves and drink each other's blood; or they might use the blood to make a written declaration. In England, halving a coin was a popular custom. A character in a play called *The Country Wake* (1696) says:

'I asked her the question last Lammas, and at Allhallows-tide we broke a piece of money.' The straw true-lover's knot was another token of fidelity, in use within living memory. A young man prepared two, one for himself and one for his sweetheart. If she pinned hers over her heart, this meant she had chosen him, and they wore the knots until their wedding day. The girl might also be presented with a sprig of the plant Lad's Love; if she threw it away, her lover had been rejected, but to smell it was a sign of acceptance.

A young man from the fens would present a fur tippet to his sweetheart. This was a narrow fur stole, prepared by the lover from animal skins, which he had obtained and cured himself. The couple stitched the hide to a silk lining, stuffed it with sheep's wool, and inside each end placed a sachet containing a little pubic hair: the man's on the right, the woman's on the left. When worn, the criss-crossed ends covered the woman's heart, and the little packets inside ensured a happy married life.

In many countries marriage is a social obligation, and anyone remaining single is frowned upon. The ancient Jews had no word in their vocabulary

A wedding takes place in the Brunei-Muara district of Brunei

for bachelor, and the Poles used to ridicule anyone unmarried beyond the proper age. Nonetheless, it was not always so easy to obtain a wife, and a young man might have to earn her by working for his prospective parents-in-law: 'So Jacob served seven years for Rachel, and they seemed unto him but a few days because of the love he had for her' (Genesis, chapter 29.20).

This ancient custom persists today. Among the Eskimos of St. Lawrence Island, Alaska, the boy works one year for his sweetheart's family, carrying water, gathering driftwood, chopping ice, assisting with hunting, and generally proving his willingness to work for them and his ability to provide for a family. But if the girl is already pregnant, the couple is usually married as quickly as possible.

Bundling and Hand fasting

Anticipation of the intimacies of marriage was not so frowned upon in the past as one might suppose, since betrothal was often considered to be nearly as binding as marriage. The early seventeenth century Puritan settlers of New England practiced bundling, a custom known variously in England, Scotland, Ireland, and Wales, as well as Holland, Norway, and probably elsewhere. The parents of a New England girl who was courting permitted the couple to spend the night together in her bedroom. The pair who were expected to behave with reasonable propriety, wore all their clothes and were occasionally separated by additional layers of bedding. This custom, which seems to have begun dying out in the United States during the eighteenth century, was still common within living memory in England in Cambridgeshire, where it was introduced by Irish labourers.

In seventeenth century Holland bundling was known as *queesten*. Suitors on Texel Island traditionally arrived through the window and, since this necessitated smashing the pane, few houses had all their windows unbroken. Although couples met in the girl's bed, it was again intended that propriety should be observed. The girl lay on the sheet, the boy between sheet and cover. Nearby an iron vessel and a pair of fire tongs were ready for her to sound the alarm if the young man became too bold. Parents usually approved of the custom since it was thought an honour for their daughter to receive these visits. The call might last all night, and if a pregnancy resulted the baby was taken along to its parents' wedding, concealed beneath the mother's cloak, though clearly visible for everyone to see. Today, in the Calvinist village of Staphorst, trial marriage is still practiced and custom decrees that a couple marry only when there is evidence of a pregnancy.

In Scotland 'hand fasting' also provided a testing period. Young men

The Peasant Wedding, by the Flemish Renaissance painter Pieter Bruegel (c. 1567).

and women chose a companion at a fair held annually in Dumfries, and lived together until the following year. If it was a success, they married; if not, they were free to take another partner. A priest nicknamed Book-in-the-Bosom, perhaps because he carried a marriage register, arrived periodically to solemnize these weddings.

There is usually no difficulty about arranging marriage for an attractive girl or man, but it may be a problem in cases of deformity or physical defect. In Poland such a man was betrothed to a relative and the banns read out in church, not with any real intention of marriage, but simply to make it known that he was eligible.

Calling the banns is an important preliminary to marriage and the English language is full of dialect expressions for this custom. In Lincolnshire it was known as 'spurring.' If the banns had been read once, people said: 'Why thoo's gotten one spur on thee!' and two banns were 'A pair of spurs.' Sometimes a peal of bells, the spur peal, was rung on the day that the first bann had been called. 'Breaking a rib' was another usual phrase. 'He's gotten one rib broke,' meant that the banns had been called once; 'fallen plump out of the pulpit last Sunday,' was a Wiltshire expression. Generally speaking it was unlucky to hear one's own banns called: it meant that children of the marriage would be deaf and dumb. Similarly in Poland, should a girl hear her first banns, her pots will break after she is married.

Gifts are always an important part of any wedding, because of the exceptional expense involved, not only in setting up the newly married couple, but in the occasion itself. If a Manx couple were badly off, it was usual to place a sieve in the kitchen so that guests could drop in a coin to help with the cost of entertainment. This custom, known as a Penny Wedding, exists elsewhere in various forms.

Bride-ale was for the same purpose; the bride sold home-brewed ale to the wedding guests, who paid her lavishly.

In Scotland and the North of England a 'Bride-wain' was arranged. This meant that carts and horses were taken round the houses of friends and relatives, who gave sacks of corn, meal, wool, and anything else they could spare. Sometimes there was a ceremonial procession from the bride's old home to the new one. A wagon, loaded with household articles and furniture, set out and, as it passed by, friends threw gifts upon the load. In Lancashire, among the very poor, everyone gathered together on the day of the wedding and built the young couple a house of clay and wood, which was known as the 'clay bigging.'

If a husband was wealthy, but nonetheless did not wish to inherit any earlier debts from his wife, there was a traditional remedy. Until about one hundred years ago in England, it was commonly believed that if a bride arrived at her wedding dressed in nothing but a shift, her husband would be freed from any such obligation. Again, if the bride walked stark naked from her house to her future husband's, the same purpose would be served. During the last century a woman tried to do this at Kirton-in-Lindsey in Lincolnshire. She had intended starting out down a ladder from her bedroom window, but her courage failed her; she partially dressed while still standing at the top.

The idea of approaching one's wedding in a state of nakedness is echoed in the custom of removing old clothes and putting on a completely new set. A Vlach bridegroom would stand in a flat metal dish and strip, preparatory to donning his pristine wedding clothes. English brides too were freshly dressed from head to foot, though the requirements of the old rhyme: 'Something old, something new, something borrowed, and something blue' were

carefully observed. Today the luckiest colours for a bridal dress are white, pink, and blue. Green is thought to be especially unlucky and in parts of Scotland even green table decorations and vegetables were omitted from the bridal meal.

Food is an important feature of any wedding celebration, and certain items are essentially symbolic. Formerly in the Netherlands the bridal couple was offered salted cream sprinkled with sugar, a confection representative of the bitter and the sweet sides of married life. English wedding cake with its icing sugar and bitter almonds is said to possess the same significance. The rich mixture traditionally used in its preparation stands for fertility and abundance. Every guest must eat some and unmarried girls are supposed to sleep with a slice beneath their pillow in order to dream of their husbands-to-be. Yorkshire folk called this 'dreaming bread.' A sliver of cake used formerly to be passed nine times through a wedding ring to achieve the same result. This form of wedding divination has always been popular. Indeed as early as 1279, the Church in Poland was obliged to issue a decree forbidding its practice.

Baking and Breaking

Polish bridal couples wear pieces of cake tucked inside their blouses throughout the marriage ceremony; they must also share the first and last pieces together. Hence the ceremony of baking the bridal cake is very important. Women known to be happily married are invited to prepare the mixture, and the bride's mother receives them with vodka, sausage, ham, pickles, and cake. Only women may be present, apart from the official matchmaker, and the cake is made without salt to signify that the young couple should live together without sorrow. If the cake rises well, it is a good omen. In Macedonia three maid-

Riding The Stang from *Picturesque History Of Yorkshire* (published c. 1900) shows the Yorkshire custom of rough music, which was used to express displeasure at transgressions such as wife beating.

ens sift the flour, and three married women prepare the dough. They may put a hook and eye into the mixture, representing the male and female elements. Sometimes the bride wears two great ring-shaped cakes on her arms as she makes her way to the bridegroom's house. She breaks one when she is halfway there and the other is broken on arrival. Women eagerly seize the pieces, which they believe will assist them in childbirth.

In parts of England it was usual to break a piece of cake over the head of the bride when she returned from church; in Ireland they used an oatmeal cake, in Scotland shortbread. This was generally done by the groom. Sometimes it was thrown over the head of the bride, plate and all, and if the plate broke into many pieces, it was a good omen foretelling many children; if it failed to smash, some-

one quickly stepped on it to avert the unlucky sign.

When people were very poor, as in Ireland during the last century, the food for a wedding simply consisted of what was available; in this case, bruised potatoes, flour, oat bread, and butter. More often it was representative of fertility and abundance. For this reason, on entering her new home, a Greek bride crushed a pomegranate—a popular symbol of fruitfulness in the East—and marked the doorpost with a butter cross. The couple ascended the stairs beneath a shower of sweets, coins, barley, chickpeas, and rice. These ideas are present in our own wedding ceremonies.

The symbolism of the cereals in wedding ceremonies arises from the fact that they are basic foods in the countries where they are used. At a Polish wedding feast a flat, plaited

wheaten loaf called *kolacze*, which has been blessed in church, represents all bread. Good, solid food is served: a traditional mixture of lentils and barley called *kasha*, peas, gravy, a bird, and *borscht*—soup made from beetroot or cabbage. Everyone cries: 'The soup is bitter' until bride and groom have kissed each other. Since the wedding feast is said to represent the couple's future married life, there is always plenty of food. For the same reason, the fiddlers are fed by the bridesmaids so that they will not stop playing.

In Scotland it was the custom to serve a fowl. Afterward, so that she and her husband would be happy, the bride was given the small side-bone called 'hug me close.' In Sunderland, as elsewhere, the bridal pair was presented with hot pots after leaving the church; these were mugs of ale that were brought by local women as a compliment to the newly weds. A stranger to the district, taken by surprise at his wedding more than 100 years ago, remarked: 'The composition in these mugs was mostly, I am sorry to say, simply horrible.'

On reaching the churchyard gate, the bride might jump, or be lifted over, what was known as the petting stone; on Holy Island the petting stone is all that remains of a lost Saxon cross. A decorated rope might be stretched across the road, and the groom had to pay a fine to obtain free passage.

Today when the ceremony and reception are over, bride and groom set off on a journey together. But this is a modern custom. Three centuries ago, in parts of Western Europe, the whole wedding party danced along with the couple to the bridal chamber, where the bride's mother was waiting to say goodbye. An English marriage, before the honeymoon came in vogue, concluded with the ceremony of 'throwing the stocking.' Bride and groom were expected to sit up in bed, fully dressed, while the bridesmaids took it in turn to stand at the foot of the bedstead and throw the bridegroom's stocking over their shoulder. The aim was to hit him on the face. The groom's men then aimed at the bride using her stocking. This was a form of divination: whoever succeeded would soon be married.

A post-marital custom recorded in 1792 in Ayrshire, was known as creeling. Two days after the wedding the married couple gathered together with friends and filled a small basket, or creel, with stones. The young men were obliged to carry this in turns until released by a kiss from one of the girls. When the groom's turn came he was expected to carry the basket for a much longer period, until his bride had pity and kissed him, as a sign of her satisfaction with the marriage. Two days however is scarcely a fair trial period, and the real question was

whether the marriage would stand the test of a longer time. At Dunmow in Essex, the ancient custom survives of presenting annually a flitch of bacon to a married couple who can swear, kneeling on two sharp stones, that they have not regretted their marriage for a year and a day.

Infidelity, like marital harmony, used to be considered a community affair and the punishment inflicted on the offender was by no means good natured. A practice called 'rough music,' known by a variety of names according to the district, consisted of a procession, generally at night, with the local men banging any suitable metal object they could lay their hands on, such as saucepans and kettles, and blowing improvized musical instru-

ments. Verses were recited and life-size effigies of the offenders were publicly paraded. Rough music could be played for a variety of reasons, the most usual being some offence against the marital code, particularly adultery or incest. The punishment was effective; as a rule the persecuted couple had to leave the district.

Cost of a Secondhand Wife

In the event of a marriage being unsuccessful, it was once a common belief that if a man disliked his wife, he could get rid of her by the simple expedient of selling her. With a halter placed round her neck, the wife would be publicly exhibited for sale for a sum not less than a shilling; the man who bought her would then become her

Jewish wedding ceremony, showing groom crushing a glass to remind Jews that despite the joy, they still mourn the destruction of the Temple in Jerusalem

husband. It was considered that he had done so, simply by virtue of the purchase. There are many recorded cases during the last couple of centuries. Some of these cases strike us today as bizarre. For example on April 7, 1832 at Carlisle, a farmer named Joseph Thomson put his wife up for sale after three years of marriage, complete with a straw halter. After waiting for almost an hour, he succeeded in getting twenty shillings and a Newfoundland dog for her. According to popular custom, this rough-and-ready form of folk divorce was legally binding.

It was commonly believed that the success of a marriage would depend upon the time at which it was celebrated. We know that the ancient Romans avoided May weddings because the month was a time of purification. The *Lemuria*, or Feast of the Unhappy Dead, was celebrated on the ninth, eleventh and thirteenth of that month, and the poet Ovid says those who married in May would soon die.

There is a curious association of death and marriage in Jewish custom, perhaps explained by the tragedies of their history. The couple must be reminded of sorrow in the midst of joy and hence a glass is broken. The pieces used sometimes to be carefully saved and used to weigh down their eyelids in death. Numerous examples from different cultures of the ceremonial smashing of objects at weddings are cited by E. Westermarck (1862–1939) in his *History of Human Marriage*. Among the southern Serbs, for instance, it was the custom, after the bride and groom had returned, to throw a wine glass at their door, symbolizing the approaching loss of virginity. The guests, with a great deal of noise, were meanwhile busy smashing glasses, crockery, and an egg in a sack. It seems likely, as Westermarck suggests, that the shattering of fragile objects was intended to ensure the consummation of the marriage, which might otherwise have been prevented by malevolent influences.

The Ashkenazim, the Yiddish-speaking Jews of Central and Eastern Europe, used to carry a hen and a rooster in procession with the bride and groom as symbols of fertility. For the same purpose was the custom among Spanish and Portuguese Jews of causing the bride to perform the Fish Dance. Russian and Polish Jews fed the couple on fish, and the woman might also jump over a bowl of live ones.

Certain Jewish wedding customs, particularly among the Ashkenazim, were not dissimilar from those known elsewhere. Bride and groom were escorted separately to the synagogue in a merry procession, and on arrival were showered with wheat or barley. To make the significance of this ritual quite clear, the celebrants called out three times to the bridal pair: 'Be fruitful and multiply,' while a wedding canopy, the *chuppah*, set out of doors, signified God's promise to Abraham: 'Thus shall thy children be, like the stars of heaven.'

VENETIA NEWALL

FURTHER READING: R. B. Outhwaite. Marriage and Society: Studies in the History of Marriage. *(London, UK: St. Martin's Press, 1982); E. Westermarck.* Short History of Marriage. *(Humanities, 1969); Ernest Crawley.* The Mystic Rose, *rev. enl. ed. (Farmington Hills, MI: Gale, 1971); Arnold Van Gennep.* The Rites of Passage. *(Chicago, IL: University of Chicago Press, 1961).*

Mayday

The great festival of rebirth and renewal, May Day, the first day of May, was an occasion of great joy in the past among the common people of Europe. As a ceremonial day it was superimposed upon the ancient festival of Beltane, the inauguration of the second half of the Celtic year. However, in the form in which it was observed by our forefathers it was a dramatized presentation of the union of spring and summer.

Very early on May morning, in the past, the young people of the community would rise from their beds and make their way to the woods. Here they would gather garlands of flowers with branches from the trees and, it is said, indulge in 'wanton dalliances.' As a symbol of rebirth, the greenery would be brought back to the villages and used as decoration for the doors and windows of the houses. This ancient rite of 'bringing home the May' was in effect a method of ritually conveying the fertilizing powers of awakened Nature into the human community.

The central figure of the celebration was the maypole or May tree; in England this was the white hawthorn, which possessed supernatural powers and symbolized the transition from spring to summer, while in the United States it was the evergreen arbutus. Like so many other magical objects the hawthorn was dualistic in character, being a force both for good and evil. As long ago as the twelfth century its sinister aspect was recorded in Ireland, and in England the once beneficent May has become a flower of evil that must never be brought into the home.

The election of a Queen of the May, one of the great May Day ceremonies, had no doubt some connection with the ancient Scandinavian custom in which a mock contest was staged between two individuals, the one representing summer and the other winter, from which the former always emerged the victor. This ceremony, which continued in the Isle of Man until early in the nineteenth century, was described in the *Universal Magazine* in 1786 as a ritual contest between the Queen of Winter (a man dressed in woman's

A Boston elementary school's students hold their annual Mayfest in Copley Square, which includes songs and the traditional maypole dance

clothes) and a female Queen of the May. The same basic idea was also represented in the better-known ritual marriage between the May bridegroom and the May bride, which has been supposed to symbolize the union of spring and vegetation. A King of the May was also elected in former times, but the crowning of the May Queen remains integral to the surviving rite in the British Isles. This is accompanied by merrymaking and ceremonial dancing around the decorated tree or maypole.

On May Day it was once the custom for groups of young people to visit all the houses in the village bearing garlands of flowers and soliciting donations, in return for which they received the 'blessing of May' to bring them good luck for the coming year.

All the characters in the May Day rites embodied the power to endow crops and women with fertility and good luck. The maypole or May bush, originally a tree brought in from the woods, was only in later times set up as a permanent fixture on the village green. The famous maypole in

As a symbol of rebirth, the greenery would be brought back to the villages and used as decoration for the doors and windows of the houses.

London's Strand, which was 134 feet tall, was later transferred to Wanstead in Essex, where it was used to support the largest telescope then known.

One feature of the English ceremony was the dance of the Morris men, the main characters being Robin Hood, Maid Marion, Will Scarlet, Little John, the Fool in cap and bells, Tom the Piper, and the hobby-horse, all symbolical of primitive ceremonial magic. The hobby-horses still play a prominent role in the May Day ceremonies at Padstow and Minehead in the west of England, where they attract visitors from all over the world, but the other characters in the play have long since made their exit.

It was perhaps inevitable that the Puritans should have taken deep offence at the May Day ceremonies, detecting in the maypole obvious fertility connotations and also a close affinity with the Roman games dedicated to the goddess Flora, which were held on April 28. To the English and US Puritan, the sight of rustics capering about an upright pole was all too reminiscent of pagan worship.

The Puritans' hostility to the superstitions of May Day apparently did not extend to the prohibition of washing the face in May dew, the traditional recipe for a good complexion as well as for health and strength; presumably they were unaware of the custom in some parts of Europe for young girls to roll stark naked in the magical dew on May morning. It is on record that Oliver Cromwell himself was not above using May dew on medical advice.

Inevitably the May Day celebrations, like many Christmas customs, were suppressed during Puritan rule, to reemerge at the Restoration. Later they became part of that gradual decline to which all the elements of 'Merry England' were now subject. The May Day rites continued throughout the eighteenth century and into the nineteenth, with May games on the village green and dancing chimney sweeps and garlanded milkmaids a common sight in the London streets. As the drab century of industrialism drew to its end, May Day underwent temporary metamorphosis as the festival of international labour, the hobby-horse and Morris men being replaced by processions of trade unionists marching behind banners. Today remnants of traditional May Day celebrations survive only in rural areas.

Midsummer Eve

Since our ancestors relied upon the sun for warmth and light, the arrival of Midsummer, which marks the passing of its seasonal apex, brought a chilling reminder of approaching darkness and cold. It was a time of uncertainty when, so it was once believed, poisonous dragons thronged the air. Excited by the heat of summer, they copulated, and their emission fell upon the earth, polluting the drinking water: 'There was soo greate hete the which causid that dragons to go togyther in to kenynge that Johan dyed in brennynge love and charyte to God and man.'

This curious reconciliation of early myth and Christian tradition explains the transfer of pagan usage from the solstice, June 21, to a celebration three days later. This was the Nativity of John the Baptist but some churchmen still voiced their objections. An entry in the Register of the Synod of Caithness and Orkney for June 21, 1708, reads: 'Johnmas fires which are commonly observed sometimes in this month are very common in many paroches. Therefore recommends to the several ministers where this or the like superstitious custome is to deal with persons and to bring them to a

Witches were said to hold their sabbath on Midsummer Eve, riding on toasting forks or a black three-legged horse.

sense of yr sin and that they continue to rebuke the same from yr pulpits.'

Bonfires, supposedly honouring St. John, are still lit in many places, such as Cornwall in England, Scandinavia, and Catalonia; at one time they blazed all over Europe, to strengthen the weakening sun and keep evil creatures at bay. The vigour and extent of the crops were believed to be governed by the distance from which the fires were visible, and the height which people reached by jumping over them. Leaping of this kind, still to be seen in some places, was once a common folk custom, intended to stimulate the crops by sympathy. Burning torches were carried through the fields to guard against mishaps, and fires were lit to the windward so that their smoke would blow over the grain. A piece of blazing turf was thrown in the growing corn or carried round the cattle, and wheels covered with burning straw were rolled downhill to imitate the

sun's descending course.

The bonfires were often a social occasion. An old English account records: 'For making the king's bonefuyr, 10s.' At Augsburg in 1497, one was lit in the presence of Emperor Maximilian, and Philip the Handsome led the first ring dance around it. Louis XIV, crowned with roses, is known to have kindled the flames himself, and he also joined in the dancing. The custom still survived of burning live animals in the fire; usually foxes or cats, probably because witches were thought to assume these forms.

Night of the Witches

Midsummer, when the sun's power began to diminish, was traditionally a dangerous time, during which malevolent beings were unusually active. Witches were said to hold their sabbath on Midsummer Eve, riding on toasting forks or a black three-legged horse. In parts of Yugoslavia, armed with tree stumps, they attacked baptized Christians on this particular night so, as a precaution, people disposed of these natural weapons in advance. The seventeenth century antiquary John Aubrey (1626–1697) wrote: 'Tis Midsommer-Night, or Midsommer-eve (St. Jo: Baptist) is counted or called the Witches night . . . of the breaking of Hen-egges this night, in which they may see what their fortune will be.' Anyone brave enough to sit in the church porch at midnight saw a procession of apparitions pass into the church; those who did not reappear were doomed to die in the course of the year. And young girls would busy themselves in various activities in order to conjure up or dream of their future husbands. Alternatively, plants were often used for a similar purpose. Yarrow, gathered from a young man's grave and laid under the pillow on Midsummer Eve, produced the shade of one's husband-to-be; or slips of orpine, a purple-flowered stonecrop, popularly known as Midsummer Men, were stuck in a convenient crack. If they leant together, the marriage omen was good.

St. John's Wort, a yellow plant blooming at this time, which resembles a miniature sun, was also known as *Fuga Daemonum* ('flight of demons') because, so people said, it repelled evil spirits. In the Middle Ages it was applied to the mouths of accused witches in order to make them confess.

Midsummer Eve fern seed was supposed to make men invisible. Shakespeare wrote of this in *Henry IV, Part 1:* 'We have the receipt of fern seed. We walk invisible.' Also a protective plant, it possessed the property of revealing treasure, glowing deep in the earth with bluish flames.

'A Very Splendid Appearance'

A branch of hazel, cut on Midsummer Eve, also guided the user to hidden treasure. It had to be obtained at night by walking backward, then cutting it with both hands between one's legs. A test was to hold it near water and, if all this had been properly done, it would squeak like a pig. This was a German idea; belief in the mystical powers of vegetation at Midsummer Eve used be common throughout Europe. The historian John Stow (c. 1525–1605), in his *Survey* (1598), describes the magic plants which at one time were hung up in London on St. John's Eve: 'On the eve of this saint . . . every man's door was shaded with green birch, long fennel, Saint John's Wort, orpin, white lilies, and the like, ornamented with garlands of beautiful flowers. They . . . had also lamps of glass with oil burning in them all night; and some of them hung out branches of iron, curious wrought, containing hundreds of lamps lighted at once, which made a very splendid appearance.'

VENETIA NEWALL

Moon

Come full moon, the face of the 'man in the moon' beams down upon the earth, his lustful air, so legend has it, attracting—and even ravishing—every woman. He is also said to influence women's fertility, and certainly the cycle of ovulation and menstruation does correspond closely to the twenty-eight-day lunar cycle. The moon takes on masculine form in Eskimo legend, being the lover of the female sun who visits her by night, and in Greenland the male moon, who sleeps on his back, demands that any woman wishing to sleep on his back first rubs his belly with her spittle.

In most mythologies, however, the moon's ruler is female, as in the Apache deity of Changing Woman who alters her form as the moon waxes and wanes. The ancient Babylonians worshipped the moon as queen of the night, ancestor of the less powerful sun. Her goddess was Ishtar, who ruled both the earth's fertility and the sexual passions of its inhabitants. Before it rises at night the moon was, to the Greeks, the realm of Hecate, the Greek's three-headed goddess of the underworld; when shining on the fields it was the embodiment of Selene, the lover of Endymion, the mortal shepherd's son. For the ancient Egyptians the goddesses Isis and Hathor both had lunar associations while to the Chinese the moon is behind everything female or Yin, being the opposite of the sun which is male or Yang.

Lunar Influence

The waxing and waning of the moon has helped to set the agenda for country folk and is still taken into account today by many growers and gardeners. It was vital to plant seeds, harvest crops, prune fruit trees, shear sheep, and slaughter animals such as pigs, for winter storage whilst the moon was

waxing. A waning moon would lead to failing crops and meat that would be hard, not plump nor succulent. Cutting hair (including the beard), nails, and even corns on the feet was never done except when the moon was on the increase. To get rid of warts, an old remedy is to rub the hands together whilst lying on the ground under a waxing or, best of all, a full moon.

To be sure of good luck, it is taboo to point at the moon or to look at it through the branches of a tree or through glass (with the exception of spectacles). The superstitious will still bow to the new moon, especially the first of the year and, at the first sight of a new moon turn the money in their pocket, whilst making a wish, to ensure future prosperity. Equally, it is deemed dangerous to sleep in the open under the moon, or even to allow moonlight to penetrate the bedroom and fall onto the face. At sea, sailors would avoid sleeping on deck on moonlit nights for fear of suffering the fate of moon blindness.

Weather Wise

The moon features in many weather predictions, some more believable than others. It is certainly true that a ring around the moon occurs at times of cold, wet weather, as in 'ring round the moon, snow soon.' That two full moons in a month bring floods is less reliable, although the second of these moons—a blue moon—can be true to its name. Most famous of blue moons in history were those that followed the eruption of Krakatoa in 1883. The saying: 'when the new moon holds the old one in her lap, expect fair weather' relates to the fact that when the air is very clear at new moon, as happens during a spell of settled weather, it is possible to see the entire moon as a dim gray ball.

The position of the new moon in the sky has also been held as significant to the weather. A new moon on its back is said to signify wind, but no rain because you can 'hang your hat on its horns.' If the new moon is on its point it said to forebode rain in summer and snow in winter.

The Roman poet Virgil, the son of a farmer and student of astronomy, was a keen observer of the weather and wrote of the new moon and its appearance:

When the moon first appears, if then
she shrouds
Her silver crescent tipped with
sable clouds,
Conclude she bodes a tempest on
the main,
And brews for fields impetuous floods
of rain;
Or if her face with fiery
flushings glow,
Expect the rattling winds aloft
to blow;
But four nights old (for that's the
surest sign)
With sharpened horns, if glorious
then she shine,
Next day, nor only that, but all
the moon,
Till her revolving race be wholly run,
Are void of tempest both by land
and sea.

RUTH BINNEY

FURTHER READING: R. Binney.
Wise Words and Country Ways:
Weather Lore. *(Newton Abbot, UK: David and Charles, 2010); Iona Opie and Moira Tatem.* A Dictionary of Superstitions. *(New York, NY: Oxford University Press, 1989).*

Mother Goddess

'Concerning Earth, the mother of all, shall I sing; firm Earth, eldest of gods, that nourishes all things in the world . . . Thine it is to give or to take life from mortal men.' These words from

Relief at the Dendera Temple, Egypt, showing Traianus, Horus, and Hathor. The temple is dedicated to Hathor, who personified the principles of joy, feminine love, and motherhood.

The Moon by Name

Most famous of all moon names is the harvest moon, the moon nearest the fall equinox, which appears very large and orange or red due to the effects of light as it travels through the atmosphere. The hunter's moon, which follows, is almost as spectacular. In folklore, the moon is designated one or more names in each month, many of them Native American designations:

- January: wolf moon, hunger moon, old moon
- February: snow moon, ice moon
- March: worm moon, sap moon, sugaring moon, crow moon, storm moon
- April: pink moon, egg moon, grass moon, rain moon, growing moon
- May: flower moon, planting moon, milk moon, hare moon
- June: strawberry moon, rose moon, honey moon, mead moon
- July: buck moon, thunder moon, deer moon, hay moon
- August: sturgeon moon, corn moon, fruit moon, barley moon
- September: harvest moon, wine moon, elk call moon
- October: hunter's moon
- November: frosty moon, snow moon, beaver moon
- December: cold moon, long night moon, winter moon

the Homeric Hymn to Earth typify a religious belief that is as old as history.

From time immemorial man has reflected in wonder and amazement on the earth upon which he lives, and that nourishes himself, his family, his tribe, and his animals. As long as man has felt himself dependent on the earth, he has personified it and worshiped or at least reverenced it, in the most potent of all images, the image of the mother.

Today in a Western society that has to a very great extent lost its hold on the realities of agricultural existence, it is said that the earth has become desacralized. Reverence has given way to ruthless exploitation. The mystery has fled, to be replaced by concrete carpets and factory farming. Nevertheless, it is still possible to see shadows and hear distant echoes of what was once an unquestioned item of faith.

Not long ago the suggestion was made that a certain bestseller in the field of religious literature would be a book entitled 'God is a Woman.' The suggestion may have been partly frivolous, but bearing in mind that it is only very recently in the history of mankind that deity has been credited with exclusively masculine attributes, the possibility of depicting supernatural power in feminine terms is far from unreasonable. In the West, God is generally spoken of as 'Our Father which art in heaven,' but the naive question 'If God is Father, then who is Mother?' still deserves to be asked. Historically the answer would be: 'The earth on which we live.'

The history of religion reveals a panorama of gods and goddesses, higher and lower spiritual beings, among whom personifications of the earth occupy a prominent place. As a rule these personifications bear all the attributes of female sexuality and motherhood.

Sometimes they are paradoxically believed to be virginal. Often, still more paradoxically, they combine within themselves attributes of generosity and grace and also those of horror and destruction. If human love is one of their areas of influence, the senseless urge that leads men into war is another.

Their icons and images may be of the order of the Venus de Milo, an idealized form of female beauty; or, equally, they may suggest a mind diseased—skinny, skull-festooned hags, their fangs dripping with the blood of generations of men. Clearly the mother goddess of human history is no romantic figure, but rather one in which opposites combine, in which the giver of life is clearly seen as the being who also takes it away, and in which promises are hollow and temporary, and hope a mockery.

The tension and paradox appear to have been almost universal. From Scandinavia to Melanesia, goddesses in which precisely these characteristics predominate have been worshipped, feared, and propitiated. This universality has led some scholars to suggest that what we are in fact seeing is the reflection of a human psychological trait that is always and everywhere

the same, though clothed in slightly different images and symbols. This psychological interpretation is not without its risks, however. The Paleolithic 'Venuses' for instance cannot simply be equated with medieval figures of the Virgin Mary. The figure of the mother goddess in India is not the same as the Great Mother of the Mediterranean world, however much they may appear to have in common. The hypotheses of Freud (1856–1939) and Jung (1875–1961) must not be made to carry more weight than they can bear. As well as similarities, there are significant differences.

Among man's earliest artefacts, dating from the late Paleolithic period, are coarse and crude figurines of pregnant women, their breasts and hips grotesquely enlarged. These, it has been supposed, represent in human form that concern with human reproduction that was a pattern of man's condition of survival on the face of the earth. It is not known whether these in any sense represent mother goddesses and there is no way of finding out. The possibility is there, but it is only a possibility.

It is interesting, though, that these figurines are seldom more than approximately human. Apart from their lack of proportion, their faces and other personal characteristics are hardly even hinted at. This same characteristic is found in female figurines from Bronze Age peasant cultures and many of the earliest urban cultures, for instance those of northwest India. Excavations made on Indus Valley sites have revealed many such artefacts, often smoke-stained in such a way as to suggest some form of household worship. If this is a continuous line of development, it would seem to suggest something more than merely 'good-luck charms' or magical amulets. The pattern is consistent, at all events: a female figure with rudimentary features, but with prominent breasts

and hips, often dressed in a girdle and necklaces, and wearing a headdress.

Even today, a visitor to an Indian village may be surprised to find that the temples of the great gods, Shiva and Vishnu, are regarded by the people as being of less importance than the little shrine of the local goddess, or Grami Devi. She may have many names, most of which are not found in the standard textbooks on Hinduism. But she is 'of the earth,' and directly responsible for the fertility of the fields surrounding the village. She may be linked mythologically with the consorts of the great gods, Parvati, a consort of Shiva, Kali his wife, or Lakshmi who was Vishnu's wife, but to all intents and purposes she is the guardian of the village and the one to whom the people turn for everyday purposes. She has her festivals and her particular responsibilities, and it is probable that her nature and function have not changed for more than 5,000 years.

A bronze statue of the mother goddess, Cybele from the second century AD

However, the most authoritative evidence concerning the worship of mother goddesses comes from the Mediterranean area, from Iran in the east to Rome in west, and covering Mesopotamia, Egypt, and Greece. Indeed, in this area, the names and functions of the great goddesses were so interchangeable as to make comparative study a highly complex undertaking. The primary identification of the goddess with the fruitful Earth is unquestionable, but starting from Mesopotamia there is an involved pattern, in which celestial elements combine with those of the underworld in such a way as to suggest that the Great Mother may be a composite figure, as complex as the human mind.

The Semitic names for the greatest mother goddess were Inanna in Sumeria, Ishtar in Babylon, and Astarte or Anat among the Canaanites. Commonly identified with the planet Venus, her most typical title is 'queen of heaven,' though she is also known as 'mistress of all the gods,' and 'the lady of the world.' In time, she gathered to herself the attributes of a host of other goddesses, so that in Mesopotamia the word *ishtar* came to mean simply 'goddess.'

She was believed to be the giver of vegetation; a hymn contains the words: 'In the heavens I take my place and send rain, in the earth I take my place and cause the green to spring forth.' She was the creator of animals, and the goddess of sexual love, marriage, and maternity. In another hymn it was said: 'I turn the male to the female, I turn the female to the male; I am she who adorneth the male for the female, I am she who adorneth the female for the male.' Her worship was frequently connected with the practice of sacred prostitution.

Two other characteristics of the Semitic mother goddess are worth mentioning in this context. The first concerned her connection with a male figure who could be described as son, brother, or husband. The best known of these figures was Tammuz (Sumerian Dumu-zi), a god of vegetation and in particular of the growing wheat. Every year a festival was held at which his 'death' and 'resurrection' was celebrated.

Naked Before the God

The vegetation god was believed to die and rise again annually, and in the myths of the descent of the mother goddess into the land of the dead, there is a dramatic image of the search of the mother for her lost son and lover, the search of the earth for the temporarily lost fertility which the new spring restores. A Sumerian version of this myth, *Inanna's Descent to the Nether World*, is one of the earliest examples.

Inanna descends, perhaps in order to free Dumu-zi; she approaches the subterranean temple of Ereshkigal, god of the dead, through seven gates, at each one of which she has to remove part of her clothing, until she stands before him naked. An interesting feature of this myth is that on her return, she brings with her all manner of evil and malevolent beings: 'They who preceded her, they who preceded Inanna, were beings who knew not food, who knew not water, who eat not sprinkled flour, who drink not libated wine, who take away the wife from the loins of man, who take away the child from the breast of the nursing mother.' Similar myths were current all over the Semitic world, for instance in Canaan, where the mother goddess Anat attacks and conquers Mot (death) in order to free the fertility god Baal.

The cult of the mother goddess moved westward, perhaps through Cyprus and Crete, into Anatolia and Greece. Significantly, the most popular image of Venus, the Greek Aphrodite, depicts her emerging from the sea on the coast of Cyprus, while her consort, Adonis, is a Semitic figure, with a Semitic name. In her purely Greek form, as Aphrodite, the goddess's cult was fairly decorous, but on the borders of the Greek world, in Corinth, sacred prostitution was practiced.

However, on entering the Greek culture, the cult of the mother goddess encountered another similar cult deriving from the Indo-European culture. In Iran, Anahita the goddess who 'purifies the seed of males and the womb and milk of females,' described in sculptural terms as 'a beautiful maiden, powerful, and tall,' was worshipped. Her cult spread through the Persian Empire, and she gradually

The Iranian goddess Anahita, who was later assimilated with the Greek goddesses Aphrodite and Athena

coalesced in various ways with Athene, Aphrodite, and the Anatolian Cybele. It was Cybele who eventually came to be honoured in the Roman Empire as the Great Mother of the gods, a temple being erected to her honour on the Palatine Hill in Rome in 204 BC.

The cult of Cybele remained, even after its adoption in Rome by the Romans, the responsibility of native Phrygians, who wore their hair long, dressed in female clothes, and celebrated the goddess in wild orgiastic dances to the point of exhaustion. It is believed their consecration to the goddess sometimes involved self-emasculation.

Although this type of worship was not unknown in Greece, particularly in connection with Dionysus, worship of the mother goddess took more decorous forms. The Mysteries of Eleusis incorporated most of the

elements already mentioned: a dying and rising pattern linked with the corn, with fertility and with the rhythm of the seasons. The rites

> *One common representation of Isis is as a mother suckling the infant Horus, thought by some to be a prototype of later Christian images of mother and child.*

of Eleusis were celebrated in honour of the mother goddess Demeter and in honour of her daughter Persephone.

Originally pure fertility rites, they gradually came to be an acted parable of the relationship of man to his surroundings, assuring initiates of the protection of Persephone in the world beyond the grave. The myth is outlined in the Homeric Hymn to Demeter.

'Demeter's People'

Persephone, daughter of Demeter and Zeus (Earth Mother and Sky Father) was out gathering flowers. The earth opened and out leaped Pluto, god of the underworld: 'He caught her up reluctant in his golden car and bore her away lamenting.' For nine days Demeter sought her; on the tenth day she learned the secret from Helios, the sun. Angry, she closed the womb of Earth until her daughter was restored to her; however, Pluto made Persephone eat pomegranate seeds, in this way keeping some hold on her. Demeter accepted the arrangement, and before leaving for Olympus, showed the people her mysteries, ' . . . awful mysteries which no one may in any way transgress or pry into or utter, for deep awe of the gods checks the voice.' The secret was well kept, and many details of the Eleusinian

The triad of the Eleusinian Mysteries: Persephone, Demeter, and Triptolemus

goddess of the dead, shared with Odin the custody of warriors slain on the field of battle. This is the same kind of ambivalence that is to be observed in most mother goddesses; because the earth receives the dead in corruption and also gives birth and sustenance to crops, men, and animals, the connection between the mother goddess and the kingdom of the dead is common. In Greece, for instance, the dead were sometimes called 'Demeter's people.'

The coming of Christianity to the Mediterranean countries and Europe had the effect, on one level, of devaluing the indigenous cults by demoting the ancient deities to the rank of demons. In the case of the Great Mother, however, popular belief reasserted itself by transferring many of her attributes to the Virgin Mary. In the same way, local deities often came to be identified with the saints. This interesting development can be paralleled in many parts of the world. Its roots are certainly psychological: the hold of the Great Mother on the mind of an agricultural people was too strong to be broken overnight. Legends and attributes came to be attached to the name of Mary, in her role as the Mother of God, which lack all scriptural support, but which clearly correspond to needs in the popular mind.

At Bethlehem for instance there is, or used to be, a cave known locally as the 'milk grotto.' Legend has it that the Holy Family once took refuge in the cave, and that as Mary nursed the infant Jesus, a drop of her milk fell on the floor. Because of this, it was believed that to enter the cave would cure barrenness in women, and increase their milk and even the milk of animals. It seems clear that this particular cave was once the shrine of a local form of mother goddess, and that the legend is merely a Christianization of the site.

It is worth emphasizing that doctrines and dogmas concerning the

Mysteries are unknown, save that the cult became established in Athens.

Another popular form of the worship of the mother goddess in the Roman Empire was that of the Egyptian goddess Isis. Originally the wife of Osiris, identified with the dead pharaoh, she was the mother of Horus, the living pharaoh, who gave birth to her son after having conceived magically on the body of her dead husband. One common representation of Isis is as a mother suckling the infant Horus, thought by some to be a prototype of later Christian images of mother and child.

Indeed, the queen of heaven, the universal mother, was known by many names in the ancient world. For example there is Artemis or Diana, the huntress and mistress of animals: in Acts, chapter 19, there is recorded a celebrated encounter between Paul and devotees of 'Artemis of the Ephesians,' a local, many-breasted form of what may have originally been a moon goddess. There was the Anatolian goddess Ma, whose priests were known as *fanatici* (servants of the *fanum* or temple) and from whose wild excesses comes the word 'fanatic.' Farther north, there were Celtic and Teutonic tribal goddesses. Among the latter, the goddess Freya was said to have had sexual relations with all the male members of the pantheon, and as

Virgin Mary have always been formulated as a result of popular religious practices. On the theological level, as long as God and Christ were thought of in terms of the dispensation of justice, both appeared remote and, the nature of man being what it is, frightening. The Virgin, on the other hand, was unquestionably human, although elevated to near-divine rank and crowned Queen of Heaven. Who better to intercede for sinful mankind at the Judgment seat? In this, she was in effect doing what the mother goddess, whatever her name, had always done from time immemorial.

Mankind's worship of, and reverence for, the divine figure of the mother, is a religious phenomenon far deeper than creeds, councils, and dogmas. It reflects man's profound need for security in a frequently unfriendly world, his own inadequacies and his own fears. In it can be seen the tension between good things and evil, between the gift of life and the fear of death, personified in the goddess who gives and takes away, who creates and destroys, but who is never as aloof and unconcerned as her consort, the sky god. As long as man retains any of his roots in the earth, reverence for the earth—whether personified or not—will remain, and the Great Mother will still have human children.

ERIC J. SHARPE

FURTHER READING: E. Neumann. The Great Mother. (Princeton, NJ: Princeton University Press, 1964); J. Preston, ed. Mother Worship. (Chapel Hill, NC: University of North Carolina Press, 1983).

The Virgin and Child

New Year

Rites in celebration of the New Year take place the world over, irrespective of differing systems of computing time. Among many nomadic and agricultural communities, it was customary to calculate the year on a lunar basis and most modern calendars continue to show this influence. Sometimes, as in the case of the Jewish faith, New Year is a moveable feast. In ancient Babylon it was celebrated in what is now March and April, and in Egypt it was linked with the annual flooding of the Nile. In Europe the New Year was celebrated at different times varying from Christmas to March, and its official celebration on January 1, is a comparatively modern innovation. Until the introduction of the Gregorian Calendar in 1752, the official New Year in the British Isles began in March, but as far as the common people were concerned, it has always been celebrated on January 1.

Many of the ceremonies associated with this turning point combine the elements of a funeral ceremony and a birth, of death and sorrow on the one hand, and on the other hope and joy. The first is represented by an old man often depicted with a scythe, and the second by a male child, the symbol of the infant year. The completion of one phase of existence and its reemergence into another has always been an occasion of ceremonial importance in human affairs, and in many ways the rites of the New Year correspond to the rites of passage of individual life. The sense of continuity is still farther emphasized in the role of the Roman god Janus, guardian of the gateway of the year, who faces both ways, looking backward into the past and forward into the future.

In keeping with the mourning element that underlies many of the rituals, obsequies for the dying year were once celebrated by English mummers who went from house to house, collecting tribute. The custom of tolling bells to mark its passing was quite literally a funeral dirge for the death of the old year. Originally, muffled bells were rung till just before midnight, and as the clock struck twelve, the wrappings were removed to permit a loud clear chime. This was to indicate that, although the old year might be weak and feeble, the new one was strong and powerful in full voice.

Time of Joy and Rebirth

The occasional appearance of a headless spectre in many places in Europe at the New Year suggests another funereal association, although whether this points to some long-forgotten sacrificial custom carried out in furtherance of the rites of seasonal death and resurrection is uncertain. It is interesting to note in this context that during Babylonian New Year ceremonies it was customary for heads to be severed from statues and that in England there is a winter solstice superstition that if the shadow of any individual sitting by the Yule fire appears without a head, it means that he or she will die before the year is out.

It is the happier and more hopeful aspects, however, which predominate throughout the world. Everywhere, east or west, the New Year is the occasion for greater rejoicing. In China the house windows are decorated with texts in honour of the most important annual festival in the Chinese calendar, a time when the gods of wealth and procreation are encouraged to visit the home, while at the same time the devils of bad luck are warned to stay away. The Japanese celebrate the day with specially baked cakes that they offer to the sun and moon. In India it is customary for new foods to be eaten and in some places for new clothes to be worn; cattle are gaily decked with flowers, and in Bengal the Ganges is worshipped. The modern Mexican ends his five days of ritual lamentation with wild rejoicings. Northern Native Americans at New Year extinguish the tribal fires, scatter the ashes, and then ceremoniously relight them. There are also sacrifices and offerings to the gods and sometimes water is sprinkled on the passerby.

In northern Europe boar-shaped cakes were baked, and in France, pancakes tossed on a griddle to bring good fortune. The European festival reveals little influence of the Christian heritage, for the introduction of the Julian Calendar in 46 BC placed the New Year in close proximity to the licentious Roman feast of Saturnalia. This gave grave offence to the Fathers of the Church who condemned it as diabolical, an attitude that received farther emphasis in a decree of the Council of Auxerre.

The superstitious aspects of the New Year festival have maintained their long hold on the imaginations

Here the baby representing the New Year 1905 is chasing old man 1904 into history

New Year is the most important festival in the Chinese calendar. The dragon is a symbol of good luck.

of people in Europe, despite religious strictures and social change. In Wales today children still maintain the quaint old custom of going from door to door asking for New Year's water to scatter on the houses. A song sung by children in South Wales on New Year's morning many years ago began:

Here we bring new water
From the well so clear
For to worship God with
This happy New Year.

The superstition that water drawn from the well on New Year's Eve turned into wine long survived in this part of the British Isles. In some places such water was drunk in the New Year as a charm against the attacks of evil spirits.

In Scotland the last day of the year is known as Hogmanay and is traditionally celebrated with cakes and ale. Fires are lit and in Galloway, Wigtownshire, there is a ceremony known as 'taking the cream off the water.' Good fortune is believed to be the lot of anyone who drinks the water on that day.

The chief feature of New Year celebrations in Scotland, however, is the custom known as 'first footing,' which is based on the principle that whatever happens in the first moments of the New Year will have a profound influence upon the events of the twelve months ahead. For this reason the first person to step over the threshold must represent good fortune and it is most dangerous should there be anything ominous about him. 'First Foot' must be male, tall, and dark haired, hair of this colour being equated with good fortune. Red-haired men are for some reason unlucky, while women threaten the New Year prospects to an alarming degree, possibly because of the age-old fear of letting a witch into the home. In Montgomeryshire in the last century, if a woman happened to gain entry into the house on that day, boys were immediately paraded through the rooms in a special purificatory ceremony called 'breaking the witch.'

First Foot, when admitted to the house, brings with him special presents that symbolize the basic needs of the household during the ensuing year,

and consist of coal, bread, and money. In parts of Wales, where a similar custom prevails, even the initials of the one selected to play the part of First Foot were considered significant. Those whose names began with an H, a J, or an R were always welcome since these initials represented health, joy, and riches; on the other hand, individuals whose initials were T, W, or S were considered dangerous since they represented trouble, worry, and sorrow.

Begin As You Mean To Go On

The same type of reasoning that lies behind first footing can be detected in many other superstitions associated with the New Year: whatever one did on this day, the most critical day of all the days in the year, continued to influence events for the whole of the succeeding twelve months. For this reason New Year is considered to be a most auspicious time for making good resolutions, since any seriously intended effort on an occasion so highly charged with magic offers the greatest hope of success. Wishes are infinitely more potent at New

Year than at the beginning of any ordinary month.

Because of the tradition that actions taken on the first day of the year determined the character of the ones that followed, the Roman tradesman of old was careful to perform a little token work on that day, since this ensured sufficient work throughout the year. The same principle appears in the old English superstition that it was extremely ominous to be unemployed on New Year's Day. Some people still believe that you must be careful to keep a piece of money in pocket or purse at this time if you hope to be assured of funds for the rest of the year. Similarly, you should always try to dine well on this day if you look forward to eating well in the months ahead.

As a result of its magical character, New Year was peculiarly favourable for divinations, sometimes by picking a verse in the Bible at random, with the eyes lightly closed.

A very ancient custom, now almost extinct, involved the giving and receiving of New Year presents that were intended to insure that the year started on an auspicious footing. Some have ascribed this to a practice current among the Druids of distributing mistletoe to the people on this day, and gift-giving at this time was common in ancient Rome. English royalty were among the principal beneficiaries of this rite for they received presents of gold from the nobility; among the most valuable of these gifts was a gold cup presented by Cardinal Wolsey to Henry VIII. Queen Elizabeth I received a present not only from the Archbishop of Canterbury but from Mr Smyth, the royal dustman. The most historically important of these presents, however, must have been the gift of a pair of silk stockings from Mrs Montague, Queen Elizabeth's silk-woman. These are said to have been the first pair to be worn in England. The Puritans were inclined to regard New Year gifts with a particularly jaundiced eye since to their eyes the custom reeked of paganism, even the innocent phrase 'Happy New Year' being frowned upon.

The one gift that nobody in his right mind would have made in the past would have been a flame for a household fire, or even a light from a candle, since this symbolized giving away the household luck, and it was supposed also to bring about a death in the family. There was even a prohibition against washing clothes on that day since, according to superstition, this was likely to wash away a life, and it was equally dangerous to part with any iron object. In the United States nothing whatsoever might be taken out of the house on New Year's Day and the chimneys had to be swept

> 'Even so, man appears on Earth for a little while; but of what went before this life or of what follows we know nothing.'

clean if the luck of the home was to be maintained, since it was taken for granted that good luck always entered the house by way of the flue.

Among the New Year customs that have survived into modern times, the most interesting is that known as 'Burning the Clavie,' which takes place at the village of Burghead at Moray Firth in Scotland, on January 12. The 'clavie' is a bonfire made of split casks, one of which is split into two parts of different sizes, probably symbolizing the unequal parts of the old and new year. An important part of the ceremony is to join the two parts together with a huge nail made for this purpose. The ceremony takes its name from the Latin word for a nail: *clavus*.

More recent is the ceremony at Queen's College, Oxford, when a needle and thread is presented to the Fellows with the injunction, 'Take it and be thrifty,' no doubt a very salutary method of introducing a New Year resolution. January 1 is also one of the thirty or so 'Collar' days when the knights of the various orders of chivalry put on their ceremonial collars.

ERIC MAPLE

FURTHER READING: T. Gaster. New Year. *(New York, NY: Abelard-Schumann, 1955).*

Night

Fear of the dark is one of the universal human terrors. Night is 'the witching time,' 'the black bat,' and its alien realms are infested by horrors and evil dreams, by spectres and goblins, by uncanny sounds in the house, and unearthly things that stalk the darkness and gather at crossroads. Day is the time when all God's creations are up and doing, and things that are active at night reverse the normal and proper order of things, like witches and demons, or the owl and the nightjar, sinister birds with uncanny cries. At sunrise the cock crows and the power of the creatures of night fades.

There is a famous passage in Bede's *History of the English Church and People* (written in the eighth century) in which a pagan Northumbrian thane likens the life of man to the flight of a sparrow across a banqueting hall in the gloom of a winter's day. Inside the hall there is warmth and firelight, outside darkness and storm. 'This sparrow flies swiftly in through one door of the hall, and out through another. While he is inside he is safe from the winter storms; but after a few moments of comfort he vanishes from sight into the wintry world from which he came. Even so, man appears on Earth for a little while; but of what went before this life or of what follows we know nothing.' The contrast between the warm fire-lit hall and the threatening darkness that hems it round is powerfully drawn in the great Anglo-Saxon poem *Beowulf* that has been described as in part 'an expression of the fear of the dark.'

It is at night that the monster Grendel, 'a black shadow of death,' prowls the misty moors and steals in to attack the Danes in the King's hall.

Night is darkness, and darkness is linked with death, the valley of the shadow, the sleep of death, the suffocating blackness of the grave, the pall that drops when the sun 'dies' in the west in the evening. Most people do not think of darkness as the mere absence of light but as something positive and almost palpable. In Homer, when a man dies we are told that 'black darkness veiled his eyes' or that 'night descended on his eyes' or that he has been 'engulfed by the unlovely dark.' The Anglo-Saxons spoke of a 'death-mist.' The idea of the darkness of death covering a man's head seems to account for the dogskin headdress of the Greek god of death, Hades, which made anyone on whom it was placed invisible.

Like death, night is inescapable. In the *Iliad* she 'dictates to gods and men alike.' Michelangelo (1475–1564) said of his famous statue of Night (in the Medici Chapel, Florence) that she was mourning the work of Time, the destroyer, and lamenting her own part in it. In Hesiod's *Theogony,* Erebos (darkness) and Night are among the earliest cosmic powers to come into existence, and it was they who gave birth to Day.

Night is also the mother of a litter of horrors—Fate, Death, the Furies, Pain, Nemesis, Deceit, Old Age,

Strife—as well as of Sleep, the tribe of Dreams, and Pleasure of Love. Her home is deep in the underworld, wrapped in dark clouds, and with her there are her twin children, Sleep who roams peacefully over land and sea, and is kindly to men, and Death, the iron-hearted, whose spirit is pitiless as bronze and who is hated even by the undying gods. Visiting Olympia in the second century AD, Pausanias saw in the temple of Hera a chest decorated with scenes. One of them showed 'a woman holding on her right arm a child asleep, and on her left she has a black child like one who is asleep . . . the figures are Death and Sleep, with Night the nurse of both.'

In many mythologies, in the beginning all was dark and chaotic, and light and order were created out of this primeval night. In Genesis there was darkness until God created light. In an Orphic creation myth, Chaos, Night, and Erebos existed in the beginning. Night laid an egg from which Eros hatched, and from him came the later generations of gods. Pico della Mirandola, the fifteenth century Italian philosopher, identi-

An illustration of Grendel by J. R. Skelton from *Stories of Beowulf*

fied the Night of this myth with the *En Sof* of the Cabala as 'the solitary cloud of the Father,' the first cause of the universe. For although night is mysterious and ominous, it is also the time of love-making, in which children are conceived, and so it has symbolic connotations of potential fruitfulness, the darkness of Earth in which the seeds ripen, the darkness of the womb in which the foetus grows. Night is the time of both death and conception. It is the name of a state of spiritual blindness and desolation, 'the Dark Night of the Soul,' regarded by some mystics as an essential stage in the progress of the soul toward God. This is a condition of inner darkness, weariness, lethargy, indecision, and misery, a condition of being far from the saving light of God that may last for months or even years.

But on the other hand, the night of love can be an image of the soul's union with God as in one of the poems of St. John of the Cross, where it is the 'night that joined the lover to the beloved bride,' transfiguring each of them into the other. Again, initiation is sometimes described in terms of a journey through the terrors of the dark, at the end of which the initiate reaches the sublime light.

Terror and love-making are combined in a different way in the nightmare, a word which used to be applied particularly to dreams which were erotic as well as frightening, and to the demon that caused them. The 'mare' is not a female horse but an incubus, a spirit that makes fierce love to sleepers at night, 'riding' them, weighing heavily on them, and causing them feelings of suffocation and evil dreams.

Opposites

'Looking back on my own experiences,' wrote the great US psychologist William James, in *The Varieties of* *Religious Experience*, 'they all converge toward a kind of insight to which I cannot help ascribing some kind of metaphysical significance. The keynote of it is invariably a reconciliation. It is as if the opposites of the world, whose contradictoriness and conflict make all our difficulties and troubles, were melted into unity. Not only do they, as contrasted species, belong to one and the same genus, but one of the species, the nobler and better one, is itself the genus and so soaks up and absorbs its opposite into itself. This is a dark saying, I know, when thus expressed in terms of common logic, but I cannot wholly escape from its authority.'

It is a common observation that man is torn between opposite tendencies, between love and indifference, dependence and independence, extraversion and introversion, intellect and instinct, and innumerable others. Similarly, the phenomena of the world outside can be classified in terms of opposites—life and death, light and darkness, good and evil, active and passive, positive and negative, matter and spirit, and many more. The course of Nature seems to swing from one opposite to the other and back again, like the pendulum of a clock. Night follows day, winter follows summer, decline follows growth, the crops are born and die and are born again. The tides flow in and out upon the shore, and the same rhythm seems to swell and ebb through all the universe.

This way of looking at things has been of great importance in religion and magic, and religious dualism is the tendency to see two powerful opposite principles at work throughout all existence. But few people who see the world in this light are so simpleminded as to leave it at that, and few systems are uncompromisingly dualistic. They look behind the opposites for something greater, in which the opposites are contained and unified as the tides are in the sea, for

This circle of the signs of the zodiac show which signs are opposite one another. It is believed that people of opposite signs are attracted to one another.

the unity into which William James's opposites 'melted,' for the One in which duality disappears.

Reconciliation and Harmony

In China the interplay of the opposites of Yang and Yin was thought to underlie everything that existed, but they were united in something greater, the Tao. The lingam and the yoni, the male and female symbols, are united in Hindu temples. The central pillar of the Tree of Life in the Cabala reconciles and harmonizes the right and left pillars. The symbol of the cross unites two pairs of opposite directions with the centre. The Greek philosopher Heraclitus (c. 500 BC) said that God is day and night, winter, and summer, war and peace, and all the opposites. In the New Testament St. Paul says, 'There is neither Jew nor Greek, there is neither slave nor free, there is neither male nor female; for you are all one in Christ Jesus' (Galatians, chapter 3.28), and in the Old Testament Isaiah (chapters 11 and 40) says that the wolf will dwell with the lamb and the leopard lie down with the kid, and every valley shall be lifted up and every mountain made low, when all opposites and contradictions disappear in the unity of the perfected world.

The Bisexual Ideal

For hundreds of years in Europe everything was believed to be made of four elements that combined two pairs of opposites—hot and cold, wet and dry. Aristotle said that the Pythagoreans saw ten fundamental pairs of opposites in the universe, and this has affected numerology ever since. Astrologers say that opposites attract each other, so that you are likely to be drawn to people born under the sign opposite your own in the zodiac circle. One of the theories of animal magnetism was that the positive and negative poles of a magnet could be used to correct an imbalance of opposite forces in

Yin and Yang and commonly shown as two halves of a whole that mirror each other

the body, and there is the same idea in acupuncture.

In some creation myths the making of the world begins with the separating out of opposites (light and darkness, for instance, or sky and earth) from a preceding totality. C. G. Jung (1875–1961) saw in this a reflection of the human mind. He says (in *Psychology and Alchemy*): 'The essence of the conscious mind is discrimination, it must, if it is to be aware of things, separate the opposites, and it does this *contra naturam* [against Nature]. In Nature the opposites seek one another

. . . and so it is in the unconscious, and particularly in the archetype of unity, the self. Here, as in deity, the opposites cancel out. But as soon as the unconscious begins to manifest itself they split asunder, as at the Creation; for every act of dawning consciousness is a creative act, and it is from this psychological experience that all our cosmogonic symbols are derived.'

What Jung called 'individuation' was the reconciliation of the opposites of human nature in a complete self ('the archetype of unity') and he was impressed by the emphasis which the alchemists placed on the union of opposites. The Philosophers' Stone itself is often described as a mysterious reconciliation of contradictions—it is made of fire and water, it is a stone but at the same time it is not a stone, it comes from God and yet it does not come from God. One reason for the importance of mercury in alchemy, and for its occasional identification with the Stone, is that it seems to combine opposites, in being a metal and also a liquid, and in being liquid but not wet. It was called 'the masculine-feminine' and was frequently depicted as a hermaphrodite.

The 'conjunction' or union of opposites in alchemy was symbolized by the marriage of king and queen, of sun and moon, of the red man and the white woman. Or it might be shown as incest between brother and sister, or mother and son, or as the reentry of the son or the king or the dragon into the womb of the mother, to indicate the mingling of opposites that had separated out from an original unity.

The Perfect Human Being

There is the same symbolism in the ideal of the androgyne or hermaphrodite as the perfect human being, who has unified all the opposites. In *The Two and the One* Mircea Eliade (1907–1986) quotes one of the German Romantics on the ideal human of the future: 'Eve was engendered by man without the aid of woman; Christ was engendered by woman without the aid of man; the androgyne will be born of the two. But the husband and wife will be fused together in a single flash.' And the poet and scholar Friedrich von Schlegel (died 1829) believed that 'the goal toward which the human race should strive is a progressive reintegration of the sexes which should end in androgyny.' The tradition that Adam was originally bisexual probably stems from the idea that God, and man as made in the image of God, must combine all opposites to be perfect.

The union of the sexes is the stock European occultist's example of a reconciliation of opposites that is physically fruitful (in the conception of a child) and also spiritually and magically fruitful. The magical ideal is 'the whole man,' the man who unites all human characteristics and potentialities in harmony, the man who is all that a human being could possibly be, and so, in effect, the man who has become the One, or God. To do this, he must bring all the opposite forces of his Nature into balance.

This is one reason for the importance of sex in magic. Richard Cavendish (born 1930) says (in *The Black Arts*): 'Many magical ceremonies are deliberately designed to summon up and unleash the animal driving forces from the deeps of human nature. The whole man is to be raised to the power of infinity, not man as civilized thinker or man as ravening beast, but man as a combination of both.' It follows that although the magician may use sex in a magical operation as a powerful source of energy, he must not allow himself to be carried away on the floodtide of desire. He must master it and subordinate it to his purposes.

One result is the importance of 'balance' in magical ceremonies, so that they can be equally blended in a greater whole. The principle is by no means confined to the West. Toga is a harmony' says the *Bhagavad Gita*. 'Not for him who eats too much or for him who eats too little; not for him who sleeps too little, or for him who sleeps too much.' The *Gita* also teaches the lesson that God is perfect peace but also its opposite, irresistible power, for it ends with a vision of 'Deity in all its blazing fury.'

Rain and Rainbows

Rain epitomizes the essence of life, for without it nothing on Earth can grow and thrive. No wonder, then, that rain was regarded by the ancients as a gift from the gods, whose wrath could cause both drought and flood. Typical were the Greek god Zeus and Jupiter, his Roman equivalent, who were believed to create rain by dipping the branches of a sacred oak into water.

Such is the value of rain that rainmakers exist in cultures worldwide, from Buddhist priests who induce downpours by symbolically pouring water into holes into temple floors, to the Druids who processed to wells and springs revered for their magical powers and beat the water surface with sticks, traditionally of hazel. In many countries, including India, both frogs and snakes are credited with the ability to make it rain and are propitiated accordingly, being ritually sprinkled with or dipped into water. To the Shawnee Indians, good rain will come for the crops if a buffalo's tail is dipped in water and the moisture then flicked onto the earth.

Rain is a variable entity, sometimes defined by its sex. For while 'female' rain is soft and gentle, 'male' rain, at least to many native North Americans, is a hefty downpour. But whatever its gender, rain is unwelcome when it falls in such quantities that it results in floods or deluges which, in ancient literature, are sent by the gods as punishment to the disobedient or sinful. The Mesopotamian *Epic of Gilgamesh*, dating to around 2000 BC, vividly described a cloud that 'rose up from the horizon . . . turning to blackness all that had been light' so that:

The wide land was shattered like
a pot!
For one day the south-storm blew

Gathering speed as it blew,
submerging mountains
Overtaking the people like a battle.

Like Noah, Atrahasis, the hero of the tale, loaded up a boat with his family, provisions, and animals to thwart the power of the god Enil, governor of all Nature, and succeeded in saving himself and the creatures.

Colours in the Sky

In the Biblical story of Noah, God sent the rainbow to signal both the end of the flood sent to destroy the sinful world and his promise that he would never inflict such a punishment on our planet's inhabitants again. Across the world, the rainbow has other meanings also. To the ancient Greeks it marked the path linking Earth and heaven, and was embodied in the form of the goddess Iris, the brilliantly clad messenger of Zeus and Hera and bringer of good news. In Norse mythology the rainbow represents Bifrost and is guarded by the sun god Heimdall against raids by the evil frost giants who, as long as the rainbow's colours—representing fire, air, and water—are still aflame, will not dare to jump astride it, in case they should melt away.

The rainbow is envisaged in many forms. In Hindu mythology, it was used as a giant bow by Indra from which he shot his lightning arrows; Indra also hurled thunderbolts. Among Native Americans and Australian aborigines, and in Iran and West Africa the rainbow is a serpent, revered as a creator and bringer of fertility, which emerges from the water to drink his fill from a sky from which life-bringing rain is falling.

Peoples of South America, including the Arawak, Witoto, and Vilela believe the rainbow to be responsible for the myriad colours of birds. Whilst the rainbow serpent was still in his infancy, so the tale relates, he was captured by a young girl who raised him at home as a pet. Once grown he escaped and went around the world devouring men and women until at last, he was attacked and killed by a huge flock of birds. To celebrate their success the birds dipped themselves into the blood of the creature, each emerging with the distinctive colouring by which we know them today.

The rainbow is feared as much as it is welcomed. The Karens of Myanmar thought it to be a malignant demon that could devour the human spirit. In Europe, rainbow superstitions have a long history, and are reliably recorded from the seventeenth century. A rainbow seen arching over a house is still, to the superstitious, seen as a sign that a death of one of the inhabitants is imminent. To neutralize the rainbow's effect, and to avoid such a disaster, children would customarily 'cross it out' by laying sticks or straws on the ground in the shape of a cross with a pebble set on each end. On no account, it is said, should you ever point at a rainbow or walk on a patch of ground on which you think a rainbow has stood.

And of course the bluebirds that fly over the rainbow, and the pot of gold at its end, remain as elusive as ever. For according to ancient Irish legend, a leprechaun hammering a shoe sits at the end of every rainbow, guarding the treasure, which was put there by the fairies. Only he, it is said, will reveal the whereabouts of the pot of gold.

Man in Mayan traditional ornamental feather headdress playing drums to please the rain god

But because he will vanish if he is ever caught, and rainbows do not actually end (because in fact they are circles), no one ever finds the gold or the magical creature.

RUTH BINNEY

FURTHER READING Funk & Wagnalls. Standard Dictionary of Folklore, Mythology, and Legend. *(New York, NY: Harper and Row, 1984); Iona Opie and Moira Tatem.* A Dictionary of Superstitions. *(New York, NY: Oxford University Press, 1989).*

Right

Whilst the left hand and foot are deemed unlucky, fortune favours the right. When being baptized or confirmed into the Christian church, good luck is believed to be conferred if the priest or bishop performs the ceremony with the right hand. To achieve Christian perfection, the repentant sinner's aim is to sit, at the last, at the right hand of God. In proper etiquette, the handshake of amiable greeting is traditionally performed with the right hand, this being for most, the one in which a sword would be drawn and used, implying that the gesture is made in peace. A right-handed fisherman will always be ensured a better catch than a 'leftie,' while to enter a home with right foot first is to bring good fortune with you.

Rites of Passage

A Flemish anthropologist working at the Sorbonne, A. van Gennep (1873–1957), was the first person to distinguish rites of passage as a distinct category of ritual, in his book *Les Rites de Passage*, published in 1909. His work immediately made a great

A groom carries his bride over the threshold of their house to mark a rite of passage

impression on all scholars working on the interpretation of the rituals of what were then called primitive and are here called tribal societies, though many of the rituals considered by van Gennep were ancient Roman, Greek or Near Eastern, and Hebraic, Christian, and Islamic. Van Gennep pointed out that many of these rituals showed a 'passage' in location or in time, and he showed conclusively that the rituals could be broken into three phases: first, a 'preliminal' phase in which the persons or groups who were the subjects of the ritual were *separated* from their previous social condition; secondly, a 'liminal' phase in which they were in a *marginal* situation; and finally a third 'postliminal' phase in which they were *reaggregated* to their previous social condition or *aggregated* to a new social condition, sometimes

in the idea of resurrection. He stressed that these three phases, found in similar form in many societies, correspond to underlying necessities of social life: all social life involves movement in space, in time, and in social situation, and certain of these movements are marked by ritual transitions.

Van Gennep began his analysis by pointing to the high significance in many cultures of the threshold of a house, and the care with which this is built with ritual or magical accompaniments, or marked by religious protection, notably in the concept of the Roman god Janus, who looked both ways; while Orthodox Jews still fix to their doorways the mezuzah, which is a small case containing religious texts. In some Jewish homes mezuzahs are placed on the doorway of each room.

The doorway to a house marked a transition from one world of relationships to another: from this developed special types of ritual that marked the crossing of the threshold (Latin *limen*, from which the word 'liminal' comes to describe such rituals).

Van Gennep then proceeded to look at a whole series of characteristic rituals present in situations that involve changes in social conditions: the erection of houses, the commencement of agricultural activities, the gathering of first fruits and harvest, birth, marriage, funerals, ordination, and the initiation of youths or girls into manhood and womanhood. These are but a few examples from the multitude of occasions that van Gennep showed to be marked by separation, marginal and aggregatory rites.

It may easily be seen how the analysis of these rites was related to his starting point, the building of the house. From our own customs we can instance the symbolic carrying of a bride by her husband across the threshold of their new home, a liminal rite which marks her movement after the wedding ceremony from her residence in her natal home to her residence in her conjugal home, with all which that movement marks in the alteration of her roles. Similarly, in some cultures a corpse cannot be carried out of a house over the sacred threshold but has to be taken out through a window, or through an opening broken in the wall.

Van Gennep's theory immediately made a profound impression on scholars studying ritual. In fact his phrase, *rites de passage*, passed in its French form into all anthropological literature. The subjects dealt with most commonly under this heading were rites of birth, puberty, initiation into manhood and womanhood (which van Gennep carefully pointed out did not necessarily correspond with puberty), and burial.

Cutting the Apron Strings

The nature of these rites can be briefly illustrated with examples: the rites, for example, surrounding the circumcision of boys of Southern African tribes on their initiation into manhood.

They first undergo separation rites, such as jumping over fire or water, which exhibit clearly the main purpose of the ritual—to separate them symbolically from the ignorance of boyhood and from the company of their mothers. These initial rites culminate in circumcision at a spot in the bush, on which no woman must look.

The boys are then segregated during a marginal period, while the circumcision wounds heal, in a lodge of brushwood built out of sight of the women. There they learn special actions, songs, and formulas, often meaningless (though said to be in an ancient language), and wear special costumes marked by special colours.

Early records stated that this symbolic cutting of the apron strings holding a boy to his mother was complete: more recent research has shown that the boys' mothers must collaborate in some of the rites of this marginal period, because they have a duty to assist their husbands in altering the tie of sons with mothers, so that the sons can grow up to be independent men. Thus, in some rites, men and boys sing songs through the cold of the winter night; and the women have to huddle in the open, on the edge of the village, around inadequate fires, ready to respond with ululations to the ending of each song. This response is said to be essential to help the boys to grow up.

When the circumcision wounds have healed, the boys are finely dressed and are allowed to appear to their mothers: these strain to get at their sons, but are driven off, often with real struggles, by the men. In some tribes the men folk are assisted by masked and clothed figures who represent ancestral spirits.

This temporary aggregation of the initiates, when their mothers can see them but not touch them, is succeeded by a less restricted marginal phase when they can be seen by the women at a distance, and even visited by their prenubile sisters. Finally, in a great celebration, the boys are brought, in smart new clothes, to dance in the village and to be surrounded by their mothers, who can now scoff at the pre-

Hamer boys before the Bull Jumping initiation ceremony, after which successful jumpers may take a wife

viously feared masked figures. Whatever their actual age, the boys emerge socially as men, who may begin sexual relationships, are forbidden to sleep in a hut with their mothers, and are allowed to sit with the men.

Time in Limbo

A second example of a rite of passage is the funeral. This often consists of an elaborate complex of rites, broken into three distinct phases. After the burial, both the mourners and the dead person's spirit enter a marginal phase. The mourners' behaviour is marked by many taboos and special modes of behaviour, dress, and adornment or lack of adornment. At this time, the spirit of the deceased may be believed to be making an arduous journey to the 'world of spirits,' or else, in societies where there is a cult of ancestral worship, it may be conceived to be wandering loose, homeless, and restless. Finally, after this marginal period, aggregation rites are held, either to mark the entry of the spirit to the world of spirits, or else to institute the spirit among the ancestors.

The 'passage' theme is evident in wedding rites, as it is in such ceremonies as initiation to special societies or the ordination of a priest or consecration of a church, even though in Western culture such rites are often much attenuated. It appears also in seasonal festivals such as the celebration of the New Year, the gathering of first fruits, and Harvest Festivals.

At the festival of first fruits the whole of a classical or tribal society might perform rituals that marked the separation of the people—often represented by their leaders—from their normal way of life, and their entry into a marginal period when they had to observe many taboos, such as not eating particular foods and not speaking loudly, save in the performance of special rites. In this marginal phase normal rules might be suspended.

Forbidden Marriage

Great festivities, dancing, and drinking, mark the aggregation into the New Year. Sometimes, in societies without well-organized government, these are the occasions when normally highly independent sections of society, potentially hostile to each other, will show their unity in common festivals: during this period, marriages, which are likely to occur between these different sections of the community and may cause strife, are prohibited.

Van Gennep was correct in pointing out that rites of this kind fall into disuse with the technical and economic development of society, though some remain. To refer this change to a decreasing interest in the

> . . . roles and relationships are materially and not ceremoniously or ritually segregated, and for this reason there is no ritualization of secular roles.

sacred, and its separation from the profane, seems inadequate. The present writer has suggested an alternative explanation, that in tribal and other societies individuals perform their roles (filial, parental, political, economic, religious, educational, etc) in the same places, with largely the same material belongings, in relationships with largely the same set of other persons. These societies are marked by highly ceremonious or even ritualized behaviour, which marks the special relationships in terms of which a person is acting, or the role he is performing, in a particular place at a particular time. The ritualization is achieved by attaching occult power to the acting—directly, or invertedly, or symbolically—of specific secular roles. The ceremoniousness serves symbolically to segregate roles and relationships where this cannot be done materially. In an industrialized society, on the other hand, people commonly interact in their various activities with a wide range of individuals, in many different buildings using different material goods: roles and relationships are materially and not ceremoniously or ritually segregated, and for this reason there is no ritualization of secular roles.

MAX GLUCKMAN

Spring

Drinking, dancing, feasting, noise-making, and love-making have been the usual ways in which men have celebrated occasions of communal happiness; the winning of a war, for instance, or an election, the birth of a royal heir, or the death of a tyrant. However, since prehistoric times man has reserved special celebratory energies for the turning of the seasons, and has reacted with perhaps the strongest surge of emotion to spring, the time when the earth is freed from the shackles of winter.

This emotion was expressed in the form of religious rites, mainly because for ancient man, no aspect of life could be kept apart from religion. Modern commentators have seen in the Paleolithic cave paintings of dancing figures in animal masks or disguises a form of hunting magic that itself was probably seasonal; but later ages brought agriculture to mankind, and the seasonal rites became of crucial importance. The celebration of returning fertility along with the magical stimulation of fertility form the basis for all ancient spring rituals and festivals, and so through them for most modern ones.

Something of their essence can be seen in the ancient spring customs of Mesopotamia in which the Babylonians performed ritual reenactments of a Creation myth, reflecting the re-creation of spring. And they staged the sacred intercourse of the king and a priestess in a room set aside for the rite and decorated with leaves and flowers.

Sex and drama also occur in the rituals of the Greeks, a festive people who took every opportunity available for some sort of celebration. And the eastern cults that were introduced during later centuries offered many opportunities. Before that the early

Greeks held a spring Festival of Flowers to praise fertility and the god Dionysus, with plenty of sacrificing, feasting, and drinking. There was also some placation of the community's dead, the ancestral ghosts, a practice that found its way into many later traditions.

In March, the Great Dionysia was celebrated, which by the sixth century BC had come to be a time not only for general revels of a wildly unrestrained Nature, but also for the presentation of drama in Athens. Evolved from older choric hymns and rites of Dionysus, the tragedies of Aeschylus, Sophocles

and Euripides developed first, but comedy followed fast. And the latter retained explicit aspects of its fertility rite origins, as in the traditional flaunting of oversize phalluses.

Rome's spring festivals took up many of these older threads and entwined them with new ones. In early Republican days there were minor festivities such as the dancing and processions of the *Salii*, in March, or the uninhibited merrymaking of the April *Parilia*, originally a shepherds' rite. Also in April was a movable feast, the beautiful *Floralia*, which in the true primitive tradition combined vegetation magic and ritual sexuality.

The better-known ceremonies of the *Lemuria* in May recall the Greek festival that paid homage to the dead: for the Romans it was also a time for laying restless ancestral spirits, and preventing them from wreaking harm. Something of the same intention functioned in another well known late Roman festive occasion, the *Lupercalia*, which was held in February, at the very start of the Roman spring. It involved sacrifices, offerings of the first fruits of the previous harvest, and the other usual basic enjoyments. But it also required some ritual flagellation of people, most usually of barren women, to stimulate their fertility and perhaps to drive off whatever evil baulked that fertility. The priests also 'beat the bounds' of the communities, or of the fields, again to set up magical protection against evil for the year to come.

The declining Empire came to know many new cults and their festivals (apart from the novel worship of Christianity). One was the *Bacchanalia*, the frenzied Roman version of the Greek Dionysia, but another more austere festival developed with the cult worship of Attis. This was the March celebration called *Hilaria*. It involved processions and sacrifices, followed by abstention from meat, and general restrictions, to accompany the ritual

Relief, showing the House of Dionysus and the Four Seasons, third century AD

mourning of the god's death. The god's eventual resurrection was followed by ritual joy and festivity. Christians will find the pattern not unfamiliar.

First and Last Flings

From the earliest Christian times, the celebration of spring tended to begin on or shortly after Twelfth Night, but to come to a head especially in the few days before Ash Wednesday and the austerities of Lent. Many pre-Christian festivals were held at this time, and again this is an example of Christianity superimposing itself onto paganism. In fact, the folk festivals, as opposed to the liturgical ones, always tended toward the secular, not to say the profane. Nevertheless, the Church's terminology took over: the final day of the festivals is invariably Shrove Tuesday, presumably so called because it was a day for priests to shrive folk in preparation for Lent. Yet, although the festivals may appear to be in the nature of 'last flings' before Lenten asceticism, they were, and are, also 'first flings,' expressing universal joy at the spring renewal. The pre-Lenten festivals were not the sole spring festivities, but for Christian Europe and the Americas, they were the first.

Some motifs are found in most of these early spring celebrations. Feasting is always important, especially for Christians who had to give up meat and any kind of rich delicacy in Lent; but sometimes the feasting is merely symbolized by the eating of some special Shrovetide food. Dancing invariably takes place, as always at times of communal joy; some special dances may be mimetic and dramatic, concerning some suitable springtime theme, while others might be processional, the ancestors of later parades. The modern idea of parades with great

The Austrian Schemen are masked dancers who perform at the Innsbruck festival the week before Ash Wednesday.

MAN, MYTH, AND MAGIC

The Portela samba school float of the 2012 Carnival parade in Rio de Janeiro

decorated 'floats' was foreshadowed in the Germanic rite praising the goddess Nerthus, which involved processions with sacred objects borne on a strange 'boat-on-wheels' called a ship-wagon or ship-cart.

Masks and costumes are always part of the festivities, perhaps recalling the prehistoric dancers in animal headdresses, and the primitive belief that fearful masks provided a way of keeping evil spirits at bay. But in more modern times the costumes are worn largely for the sake of competitive splendour, and the masks have always helped the celebrants to shed their inhibitions in relative safety.

The motif of warding off or driving off evil crops up in many places in forms other than masking. Sometimes it is a magical ritual to protect the crops, at other times it appears as a magical destruction or exorcism of the demonic winter or some other ap-

propriate symbol of evil. Noise plays a large part in the expulsion, as it does in many primitive rites; often an effigy figure is burned or suitably destroyed.

Mock battles of one kind or another occur frequently, and are probably linked with the motif of driving off evil. For while they may have taken on special colourations, such as reenactments of historical combats, or riotous sport, their presence in a spring festival links them with more ancient ritual battles symbolizing the conflict of winter and summer.

Spring festivals all naturally incorporate some form of sexuality—not only private sex activity, which has always accompanied drinking, feasting, and dancing, but also ritual sex that long predates the Christian traditions. Some traditions incorporate variants of the sacred marriage; others merely bring in rude songs, the coarse antics of clowns, and earthy folk drama.

Drama, on any level, is a spring motif of its own. The incomparable Greek drama grew from much older, primitive rites; and the high traditions of English drama had their roots in choric liturgical rites of the Church at Easter that gave rise to later mystery and miracle plays, and the folk dances, mimes, and mummery of the people, performed at Shrovetide, which developed the morality thread of the English tradition. Many lands still have special folk dramas and masques that are performed before Lent as they have been for centuries.

The sexual and dramatic aspects of the revelry sometimes overlap with another common motif, in which the normal order of things is overturned. Servants or fools become rulers, Lords of Misrule dominate the festivities of many countries, men dress as women.

It may seem odd that countries of the far north start their festivities to celebrate spring and fertility at a time when the snow is usually no less deep than at Christmas. Similarly, it may seem strange that customs left over from Catholic observances of Lent still survive in primarily Protestant countries. The latter fact may be accounted for simply because the old ways die hard, especially when they are enjoyable, and the former may be because the combined pagan and Christian jollity, though perhaps imported to the northern lands, proved able to overcome the frost and ice of February.

Indeed, a Finnish tradition makes use of the snow: outdoor games are part of the holiday, and old lore says that if the children's sleds can coast long distances on Shrove Tuesday, the year's crops will be bountiful. Elsewhere in Scandinavia, feasting, processions, games, and dances are hallmarks of the pre-Lent time as is the custom of playful ritual flagellation with birch or willow switches, recalling the old purification theme, the driving off of winter and evil.

Driving off demons also seems all-important in Teutonic traditions, especially in the great *Fastnacht* celebrations of Germany, known as *Fasching* in Austria. The Austrian *Schemen*, a wild assortment of masked demonic dancers that form the centrepiece of the Innsbruck festival the week before Ash Wednesday, are especially notable. Cologne's revelry features a Prince of Fastnacht with a court of fools, while Saxony was given to staging a mock battle between the forces of winter and summer. Munich's gorgeous pageantry is world famous, but seems to dwell more on the city's medieval history than on folk custom or ancient rite; the German-speaking Swiss of Zurich have a tradition of killing an effigy of winter in their spring festivities.

British customs generally seem to have missed out the parades and pageantry so favoured in other lands,

but some of the old spring motifs make their appearance. Shrove Tuesday is still Pancake Day in Britain, symbolic of the coming abstention from meat. Apart from this special food, Shrovetide for Britons once meant a time for rough games and hooliganism. In the past, apprentices were given a holiday on the Tuesday, and showed their appreciation by all kinds of happy rowdiness. A special sort of Shrovetide football was played in many towns and rural villages.

The sexuality theme seems to be lacking in the British Shrovetide, though the traditional post-Easter fun, and especially the Maytime delights of the past, tended to make up for this lack.

In other countries pancakes are eaten as in Britain, and there are also splendid parades or dances. In Belgium where pancakes and door-to-door begging are both part of the tradition, glorious processions were staged. These were dominated by the Gilles, who wore beautiful costumes of silk embroidered with lace, and ostrich-plume headdresses, and who used to pelt onlookers with oranges.

Old Russian and Eastern European customs included eating special cakes: the Russians called them *blini*, and the time of celebration was known as *Maslenitza*, 'butter week.' Apparently the Soviet Union has retained some of these traditions—especially the blini—though stripped of any religious associations. However, it is unlikely that other Slavic customs have lasted; the Eastern European dance where the women had to leap high, so that the crops would grow tall, for instance, or the Bulgarian processions with men, dressed as women, performing mimetic ploughing and sowing dances.

Farther south in Europe, terms meaning 'Shrovetide' are replaced by the word 'carnival,' which has come to mean unrestrained festive gaiety. Italy sometimes begins its *carneuale*

in mid-January or earlier, and keeps up the feasting, dancing, and pageantry until Shrove Tuesday. Venice crowns an overweight effigy, the spirit of fleshly indulgence, as King of Carnival and ritually burns him to bring in Ash Wednesday. Florence, among other centres, is noted for the delightful rudeness of traditional carnival songs.

The Spanish carnival spirit produces most of the usual traditions, especially public dancing and masked processions. In northern Spain, a stuffed effigy again acts as the emblem of carnival license; it rides in a cart decorated with greenery, reflecting the ancient belief in vegetation magic, and is duly burned. Elsewhere in Spain an effigy representing the King of Evil is ritually buried; and the spring *fiesta* also includes many folk dramas on sacred marriage or Resurrection themes, or on the symbolic battle theme, which is sometimes in the form of dramatic dance battles between Moors and Christians.

The Spanish concepts of pre-Lent fiesta were widely adopted in Latin and South America, and there, too, the motif of the mock battle seems to be strong. A Mexican drama ritually depicts the capture of a famous bandit by soldiers, while in southeast Mexico a mock battle dance concerns 'priests' and 'devils.' Throughout Latin America maskers represent devils and the dead, signifying the supernatural forces that are to be warded off.

But the Spanish ex-colonies take fiesta to its heights in their immense variety of special dances, such as the quadrille-type dance of central Mexico, for instance, in which participants wear medieval garb. Many of the dances incorporate elements of pre-Columbian Indian dances and rites. In Mexico, for instance, the time that is now carnival was once given to revelry in praise of the Aztec god of agriculture.

Portugal's carnival spirit rivals that of Spain. It was once especially famous for the extreme coarseness of the songs, dances, and jokes of the masked Fools who dominated it, though this feature has diminished in recent times. The mock battle theme recurs abundantly: in the town of Louie, for instance, the ritual conflict is fought out with flowers.

Portuguese carnival traditions were naturally exported to Brazil, where in 1840 the urban carnival of Rio de Janeiro began; it is now regarded as the most lavish on the continent. All the expected features of carnival can be found in costly abundance, especially parades with vast resplendent floats and ornate costuming, in which various societies and clubs ruthlessly compete. Otherwise, besides the street dancing, music, noise, drinking, and wild revelry, Rio finds some quiet corners to stage a major song contest, with rich prizes. And the whole festival culminates in a masquerade ball in the Municipal Theater.

'Fat Tuesday'

The French have always enjoyed many different kinds of carnival, including a now extinct festival of butchers in Paris, which featured *Le Boeuf Gras*, a fattened ox decorated with ribbons, which was probably another emblem of the indulgence to be forsworn in Lent. But the chief festival is the carnival of Nice, with glorious parades and pageants, dominated by King Carnival and his court of clowns and harlequins, embodying the free wild spirit of the season. This spirit flourished especially in the French colony that is now the US state of Louisiana. There the significant French name for Shrove Tuesday took on new meaning as the general term for the whole festive time. The name is Mardi Gras, 'Fat Tuesday.'

Mardi Gras traditions date from the mid-eighteenth century, in New Orleans, when private masquerade balls often exploded onto the streets to become public, sometimes violent, merrymaking. By the early nineteenth century the city's revelers had taken to parading through the streets on horseback or in carriages to display their finery; and tableaux, masques and similar light dramas had become a part of the occasion.

By the mid-nineteenth century, the Creole domination of this essentially

The colourful Mardi Gras Parade of New Orleans, Louisiana, in 2005

French tradition had begun to be eclipsed by the eager 'Saxons.' Then in 1857, a group of the latter formed a theoretically secret society called the 'Mystic Krewe of Comus,' and staged a colourful street parade depicting the demons from Milton's *Paradise Lost*. So the modern Mardi Gras was born.

The Civil War interrupted the tradition but the Krewe of Comus formed itself again afterward and continued its parades, always with a special theme that might be allegorical or sometimes satirical. There was always a torchlit night parade on the Tuesday. The Krewe also staged tableaux, and topped off the night with a grand ball that rapidly became a major social occasion.

The festivities were often marred by Creole-Saxon conflicts and general riotous behaviour, but the protests of some citizens could not stem the Mardi Gras tide. In 1872, the day was declared a legal holiday, though by then the festival had been getting under way much earlier. Indeed, in 1870, a Lord of Misrule figure had briefly appeared, with a parade of his own, on Twelfth Night. But in 1872 he faded out, for Rex, King of Carnival, and his court of Dukes, came into being partly to impress the Russian Tsar's younger son, who was visiting the city. The parades were enormous that year, the decorations lavish, the merriment frenzied. On the Tuesday more than a dozen bands played a song called *If Ever I Cease to Love*, supposedly a favourite of the royal Russian; and though he must have been heartily sick of it by the end of the day, it remains a traditional tune of Mardi Gras. That year also there was a Boeuf Gras in the old French tradition. Rex, whose parade was at noon on the Tuesday, initiated the now fixed custom of acquiring a Queen, usually a pretty society debutante, and escorting her to the 'court' of Comus at midnight, to pay

respects to the first lord of Mardi Gras.

Soon other krewes, as the clubs and societies are still generically known, began to take part. The Knights of Momus led the newcomers, and at first paraded on New Year's Eve, later switching to the Thursday before Fat Tuesday. In 1882, the Knights of Proteus began parading on the Monday; the Krewe of Hermes took over the Friday; and krewes of Orpheus, Osiris, Mithras, Elves of Oberon, the Harlequins, Pierettes, Marionettes, and dozens of others found room where they could for their own parades and displays.

Some citizens thought it was all getting out of hand. Sometimes the festivities began before Christmas, as they still do: in 1965 the society balls began on December 23, and there had been 62 of them by Fat Tuesday. From the start, the inter-krewe rivalry had been lavishly expensive and there was no stopping the flood. Neighbourhood parades began to spring up and on the Saturday, schoolchildren organized their own parades. After the First World War the Negroes of New Orleans introduced a parade on the Tuesday itself, before Rex's parade began. The black contribution was headed by the Zulu King, with a ham-bone as scepter, who was clearly in the Lord of Misrule tradition of overturning the usual order of things. He parades still, though black militants deplore his presence.

Others now tend to deplore the New Orleans' Mardi Gras, feeling that its French antecedents and the pre-Lent gaiety have been forced into a back seat by the more modern spirit of public relations. Mardi Gras remains the high point of the social calendar, with an invitation to the Comus ball being a testimonial to social success; otherwise, the ruling theme is not snobbery but civic promotion and commercialism. The two may

overlap, of course, for many of the krewes are somewhat identified with businessmen's lunch clubs.

Mardi Gras has been taken over by the promoters because it is a successful tourist attraction. Though the carnival spirit of the citizens is supposed to be the mainspring of the festivities, the Chamber of Commerce is in fact a more likely one, and the city itself pours hundreds of thousands of dollars into the occasion. Nor are private promoters far behind: the trinkets traditionally thrown to the crowd from Rex's parade, once considered luck-bringing souvenirs, now carry advertising matter.

Citizens are calling for the abandonment of the celebration because, they say commercialism and violence have distorted the spirit of Mardi Gras. However, it is doubtful if that folk spirit truly survived much past the 1850s. After all, the originators, with their self-conscious title of a Mystic Krewe, their high literary themes from Milton, and their expanding sense of their own social cachet, could hardly be said to have represented a spirit that had much to do with the simple, age-old human urge to celebrate the earth's renewal in spring.

DOUGLAS HILL

FURTHER READING: E. O. James. Seasonal Feasts and Festivals. (New York, NY: Barnes and Noble, 1961); Errol Laborde. Mardi Gras!. (Picayune Press, 1981).

Summer

The true start of summer coincides with the longest day of the year, the summer solstice, on June 21. Under the influence of Christianity much of the time-honoured celebration was transferred, over the years, to Midsummer Eve, two days

Revelers gather as druids and pagans celebrate the summer solstice at the megalithic monument of Stonehenge, England

later and St. John's day on June 23, but celebration of the solstice retains it connection with traditional fertility rites and rituals, when it was once believed that the gods would confer sexual powers. South of the equator, where the summer solstice occurs in on December 21, celebrations have similarly become combined with those of the Christmas season.

At Stonehenge, on Britain's Salisbury Plain, thousands gather each year to mark the summer solstice. Central to this choice of venue is the belief, still held by many, that this extraordinary megalith was constructed in around 3100 BC as an observatory designed so that, on the dawn of the longest day, the sun rises directly over its Heel Stone, when this is viewed from the centre of the stone circle. So strong is the draw of Stonehenge that in 2013, more than 20,000 New Age and Pagan followers gathered on the morning of June 21 to witness the sun rising at 4:52 am, celebrating with dancing and singing.

In Mexico, a similar ceremony, complete with crowds, takes place at Chichén Itzá. Here on June 21, at the ancient Mayan centre of science, culture, religion, and trade, the sun strikes the north and east sides of the Temple of Kukulcan—a precisely built four-sided step pyramid, casting such a deep shadow on the south and west sides that the temple appears to be split exactly in half. In ancient times the solstice was also here, as elsewhere, a time for rituals designed to bring fertility and prosperity.

Across the Americas, solstice celebrations amongst native peoples include ritual dances. The Sioux would cut down and then raise up a tree to form a link between heaven and Earth, and place their teepees in a circle representing the cosmos. Dancers would paint their bodies or wear costumes in colours representing different aspects of the natural world—red for the sunset, blue for the sky, yellow for lightning, white for sunlight, and black for the night.

Predicting Summer Weather

Rain or shine—deluge or drought? Predicting the summer's weather in both the short and the long term has for centuries been a preoccupation in temperate climes, particularly for those tending crops and animals but, more recently for vacationers and sportsmen and women. Most famous of the short term summer predictions is that of St. Swithin's day—July 15:

St. Swithin's day, if thou dost rain,
For forty days it will remain.
St. Swithin's day, if you be fair,
For forty days 'twill rain no more.

In Europe St. Swithin's day is customarily associated with the health of the apple crop and rain on that day is said to 'christen' the apples. In Germany, June 27, or *Siebanschäfertag* (Seven Sleeper's day) is a similar prediction date, the weather on that day being believed to last for seven weeks. Modern meteorology confirms that there is some truth in the saying, since by mid-July the jet stream, which largely controls Europe's summer weather, is likely to be set in place for the season.

Keeping a watchful eye on the natural world is a favourite way of predicting summer's weather, and while some have an element of the truth, many are unreliable. It is not true, for instance, that cows lie down when it's going to rain—they lie down to chew the cud, whatever the weather—nor that rooks build their nests high when a fine summer is on the way. It is true, however, that dandelions and scarlet pimpernels close their petals ahead of rain (although the pimpernels always close at 2 p.m. whatever the weather). And swallows do indeed fly low when rain is on the way, since their insect food drops nearer the ground when the air is damp.

Heights of Heat

The hottest days of summer were dubbed by the Romans *caniculares dies,* or dog days, because, according to the naturalist Pliny the Elder (AD 23–AD 79), these were the times when dogs were 'most ready to run mad.' Equally, it was believed that the heat was caused by both Sirius, the dog star, and the brightest in the constellation Canis Majoris (the big dog) rising at the same time as the sun. The actual dates are vague, but dog days were usually said to occur between July 3 and August 18, when Sirius entered Leo and rose at the same time as the sun, thus accentuating the heat.

Dog days were a cause for great wariness, for the Romans thought that they coincided with calamities of all kinds. The seventeenth century author Godfridus set out the strict rules of behaviour expected during dog days, forbidding bloodletting, the taking of medicines, and sex. Warnings were also sounded against attacks from flies and snakes, which in hot weather could be

The thirteen at the Last Supper as depicted by this nineteenth century Russian painting

fatal, and against 'feeding violently.'

Picking up on the canine connection, town magistrates often ordered dogs to be muzzled at this time, for fear that they would become over aggressive.

RUTH BINNEY

FURTHER READING: B. Blackburn and L. Holford Strevens. The Oxford Companion to the Year. *(New York, NY: Oxford University Press, 2003); R. Binney.* Wise Words and Country Ways: Weather Lore. *(Newton Abbot, UK: David and Charles, 2010).*

Thirteen

That the number thirteen is unlucky is one of the most common and persistent of superstitions and one

of the few that is openly catered to. Hotel managements still frequently take care to have no thirteenth floor and some builders and local authorities do not number a house thirteen, because if they do it will be difficult to dispose of. Gustav Jahoda records in his book *The Psychology of Superstition* that in 1965, when the Queen paid a visit to West Germany, the number of the platform at Duisburg railway station from which her train was to leave was changed from 13 to 12a.

Thirteen to Dinner

A great many people dislike parties of thirteen and it is thought to be extremely unlucky for this number of people to sit down to a table. One of them, sometimes said to be the first person to rise from the table, or sometimes the last, will die or suffer some damaging misfortune before a year is out. The belief was recorded, in Oxfordshire, England, that it was ominous for thirteen people to be together in one room, especially for the one who was nearest the door and, in London, that if the number on a bus ticket added to thirteen it brought bad luck.

The thirteenth day of the month is widely regarded as a most unpropitious day for beginning any new undertaking (although there seems to be nothing unfortunate about being born on it) and even people who think of themselves as entirely unsuperstitious have been known to show slight symptoms of unease when the thirteenth falls on a Friday, which is an unlucky day in its own right.

The reasons for this uneasiness about thirteen are obscure. Though it has probably been strengthened by the fact that thirteen sat down to the Last Supper—the first person to rise from the table being Judas, who went out to betray Christ—the uneasiness is older than Christianity, for even the Romans associated thirteen with death and misfortune. The root reason may be that thirteen is one more than twelve, which is a number of completenes—the whole year consisting of twelve months, the whole day of twice twelve hours—and so it has the connotation of dangerously exceeding proper limits, of going beyond a natural cycle or starting on a new and uncertain course.

In early Christian numerology thirteen was sometimes categorized as the number of sin because it goes beyond the twelve apostles, though it could equally be a holy and admirable number that adds faith in the Trinity to the Ten Commandments. In the European magical tradition thirteen is the number of necromancy, of bringing the dead back to temporary life, which again implies transgressing natural and proper limits.

Submitting to the Magician's Will

One of the Graeco-Egyptian magical texts of the early centuries AD provides a method of animating a corpse that can then be forced to obsess a woman until she submits to the magician. It involves making a doll to represent the woman, piercing it with thirteen needles, and putting it on the grave of someone who died young or by violence, and then conjuring the corpse by incantation to rise up and stalk the streets to the woman's house, there to prey on her mind until she does the magician's will.

The Tarot trump—unnumbered in the traditional packs, but the only number missing is thirteen—is Death, a skeleton who is mowing a field of human heads with a scythe, while hands and feet grow in their place, a symbol of death and new life.

The fact that thirteen is the traditional number of a coven of witches, with the thirteenth being the Devil or the local leader, may also have contributed to the number's evil reputation. Margaret Murray (1863–1963), in *The Witch Cult in Western Europe* and *The God of the Witches*, maintained that witches were in fact organized in groups of thirteen, each with a leader and twelve followers. Modern witches generally regard thirteen as the proper number for a coven, though many real covens are smaller. The famous witch Isabel Gowdie said that there were thirteen in each coven, and in 1673, a woman named Anne Armstrong, of Morpeth in Northumberland, England, said that every 'covey' of witches had thirteen members and 'every covey of thirteen had a Devil, who danced first with those boasting the most evil.' But in general the evidence for real covens of thirteen is slight and unconvincing.

It has been suggested that a 'baker's dozen' of thirteen really means 'the Devil's dozen' and is derived from 'Boucca's dozen,' Boucca being an old name for a god or spirit, surviving in the buccas of Cornish lore. Margaret Murray, who, to the mingled scorn and amusement of more orthodox historians, connected the founding of the Order of the Garter by King Edward III with the 'old religion' of witchcraft, noted that there were twenty-six knights, equivalent to two covens, and that Edward's mantle as head of the order was decorated with 168 garters which, adding the one he wore on his own leg, makes 169, or thirteen times thirteen, equalling thirteen covens. However, it seems more likely that the number thirteen here was drawn directly from the model of Christ and the twelve apostles.

Three

Three is generally considered the luckiest of numbers and if your name adds to three, you will be described by numerologists as being fortunate. Creative, clever, charming, lively, and entertaining, extremely successful, a three has a natural attraction for both money and the opposite sex. He is one of those people to whom everything seems to come easily, who succeeds without really trying. Rarely worried or depressed, he takes life as it comes and may have difficulty in taking anything seriously, though he will have a strong underlying sense of his own value and importance. One of the key ideas attached to three in numerology is 'expression,' and those whose number it is express themselves wittily, effectively, and with frequency. Imaginative and optimistic, cheerful, generous, and agreeable, they get on well with everyone, but perhaps more because they are anxious to be liked than because of any deep concern for others.

A three enjoys the limelight and detests obscurity. Active, energetic, and proud, he may have a commanding air about him and he will make a bad subordinate. He likes to show off and to be admired, but is probably more nervous and sensitive than his assured and brilliant exterior suggests. He has a tendency to expend his energies wastefully in too many directions and, since he loves pleasure and luxury, to scatter his money about. Though always the life and soul of the party, he can sometimes be exasperatingly vain, gossipy, and superficial.

The Manifest Creator

Behind this picture of the creativity and self-expression of three are a number of converging numerological theories. To begin with, the number one, though potentially all-creative, is regarded as barren by itself, for however many times it is multiplied (fertilized) by itself, it remains one. The number two introduces a pair of opposites, but two multiplied by one remains two. It is three that fruitfully reconciles these opposites and creates more numbers (3 x 2 = 6). As the French magician Eliphas Levi (1810–1875) put it: 'Were God only one He would never be creator or father. Were He two there would be antagonism or division in the infinite, which would mean the division also or death of all possible things. He is therefore three for the creation by Himself and in His image of the infinite multitude of beings and numbers.'

Again, one is assigned to the point and two to the line, both of which are theoretical constructs. When three points are connected, in the triangle, the first plane figure is constructed, the first that has surface and is therefore observable. So one is regarded as the number of God as alone and complete in himself but hidden and unmanifested. In two something emanates from within God's wholeness to create the opposite forces that run all through the universe. In three the opposites are reconciled and God is for the first time manifest, for the first time comprehensible to human experience in having, as it were, a surface. This is followed by the creation of solidity in four, when a fourth point is added above the triangle and a pyramid constructed. Then the three of spirit and the four of matter, added or multiplied, produce seven and twelve, the numbers that govern the rhythms and cycles of life in the universe—the seven planets and days of the week, the twelve zodiac signs, months, and hours of the day.

Added to all this is the sexual symbolism of three. It is the first of the masculine numbers and the number of the male genitals, which are threefold. The triangle is a natural symbol for the male genitals (though it can also be a symbol for the female). Where God as one is the hidden and unknowable Absolute, God as three is the manifest creator of 'the infinite multitude of beings and numbers,' and this is the basic numerological interpretation of the Trinity, the three-fold godhead.

It follows that three is the number of creativity and self-expression on the human plane, as it is the number of God making himself known on the divine plane. The connection with 'surface' accounts for some of the

The illustration from an edition of the story of Goldilocks and the Three Bears (1900)

other characteristics of three—sparkle and glitter, showing off, a tendency to superficiality. The triangle, facing three ways, accounts for the tendency to expend effort in many directions, but this and other traits allotted to three also have a genital reference—attractiveness, need for approval, pride, energy, love of pleasure. The idea of three reconciling the opposites in a third term which harmonizes and transcends them accounts for the harmonious progress through life attributed to three, easy money and success, getting on well with everyone.

The tomb of Prince Alexander of the Mark, showing the Three Fates

Three Blind Mice

As the number of the Trinity, in Christian numerology, three is linked with the most holy, the most perfect, the best. However, the number's connection with the superlative is older, and is expressed in the Greek word *trismegistos* ('thrice-greatest,' superlatively great) and the Latin *ter felix* ('thrice-happy,' happiest). The notion of the superlative itself involves the third term in a series of three—good, better, best. And three is not only connected with 'best' but also with 'all,' and is the most important of the numbers of completeness. Time is made of three ingredients (past, present, and future) and so is space (length, breadth, and thickness). All created things have a beginning, middle, and end. The feeling that three is the basis of everything we experience may account for the belief that runs of luck, good or bad, tend to happen in threes. 'Third time lucky' is a common phrase and, on the other hand, if two unlucky things happen one after the other, some people will deliberately break a dish or do some other minor piece of damage in the hope of ending the run of ill luck.

Three of anything is somehow 'all' of it and 'enough' of it. 'I'll give you three guesses,' we say, with the feeling that three are enough. The hero of a folktale frequently has three wishes or three tries at a task, the heroine has three suitors. Three frequently bobs up as a number of completeness in nursery rhymes. Goldilocks met three bears, there were three blind mice, and three little kittens who lost their mittens.

In the distant past behind all this there may lie very early methods of counting which used special words for one and two, but for three or more

As the number of the Trinity, in Christian numerology three is linked with the most holy, the most perfect, the best.

simply said 'many.' The Babylonian term for a constellation, for instance, regardless of how many stars it might contain, was 'three stars,' meaning 'many stars.' In this way the connotations of three may have come to include 'many,' 'all,' 'abundance,' 'best,' and so 'lucky.'

Numbers of completeness are always important in magic because they prescribe how many times an action must be repeated to be effective. To chant an incantation three times is magically to chant it 'enough' times or 'all possible' times.

The Threefold God

Medieval Christian numerologists remarked on various uses of three as a number of completeness in the New Testament, including the three gifts of the magi to the infant Jesus, the three temptations in the wilderness, the three denials of Christ by Peter, the three falls on the road to Golgotha, the three days between Christ's crucifixion and resurrection, and the three appearances of the risen Christ to his disciples. These could all be taken as foreshadowings or reflections of the Trinity.

The period of thirty-three years is also regarded as significant by some modern occultists. A. E. Abbott observes in his *Encyclopaedia of Numbers* that 'important phenomena of history receive their special imprint through the fact that they unfold in a cycle of thirty-three years from their origin to maturity and fulfilment or to rebirth . . . The life of Christ, occupying thirty-three years on Earth, has impressed its forces and rhythms into the earth-organism and into time, thus giving form to world history.'

The doctrine of the Trinity was officially recognized by the Council of Constantinople in 381. The earliest Christians were Jews who believed that God is One and though of him as the heavenly Father. But in recognizing Christ as divine they introduced a second person into the godhead, the Son. In their confidence that the spirit of God, which had descended on the apostles after Christ's death (Acts, chapter 2), was with them and working in them, they added a third divine personage, the Holy Spirit. The Nature of God as Three-in-One, and of the relationship between the persons of the Trinity, caused great philosophical speculation.

Occasional groupings of deities in threes can be observed in pre-Christian religions: Osiris, Isis, and Horus as father, mother, and child in Egypt, or the triad of Serapis, Isis, and Harpocrates (Horus) at Alexandria, or the three universal gods at the head of the pantheon in Mesopotamia. Numerous other examples come from the Celts, to whom three was a sacred number. They sometimes portrayed their deities in groups of three, or with three heads or three faces, as a way of emphasizing their power and perhaps with the same basic idea of a single god making himself known in terms of three that underlies the numerological approach considered earlier.

Groups of three can also be found in Greek mythology—three Graces, the three Fates, and the three Furies. Early in this century a German scholar counted more than 120 triads in Greek myth and ritual. His conclusion was that three meant 'all' or 'many.' Greek triads attracted the interest of Renaissance humanists, who connected them with the Christian Trinity (even the three heads of Cerberus, the dog of the underworld, becoming an emblem of the Christian doctrine) and who saw them, again, in terms of a unity manifesting itself by displaying its three components, the opposites and the factor that reconciles them.

In Hinduism the concept of God as both one and three appears in Brahman, which in itself is One but which as it presents itself to the world is Three—Being, Consciousness, and Joy, or the godhead that originates, sustains, and destroys the universe, personified as the triad of Brahma, Vishnu, and Shiva. In his book *Mysticism Sacred and Profane* R. C. Zaehner comments on the remarkable closeness of the concept of the threefold Brahman as *Sat* (Being), *Cit* (Logos or Reason), and *Ananda* (Joy or Love) to that of the Christian Trinity of the Father (Being), the Son (Logos), and the Holy Spirit (Love).

That God must be both one and three, One as he essentially is, Three as he is manifested and known, has been observed by mystics of Christian and other traditions on the analogy, to put it simply, that a sentence must have a subject, a verb, and an object. If there is divine love, there must also be a lover and a beloved, if there is divine knowledge there must also be a knower and what is known. Zaehner quotes the thirteenth-century Jewish mystic Abraham Abulafia, who said that the Master 'is called . . . the knowledge, the knower, and the known, all at the same time, since all three are one in Him;' and a Sufi mystic, who was asked about the divine Union, and replied, 'Union, He Who unites, and He Who is united—and that is three.'

FURTHER READING: A. E. Abbott. Encyclopaedia of Numbers. *(Divernon, IL: Emerson Press, 1962); E. Wind.* Pagan Mysteries in the Renaissance. *(London, UK: Penguin, 1967 reprint); R. C. Zaehner.* Mysticism Sacred and Profane. *(New York, NY: Oxford University Press, 1967 reprint).*

Time

The mysterious Nature of time, as it is presented to human experience, has been described in a celebrated passage by St. Augustine of Hippo (354–430). He writes in his *Confessions*: 'What then is Time? If no one asks me, I know; but if I wish to explain it to one that asketh, I know not. Yet I say boldly, that I know that if nothing passed away, Time past were not; and if nothing were coming [into existence], a Time to come were not; and if nothing existed, Time present were not. These two Times, then, past and to come, how are they, seeing the past now is not, and that to come is not yet? But the present, if it were always the present, and never passed into Time past, would surely not be Time, but Eternity.'

The enigma of time is of fundamental importance, for time is one of the two dimensions of our consciousness, the other being space. We are aware of time through the change of phenomena presented to our senses; for, as Augustine saw, if the present pattern of our experience did not change, we should have no sense of time, but be in a state of timelessness or eternity. In other words, normal human consciousness consists of awareness of the three temporal categories: past, present, and future.

The Consciousness of Time
On analysis, it is impossible for us at any given moment to define exactly what is the present. The 'here-now' of the present is an ever-moving point separating our past and future. Indeed, psychologically our 'present' includes our immediate past experience and anticipates the continuance of our experience into the immediate future. However, when we reflect on our experience over a longer period, we can distinguish more clearly what is

Melted clocks, similar to these, are shown in Salvador Dali's 1974 painting, *The Persistence of Memory*. **They represent time moving slowly.**

'past' and what is 'future,' although the existential reality of what is past and future constitutes problems of great metaphysical subtlety and complexity.

Enigmatical though time is and replete with problems beyond the comprehension of most persons, it constitutes a factor that has affected the evolution of humans. For man, in contradistinction to all other species, is endowed with an acute time-consciousness that he has exploited with amazing results. Because man is so acutely aware of time, he is by nature a 'planner:' he is forever drawing upon past experience in the present to provide for future needs.

This trait finds expression in the earliest evidence we have of mankind. For the Paleolithic peoples were tool-makers, and the making of a tool, for example, a stone axe, involves the anticipation of the future need of such an axe and busying oneself in the present to make it. Through the ability to anticipate and so provide for future needs, humankind has succeeded, since Paleolithic times, in dominating the world and eliminating or enslaving all animal competitors. The complex scientific and technological civilization that we now enjoy is a sophisticated product of our time-sense. And its range is enormous: from the planning of a nuclear power station to the taking out of an insurance policy, past experience is being utilized in the present to meet future contingencies. In short, the time-consciousness of men and women has been, and is, a primary cause of their success in the struggle for existence.

But this endowment has a kind of debit side. Men's and women's time-consciousness has not only enabled them to plan ahead to ensure their physical well-being; it has also made them acutely aware that they are subject to the flux of time that brings change, decay, aging, and finally death to every form of life. Accordingly, every human being learns early in childhood to anticipate his or her own death. In this sense, it has been truly said that mankind has invented death. For whereas the animals suffer the experience of dying without the long anticipatory knowledge of mortality, men and women contemplate their end from the moment of their first discovery that all life dies.

This awareness of mortality, which stems from the ability to project oneself mentally into the future, produces in mankind a fundamental sense of insecurity. It prevents people from immersing themselves wholly in the enjoyment of present well-being. They ever fear that changing time will bring misfortune; and they know that it is surely bearing them toward that dreaded moment of personal

An elaborate Wheel of Fortune allegory from the late fifteenth century, in which Fortuna's wheel is turned by Time, while Death takes the figure at the bottom of the wheel.

extinction to which they have seen so many of their fellow-beings come.

This ambivalent endowment of acute time-consciousness has found expression in human history in a twofold quest for security. As we have seen, the complex structure of civilization is designed to ensure constant and adequate provision for the material needs of mankind. But beyond the satisfaction of these needs, the prospect of death has remained as the ultimate menace. Mankind's reaction to this grim fact has found expression in religion.

In Search of Security

It can be reasonably shown that all religions are basically concerned with the problem of security after death. The logic of experience has precluded any serious attempt to provide immunity from physical death in this life (the quest of some Taoist magicians in China to find an elixir of immortality is notable only for its persistence against all evidence of failure). Though forced to accept the inevitability of death, mankind has generally believed that some part of the personality survives physical disintegration and needs to

be secured against postmortem perils. In conceiving such security, mankind's fear of the destructive process of time is reflected in a variety of imagery expressive of the instinct to transcend time. Behind this imagery certain distinctive forms of belief and action can be discerned by the comparative study of religion.

What is one of the most complex attempts, so far as thought and action are concerned, to gain everlasting postmortem security from the destructive process of time occurred in ancient Egypt. There the elaborate mortuary ritual, including mummification, was designed to effect two things. By embalming the corpse, it was hoped that physical decomposition would be stopped and the body preserved intact forever. Through the magical efficacy of the ritual 'Opening of the Mouth' it was believed that the ability to see, breathe, and take nourishment was restored to the mummified remains, so that the deceased might live, together with his *ka*, a kind of double or second self, and revisited by his *ba*, an entity separated from the human body at death, in his 'house of eternity,' the tomb, forever. Arrangements were also made for the perpetual offering of food at the tomb and it was hoped that the dead, revivified, and immune from decay, and 'perfectly equipped' with magical spells, would be eternally secure, 'coming forth' each day to the portal of the tomb, to see the sun and feed on the mortuary offerings. The other purpose of the mortuary ritual was to assimilate the dead person to the god Osiris, and among the various virtues that would accrue from such assimilation was transcendence of time. This was achieved, as a text in the Book of the Dead shows, by magically incorporating time into one's own being. The dead person, who had become one with Osiris, exclaims: 'I am Yesterday, Today, and Tomorrow.'

Flight to Heaven

The idea of gaining immunity from the destructive flux of time by union with a supernatural being regarded as eternal, which lies behind this passage in the Book of the Dead, finds various forms of expression in many religions. It appears in a non-Osirian context in Egypt as far back as the *Pyramid Texts*. The dead pharaoh is imagined as flying up to heaven to join the sun god Re in his solar boat, in which the god daily crossed the sky; as Re's companion on this unceasing journey the pharaoh would be beyond temporal change.

In Christianity, the 'beatific vision,' which constitutes the final reward of the redeemed, is an eternal communion of the individual soul with God.

In the Apocalypse of St. John, an attempt is made, in an esoteric imagery, to represent the transcendence of time in the eternity of worship. The four living creatures about the throne of God 'never cease to sing, "Holy,

'. . . there is neither coming nor going nor staying nor passing away nor arising. Without support or going on or basis is it. This indeed is the end of pain.'

holy, holy, is the Lord God Almighty, who was and is and is to come!"'

In Indian thought there is a similar conception of the effect of the individual's ultimate realization of Brahma: 'Verily, for him who knows

thus, this mystic doctrine of Brahma, the sun neither rises nor sets. For him it is day forever'—in other words, he is beyond time, whose passage is marked by the succession of day and night.

Nirvana, in Buddhist imagery, is likewise a state beyond time's changing phenomena. The Buddha is represented as teaching: 'There, monks, I say there is neither coming nor going nor staying nor passing away nor arising. Without support or going on or basis is it. This indeed is the end of pain.'

'Know I Am Time'

Concern about time has not only expressed itself in religion by imagining states of beatitude beyond its range. Since man is so disturbingly aware of

The 'ba,' depicted as a human-headed falcon, was a spiritual aspect of one's personality.

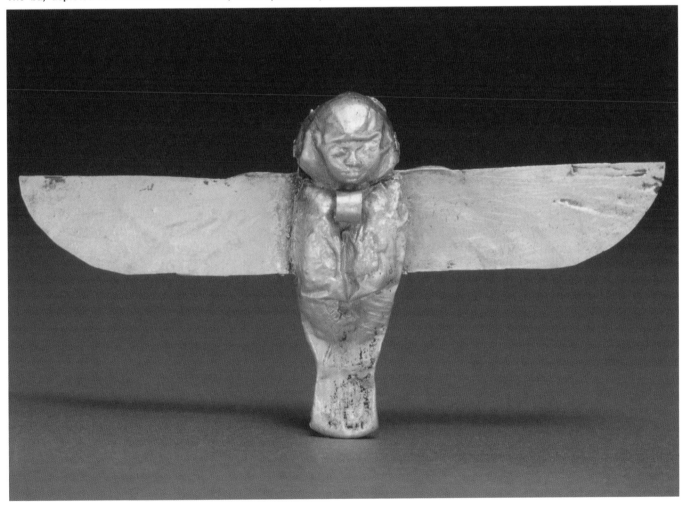

his subjection to time in this world, his religions reflect his preoccupation with its Nature and the significance of its operation throughout the universe. This preoccupation has led to the deification of time among some peoples. The rich imagery of Hinduism provides examples that are both impressive in their dramatic portrayal and significant in their theological implication. In the *Bhagavad Gita,* which is one of the foundational documents of Hinduism, the god Vishnu, in his form of Vasudeva, is equated with time.

This aspect of Vishnu is revealed in the culminating vision given to the prince Arjuna. At first Vishnu had revealed himself as the Creator and sustainer of the world. This was a revelation of the beneficent providence of the deity. Arjuna was impressed; but feeling that he had not seen all, he asks that a full revelation be made. His request is granted, but he is appalled by what he then beholds. Vishnu appears as a monstrous being, into whose awesome mouths, beset by hideous fangs, all forms of life are seen passing swiftly to destruction. Vishnu announces: 'Know I am Time, that makes the worlds to perish, when ripe, and come to bring on them destruction.'

This account is significant both for the ambivalence of its concept of deity and its identification of the supreme deity with time. It reflects the Indian conviction that creation in the empirical world inevitably entails destruction, that life involves death, and that time governs this alternating rhythm that never ends. This Vishnavite theology is paralleled by a similar conception in Shivaism. The god Shiva, on one side of his being, personifies the dynamic persistence of life, in all its teeming abundance and complexity of form, which is symbolized by the *lingam,* the mighty generative organ of

the god. In his other aspect, he is Bhairava, 'the terrible destroyer' and Maha-Kala (great Time), and Kala-Rudra (all-devouring Time).

An even more remarkable conception is that of *Kali,* the goddess who personifies *kala* (time). She derives from the concept of Shiva's *shakti* or activating energy. Her iconography is

> *For Time no limit is apparent, and no height can be seen nor deep perceived, and (Time) has always existed and will always exist . . .*

horrific, being thus designed to portray the baleful nature of time. She is depicted as black in hue, and wearing a chaplet of severed heads; her many hands hold symbols of her destructive power—the exterminating sword, scissors that cut short the thread of life. Yet, like Shiva, her lord, from whom she emanates, Kali is of ambivalent character; for she also holds the lotus of eternal generation and her body is expressive of vigourous fecundity.

This deification of time is related to the Indian view that the empirical world is not ultimately real. It is a view designed to account for human destiny, and it involves a belief that time moves in cycles.

The Infinite and the Finite

The ancient peoples of Iran had a god of time called Zurvan. How old this deification of time may be is unknown; there is some evidence that such a god was worshipped as far back as the twelfth century BC. The earliest reliable information, however, comes from a Greek scholar, Eudemos of Rhodes, who explained in the fourth century BC that the well known gods of Persian dualism, Ohrmazd and Ahriman, were derived by the Persians

from time and space. Although the native Iranian writings that witness to this deification of time are comparatively late, they are definite about the primordial Nature of time and its religious significance. Thus in the *Rivayat* it is stated: 'It is obvious that, with the exception of Time, all other things have been created. For Time no limit is apparent, and no height can be seen nor deep perceived, and (Time) has always existed and will always exist . . . Time is both Creator and the Lord of the creation which it created.'

The Iranians, however, distinguished between two forms of Zurvan. Zurvan *akarana* was Infinite Time; Zurvan *daregho-chvadhata* was 'Time of the long Dominion' or Finite Time. This latter form of Zurvan represented the time that rules in this world, and which brings age, decay, and death to all men. Although its dominion was believed to be long, extending to 12,000 years, it was finite. During the Sassanian period (AD 226–637), it appears that a cult of Zurvan developed, which explained mythically the relation of Zurvan to Ohrmazd and Ahriman, who personified the opposing forces of good and evil in Zoroastrian dualism. According to this myth, Zurvan, as the primal being, desired to have a son who would create the universe. To this end he offered sacrifice for 1,000 years. Before the millennium had been completed, Zurvan doubted for one brief moment the efficacy of the sacrifices. This momentary doubt had a fatal consequence; for it caused a second son to be conceived, who was to be Ahriman. And so, when the time was fulfilled, two sons were born to Zurvan: Ohrmazd, radiant with light; Ahriman, dark and foul. When Ohrmazd created the good and beautiful, Ahriman countered by creating the evil and the ugly.

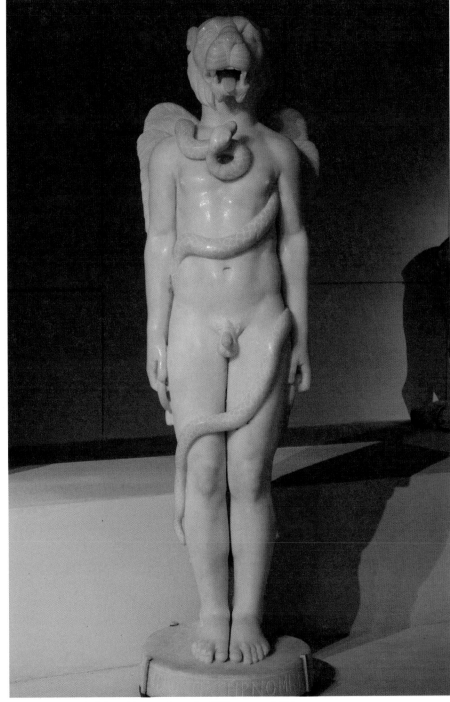

The Iranian god of time, Zurvan from the Mithraeum at Sidon

signified the sovereignty of 'Time of the long Dominion' over mankind in this world. It is possible that the devotees of Mithras thus recognized the cosmic dominion of time, but looked to Mithras for salvation from its baleful tyranny.

The influence of this form of Zurvan can be traced also in the figure of Phanes in the Greek Mystery religion known as Orphism. The Persian concept of Infinite Time was also carried into the Graeco-Roman world, where it was identified with the supreme deity under the names of Cronus and Aion. In Egypt, the cult of Cronus was closely associated with that of Serapis and, according to the Latin poet Macrobius, the cult image of Serapis in Alexandria symbolized this connection with time in a curious way. Serapis was portrayed accompanied by a three-headed monster: the middle head, that of a lion, represented time present; the wolf's head to the left signified time past, and that of a 'fawning dog' to the right depicted future time.

Janus, the ancient Roman god associated with beginnings, has sometimes, erroneously, been regarded as a time god, his two faces being interpreted as looking to the past and the future. So far as the Romans did deify time, it was in the form of Aeternitas, which derived from the Alexandrian concept of Aion. The most notable depiction of Aeternitas is in a bas-relief that adorns the base of the column of the Emperor Antoninus Pius in Rome. Aeternitas is represented as a heroic male figure, nude, with eagle's wings, and holding a serpent-encircled globe in his left hand: he bears the dead emperor and his wife Faustina to heaven.

The Sorrowful Weary Wheel

In contrast to these personifications of time, in other religions time has been regarded as an impersonal cyclic pro-

This Iranian deification of time appears to have been incorporated into Mithraism, which originated in Iran and gradually spread westward into the Roman Empire. The form in which it found expression was strange but significant. Images were set up, in the cave sanctuaries of Mithras, of a nude man with a lion's head, the mouth being open in a menacing grimace. About the body a huge snake was entwined, and on the body the signs of the zodiac were carved. The monster was winged, and usually held a staff and keys. These images undoubtedly represented Zurvan *daregho-chvadhata*, with whom Ahriman appears to have been identified. Of the significance of such images in the cult of Mithras no certain evidence survives. However, there is reason for thinking that they

cess, to which all life in this world is subject and obliged to conform. This view of time is linked with the idea of metempsychosis, or the transmigration of souls. It forms a basic concept of Hinduism and Buddhism, of Orphism, and some forms of Gnosticism.

The impression that time is cyclic in its movement, and unceasingly reproduces the same pattern of events, is an obvious deduction to make from natural phenomena. The succession of day and night, the rotation of the seasons, and the movements of the heavenly bodies, all suggest that time moves in cycles. This view has sometimes led to a cynical evaluation of life such as finds expression in the book of Ecclesiastes (chapter 1.9–10): 'What has been is what will be, and what has been done is what will be done; and there is nothing new under the sun. Is there a thing of which it is said: "See this is new?" It has been already, in the ages before us.'

It has been in connection with the idea of the transmigration of souls that the cyclic pattern of time has been most impressively utilized. The Indian sages taught that the individual self or *atman*, by mistaking the phenomenal world for reality and becoming attached to it, is involved in the stream of time. By the process of *samsara* or rebirth, the atman is continually reincarnated in a form determined by its previous actions or *karma*. Hence it becomes subjected to an unceasing process of births and deaths, with all their attendant pain. To emphasize the unending misery of such existence and impel the self to seek salvation, Indian thinkers invented an elaborate chronology based on the cyclic nature of time. A *mahayuga*—a period of 12,000 years—was conceived, but these were reckoned as years of the gods, each being equal to 361 human years. One thousand of such mahayugas made up one *kalpa*, which represented one day of Brahma, and that one day spanned the whole period from the creation of a world to its destruction. On the dawning of the next day, Brahma creates the world anew and the dreary wheel of existence begins to turn for another kalpa, through which the unenlightened soul is doomed to a farther succession of births and deaths. Hinduism and Buddhism claim to provide salvation from this 'sorrowful weary wheel' of time.

The expression 'sorrowful weary wheel' comes from an Orphic text; for a similar view of the fate of the uninitiated soul was held in ancient Greece by the members of the Pythagorean and Orphic Mystery cults. Plato also conceived of the errant soul as having to endure a series of incarnations for 10,000 years before it could return to its former state of happiness. And the philosopher and poet Empedocles tells of having for 'thrice 10,000 seasons' wandered 'far from the blessed, being

Tree of life wall relief carved in 1424 at Ahmedabad Gujarat, India, shows time's movement as linear

The Timeless Gods

All we wax old and wither like a leaf.
We are outcast, strayed between bright
   sun and moon;
Our light and darkness are as leaves
   of flowers,
Black flowers and white, that perish;
   and the noon
As midnight, and the night as
   daylight hours.
A little fruit a little while is ours.
And the worm finds it soon.

But up in heaven the high gods one
   by one
Lay hands upon the draught that
   quickeneth,
Fulfilled with all tears shed and all
   things done,
And stir with soft imperishable breath
The bubbling bitterness of life and death,
And hold it to our lips and laugh; but they
Preserve their lips from tasting night
   or day,
Lest they too change and sleep, the fates
   that spun,
The lips that made us and the hands
   that slay;
Lest all these change, and heaven bow
   down to none,
Change and be subject to the
   secular sway
And terrene revolution of the sun.
Therefore they thrust it from them,
   putting time away

Swinburne
Atalanta in Calydon

---

born throughout that time in the forms of all manner of mortal things and changing one baleful path of life for another.' For those who thought thus, salvation was to break out from time's inexorable process, or, as it is eloquently phrased on an Orphic grave tablet by one who thought that he had achieved deliverance: 'I have flown out of the sorrowful weary wheel; I have passed with eager feet to the Circle desired.'

Time's Winged Chariot

To believe that the course of time is cyclical has been the more common view; but the idea that time's movement is linear has been a basic concept of four great religions—Christianity, Judaism, Zoroastrianism, and Islam.

Both Judaism and Christianity (and the Islamic view has essentially followed the same pattern) equate the process of time with the unfolding of the purpose of God. This view finds expression in the Old Testament in what is virtually a philosophy of history. The main theme is the gradual revelation of Yahweh's providence for Israel, which starts with the call of Abraham (Genesis, chapter 22). Christianity took over this interpretation of the temporal process, but adapted it to its own recognition of Jesus of Nazareth as the promised Messiah, and of the Church as becoming the true Israel, consequent on the rejection of Jesus by historic Israel. From these basic notions there was gradually evolved the great synthesis of medieval Christianity, in which the destiny of mankind and its individual members were related in a timescheme that commenced with the Creation and would end with the Second Coming of Christ. The theme of this cosmic drama was the redemption of mankind after the Fall of its original parents, by the vicarious sacrifice on the cross of the incarnate Son of God.

This view of time has found significant expression in the division of its process into two parts, labeled respectively the era 'Before Christ' and the era *Anni Domini*, the 'years of the Lord.' In medieval iconography the end of time was symbolized by the destruction of the world, and its replacement by a new and eternal order. However, the most impressive statement, as it is also the most concise, of the Christian view that God incorporates and transcends time is given in Revelation (chapter 22) when Christ says: 'I am the Alpha and the Omega, the first and the last, the beginning and the end.'

It is interesting, to notice briefly the evolution of the idea of Father Time. The Christian view of God precludes any deification of time, but it did not prevent its personification. In the Middle Ages there were two lines of tradition concerning human destiny that finally coalesced during the Renaissance period, in the figure of Father Time. One tradition was astrological, through which the image of the pagan god Saturn survived as an old man, armed with a sickle and hour-glass: symbols of the termination of human life. In the other tradition, Death was personified as a skeleton, armed with a scythe or dart, with which he gave the death-blow. These two figures were eventually fused into the figure of Father Time, complete with hour-glass and scythe. In the iconography of Western mythology his figure still symbolizes man's ancient association of time with death.

S. G. F. BRANDON

The Golden Age

Strictly speaking, the Greek myth was not of a 'Golden Age' but of a Golden Race that was the earth's first human population. Hesiod (c. 700 BC) tells the story in his *Works and Days*. They lived when Cronus was king of the gods, and they lived like gods themselves, free from pain and toil and old age. The earth bore them its fruits untilled, and death came to them gentle as sleep. Now they have become invisible spirits that watch over men and bring them prosperity. They were succeeded by a Silver Race, foolish, violent, and irreligious: their childhood lasted 100 years, but then they aged rapidly. They have become spirits of a lower order—the Mortal Blessed.

The gods next made a Bronze Race, out of ash trees, more stern and brutal still, who destroyed themselves and left no trace. They were the first to kill animals for food. Then the succession of metals and the moral decline was

Statue of Cronus, the Titan god of time and the ages carved in c. 1765–75 is housed at the Bavarian National Museum, Munich, Germany.

interrupted: the fourth race was that of the noble heroes who fought at Troy and elsewhere, and who now live in the Isles of the Blessed and are revered as demigods. Now we have an Iron Race, that is doomed to toil, suffering, and eventually destruction, as their wickedness increases and children begin to be already gray-haired at birth.

The metal names do not have a single consistent significance. Of the Bronze Race, Hesiod says that their armour, tools, and houses were of bronze, for there was no iron then. This evidently represents a memory of the 'Bronze Age' of our archeologists, which in Greece gave way to the Iron Age about 1100 BC. At the same time, the Iron Race's name is appropriate to its inhumanity, while gold and silver join up with bronze to form a scale of absolute value. (Iron, however, ranked

as a precious, not a base metal.)

Thus the myth represents a compromise between abstract theory and a genuine memory of the past. The conflict shows itself again in the way the Heroic Age is accommodated between the Bronze and Iron Races. It has often been assumed that Hesiod was adapting a mythical scheme in which there were four races instead of five: Gold, Silver, Bronze, Iron, each worse than its predecessor. It may have been of oriental origin. Medieval Persian texts, which certainly contain some ancient material, tell how Zoroaster saw in a vision a tree with four branches, of gold, silver, copper, and iron, and Ahura Mazdah explained to him that these were the four kingdoms of Iran that were to succeed one another, each worse than the last.

We recall, too, Nebuchadnezzar's dream in the book of Daniel (chapter

2) in which four successive kingdoms are represented by the gold, silver, brass, and iron, and clay parts of an effigy in human form. The metal symbolism has been thought to point to Babylon, where alchemy was practiced and metals were assigned to each of the planets.

In India, there developed a theory of four world ages, of advancing badness and decreasing length, associated with different colours of Vishnu, though not with metals. Here too the last age is characterized by encroachment of old age upon youth.

Hesiod's poem has a double theme—honesty and industry. The myth serves to show how human morality has declined from a perfect state, and also how it has become necessary to work for a living as the earth has withdrawn her bounty. In the time of the Golden Race, righteousness went together with leisure. The general conviction of mankind that the times are growing worse, that today's men are inferior to yesterday's, here finds systematic expression. The details of the idyll follow from a negation of all that is most bothersome at the present day: toil, pain, war, want, worry, old age. Even the residual guilt over animal sacrifice is purged away in the recollection of the time of innocence when men lived in amity with each other and their fellow creatures. The statement that Cronus was king may be connected with the fact that he presided over a summer festival at which conditions approached those enjoyed by the ideal race.

The Philosophers

Later Greek and Roman accounts all derive ultimately from Hesiod, but show a perspective that gradually changes with the times. Philosophers and moralists constructed their own accounts of the development of human society. Reflection, and observation of more backward peoples, brought a new awareness of the fact of technical progress. In fifth century BC accounts, the blessed vegetarians of the earliest age have been replaced by shivering cave-dwellers subsisting on acorns and whatever else they can find. So far from declining, on this view, man's state has constantly improved.

This has little in common with Hesiod's picture, and at first there was no attempt to reconcile the two. Plato more than once makes use of Hesiod's metal races, adapting them freely in myths of his own. In his Republic, he proposes justifying his strict class structure to the citizenry by persuading them that God has fashioned them with different metals in their constitutions—gold, silver, bronze, or iron. Here the metals keep their qualitative significance, but there is no idea of temporal succession. Elsewhere, too, while he allows the idea of world cycles, Plato is disinclined to link virtue and happiness to them firmly.

Later in the fourth century BC, the philosopher Dicaearchus gave a rationalistic interpretation of Hesiod's description of the life of the Golden Race. Naturally their food grew of its own accord, because they had no agriculture, and that was why they were free from toil and care. They did not fall sick, because their diet was sparse and simple. There was no warfare, because there was nothing worth taking. So the myth is brought into harmony with more recent speculation about how early man's life must have been.

As yet there is no exaggerated insistence on the virtue and nobility of the primitive, no connection is seen between technical progress and moral regress. The influential Stoic writer Posidonius (135–50 BC), praising the benefits that philosophy had conferred on mankind, claimed that in the Golden Age the rulers were philosophers, who taught their subjects wisdom, restraint, and justice, besides providing for their wants. It was the passing of power to tyrants that brought about the decline, and the need for laws. But the philosophers remained active as makers of these laws, and in developing the arts and crafts.

It is when we pass to Rome that we find the Golden Race turned into a Golden Age as a result of the ambivalence of the Latin word *saeculum*. Other developments can also be explained from Roman conditions. The myth is given political applications.

In his famous fourth Eclogue (40 BC), Virgil announces that the wheel has come full circle, and that a return of the Golden Age is imminent. Within twenty years or so, he says, the earth will become generous again, fruit and crops will grow of their own accord, honey will run from the oaks, the snake will bite no more, warfare and commerce will disappear, the sheep will even grow coloured wool to save us dyeing it artificially. Obviously Virgil did not believe all this literally, and it is hard to say what he meant by it. But later, in the *Aeneid*, it becomes the reign of Augustus that he celebrates as the new Golden Age. His enthusiasm was sincere, but he was setting a bad precedent. To speak of 'this golden age' became a commonplace in the art of emperor-flattery.

Freedom of the Primitive

Virgil has a new concept of the connection between the end of the Golden Age and the growth of civilization. In the *Georgics*, he explains that Jupiter put a stop to the life of ease in order to stimulate mankind to resource and discovery, and 'so that his kingdom should not bask in torpor.' Deprived of automatic sustenance, they were forced to find out how to grow crops, strike fire from the flint, navigate, hunt, saw wood; harsh necessity was the mother of invention.

This favourable view of human progress was soon to be challenged. The complexity of life in the big city, and the diversity of luxury and ostentation that flourished there, increasingly provoked the censure of moralizers and satirists. Hence the advances of material civilization finally came to be identified as the symptoms and concomitants of moral degeneration. Seneca (AD 60) voiced the opinion that it was better to live in caves and hollow trees than in towering tenements that threaten to collapse, with locking doors that can only encourage avarice; the primitive's freedom was more valuable than our pastry cooks and ornamental ceilings. Man's essential needs can be easily satisfied in simple ways. Thus mankind is made fully responsible for its own fall. It was not the gods' will or the exhaustion of Nature that put an end to the Golden Age, but man's folly.

M. L. WEST

Alice And The Angry Queen Of Hearts from Lewis Carroll's *Through the Looking Glass*

FURTHER READING: S. G. F. Brandon. History, Time and Deity. *(Manchester, UK: Manchester University Press, 1965); P. T. Landsberg, ed.* The Enigma of Time. *(Bristol, UK: Adam Hilger, 1984); P. Coveney and R. Highfield.* The Arrow of Time. *(London, UK: W. H. Allen, 1990); M. Gardner.* The Ambidextrous Universe. *(London, UK: Bantam, 1988); C. H. Hinton.* Selected Writings. *(Mineola, NY: Dover, 1980).*

Weather Magic

There has been no time in human history when people have not needed to know something about the weather. Probably under modern conditions we have less knowledge of the weather than ever before. In the great urban cities of the world, the red sky at night is no longer a warning that the cloud will disappear and fine weather will come on the morrow, but it tells us of the glare of neon signs in peace and of the burning of cities in time of war. We fill our world with artificial light so that it is only in the more remote areas that one can take a walk at night to admire the moon and the stars. Within the great city the moon is less brilliant than the street lights.

To our ancestors the world was a place full of magic, and most impor-

tant of all the phenomena of Nature were the coming and going of rain and snow, which determined the growth of the food crops for the farmer; and for the hunters the rainfall determined the amount of fresh grass available for the migrating herds of deer and bison. Sometimes quite alarming falls of coloured dust of unknown origin caused red rains, white rains, and black rains which were carefully noted in the historical annals of past times. Hail storms occurred with sudden changes of temperature, sometimes blighting new crops by a layer of thin

Living Backward

Alice was just beginning to say 'There's a mistake somewhere—,' when the Queen began screaming, so loud that she had to leave the sentence unfinished. 'Oh, oh, oh!' shouted the Queen, shaking her hand about as if she wanted to shake it off. 'My finger's bleeding! Oh, oh, oh, oh!'

Her screams were so exactly like the whistle of a steam-engine, that Alice had to hold both her hands over her ears.

What's the matter?' she said, as soon as there was a chance of making herself heard. 'Have you pricked your finger?'

'I haven't pricked it yet,' the Queen said, 'but I soon shall—oh, oh, oh!'

'When do you expect to do it?' Alice asked, feeling very much inclined to laugh.

'When I fasten my shawl again,' the poor Queen groaned out: 'the brooch will come undone directly. Oh, oh!' As she said the words the brooch flew open, and the Queen clutched wildly at it, and tried to clasp it again.

'Take care!' cried Alice. You're holding it all-crooked!' And she caught at the brooch; but it was too late: the pin had slipped, and the Queen had pricked her finger.

'That accounts for the bleeding, you see,' she said to Alice with a smile. 'Now you understand the way things happen here.'

'But why don't you scream now?' Alice asked, holding her hands ready to put over her ears again.

'Why, I've done all the screaming already,' said the Queen. 'What would be the good of having it all over again?'

Lewis Carroll
Through the Looking Glass

frozen ice, but more often actively destroying crops through the massive battering of larger hailstones crashing to the ground and beating everything flat beneath them.

Demons of the Desert

Then there were the winds; to most of us the winds have simply come from the four directions of north, south, east, and west. Those who live in the cities just notice whether a day is windy or not, but to the seaman and the farmer each wind still has its own character, bringing its specific blessing or danger to the crops and animals. In addition to the normal winds there are the sudden and more violent winds, the waterspouts and the hurricanes; terrible things that cause tremendous damage as they sweep across the country. Sometimes, after a waterspout has passed, the ground is seen to be covered with small frogs or even fishes. Sometimes leaves of trees from far distant places are cast down as the storm passes.

All around the skies of the world lightning plays from time to time. To the Northern Native Americans this is the flashing beak of the great thunder-bird as she flies through the storm. To Europeans these were the thunderbolts cast by the king of the gods. Even Mahayana Buddhism involves the use of the metal *Dorje*, which represents a thunderbolt, in the temple services.

Winds in a Bag

Among the greatest weather watchers in ancient times were the Etruscans of northern Italy. Their diviners, who cast prophecies from the state of the sky, achieved great fame, and it was customary in the early days of Rome for the Senate to send deputations to Etruscan cities to ask for advice when their own oracles seemed doubtful. The Etruscan soothsayers preferred to work from a high, clear mountain

with an even view of the sky in all directions; if it was situated above oak woods, so much the better. There were sixteen wind directions to be regarded.

Particularly in thundery weather, the observers would wait on the hilltops, marking the direction of lightning flashes exactly, taking note of their brilliance and of the places where they appeared to strike. From this study they calculated the incidence of danger, and of blessings coming from the different directions. The augurs then assessed their particular meanings for the person or city on whose behalf they were consulting the elements.

For most people, knowledge of the sky sufficient to give a clue to tomorrow's weather is enough. But often a much fuller knowledge is demanded, even in primitive society, and this is expected from the weather specialists, the shamans who have watched the skies sufficiently long and thoroughly to form judgements. They make their estimates from wind, cloud, the flight of birds, and the colour of the sky, particularly at sunrise and sunset.

Such specialists included the magicians of northern Europe, who were said to have the power to tie the winds in a length of rope. This power might

Fūjin, the God of Wind, at Taiyū-in Reibyō, Nikkō, Japan.

be used for evil magic, by pulling the knots tight, when it was believed that the winds would be stopped and ships becalmed, with consequent loss of business and even health, if the calm lasted for a long time. The knots were used to tie up the bag in which the wind was symbolically trapped; the magician would use it like the bellows of a bagpipe for sympathetic magic, thus inducing the real winds to follow the example of the air being expelled.

Continual Rain in Paradise

Perhaps the most difficult of all forecasting performed by people living the simple life was that of predicting the coming of rain in semidesert areas. Some successful meteorological observers probably possessed clairvoyant powers; in Africa, Masai shamans

would sit on the hilltops near Mount Kenya and look at the sky, knowing from the position of the stars what season of the year it was. By the colour of the sky, by the appearance of little drifts of clouds forming near the snowcap of the mountain, they would estimate whether the rains would be early or late, in order to give the farmers a few days' warning so that the planting could be achieved in time. When the forecasts proved wrong the rainmaker would be considered to have been abandoned by his spiritual helpers and therefore of no farther use. He would be lucky if he escaped simply with insults and a beating.

Among the Pueblo Indians there were also many wise shamans who observed the weather. In their semidesert country, where the water supply was

dependent largely on seasonal thunderstorms, it was important to know whether the storms were likely to be light or heavy, early or late. All good observers in the hilltop villages could detect at a glance that way a stormcloud was moving, and by looking at the shadows of rain or hail falling from its base, they would be able to estimate any danger to their crops.

In central Mexico the weather gods were very important. Tlaloc, the lord of the rain and master of thunder, was a spirit who controlled the four kinds of rain and brought life and fertility to the Earth. His importance was so great that the high priest of the Aztecs was called the Tlaloc Tlamacazqui.

The consort of the rain god was the beautiful princess Chalchihuitlicue, who was the spring rains, the whirlwinds, the whirlpools in the water, and all young growing plants. Between them they looked after the fertility of the material Earth. People who had been struck by lightning or drowned were believed to have been claimed by these deities, and their souls would live in the wonderful paradise where flowers bloomed continually, there were myriads of butterflies, and thin rain fell constantly amid the rainbows. To the Mexicans of the semidesert highland, this indeed was the most beautiful place that could exist.

The Celtic Druids were skilled in weather magic. Their traditional knowledge has been preserved for us in many little nursery rhymes and riddles that refer to the wind and the sky. Like all people concerned with the natural growth of crops, the Druids realized that the power behind the weather had spiritual connotations, that the life of man was closely linked with the movements of wind and rain.

Splitting a Cloud

At all times magicians, witches, and ecstatics of various kinds have been credited with influencing the weather

Mask of Tlaloc, god of the rain

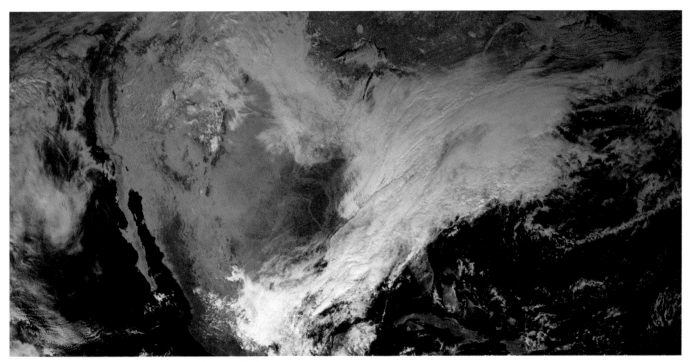

A modern satellite image used for weather predictions

—not only the shaman tying knots in his rope, but also the witches in their magical rituals, flying through the air on their broomsticks. They swept along among the clouds, they brought mists, they threw the hail, they were able to charm the winds on the ocean so they could float to sea in a sieve.

Even under today's conditions, there are various curious phenomena to be found in the experience of witchcraft. In periods when the atmosphere is highly charged with electricity and the skin is dry, a group of naked dancers in a circle may find themselves producing sudden little flashes of fire all over their bodies. This is due entirely to the electrical static discharge between the atmosphere and their skins. These discharges may often be very beautiful in the dark, like veils of flashing pale blue diamonds appearing all over the dancer. Such things in the past must indeed have seemed magical and mysterious, although to a modern mind they are simply curious and beautiful.

Although nothing has been reported in recent years to compare with the storm-raising powers credited to medieval witches or with the bringing of thunder and lightning from the heavens that was attributed to priests and magicians in classical times, in practice it has been found possible to split a small cloud in unstable weather conditions. A few years ago, three friends walking along a path in thundery weather observed a small cloud blowing up directly toward them. On looking toward it and wishing that the cloud would divide, they witnessed the actual splitting of the cloud into two portions as it approached and then passed in its separate halves overhead.

Unimpressive as this experiment may seem, it did give a clue to the possibility that people much more devoted to such activity, and with a deeper occult knowledge, could have caused clouds to disperse.

The whole of this field of weather control by magic is insufficiently explored in modern times. Nevertheless, it is still possible for ordinary people to look at the sky and say what tomorrow's weather will be. That in itself is a phenomenon worth noting as an achievement of the human personality.

C. A. BURLAND

Winter

In northern lands the season of cold, wet, and darkness has also traditionally been the time when the freest rein is given to fantasy. It was in winter that whole families in bygone ages huddled together in smoky huts listening, as the storms raged outside, to sagas and folktales. In winter, more than any other season, ghosts stalk abroad, and in the countryside a solitary light, glimpsed in the distance by a lone wayfarer, can flood the soul with emotion. Winter has also always been a time for feasting and celebrating. When harsh weather made warfare and even trivial disputes between neighbours impossible, and the concerted hostility of the elements made men mindful of their own essential brotherhood, it was natural to think of winter as the season of goodwill. There was also the gloom and tedium of long nights crying out for relief, and when the days began at last to lengthen, however imperceptibly, men looked upon it as the rebirth of the sun, and celebrated the nativity of a god.

The earliest of these winter festivals about which we know anything was the Sacaea in Babylon, a celebration of the New Year, lasting several days. From the third millennium down to the very end of Mesopotamian civilization, a few centuries before the Christian era, mock battles were held every year, in which the king impersonated the god Marduk, who had won a mighty victory over Tiamat, the watery goddess of chaos, on the very first New Year's day, when the world had been created. In Babylonia new temples were inaugurated only on New Year's day, and from this day a king officially dated the beginning of his reign. According to later Greek writers, the Babylonian Sacaea was a time of sexual license, feasting and disguising. Slaves gave orders to their masters during the days of the festival, and a criminal was chosen to have royal rights conferred upon him, only to be executed at the end of the celebrations. Whether these Greeks are reading contemporary practices in the Roman world into the Babylonian setting it is impossible to say, but if their reports are accurate, then the Babylonian festival must have been the ancestor of a number of similar celebrations in the ancient world.

The Roman Saturnalia, celebrated at the end of December, was a festival of merrymaking and exchanging gifts that left its mark on today's Christmas celebrations. All work and business was suspended, originally for three days, but eventually for seven, and slaves were free to say and do what they liked. Gambling, usually punishable with a fine fixed at four times the value of the stakes, was officially permitted on these 'best of days,' as the Roman poet Catullus calls the Saturnalia. Rich men gave their 'clients' presents of silverware, and children received little wax dolls.

A Greek writer of the fourth century AD, the sophist Libanius, has left a description of the winter festival as it was celebrated in his own city of Antioch: 'There is food everywhere, heavy, rich food. And laughter. A positive urge to spend seizes on everyone, so that people who have taken pleasure in saving up the whole year, now think it's a good idea to squander. The streets are full of people and coaches, staggering under the load of gifts. Children are free of the dread of their teachers, and for slaves the festival is as good as a holiday. Another good thing about it—it teaches people not to be too fond of money, but to let it circulate from hand to hand.'

Libanius was an early opponent of Christianity who nevertheless had Christians among his pupils, one of them St. John Chrysostom. He is here describing pagan festivities in general, though he seems to have had the Saturnalia particularly in mind. The corresponding Greek festival, the Kronia, was celebrated at harvest time, but the Greeks had winter festivals, including the rustic Dionysia, held in December, and celebrated in villages with a burlesque procession; the Lenaea, or feast of the wine vats, celebrated in January with a procession, sacrifice and competing plays; and the Anthesteria, held during three days about the time that we call February, when the casks were opened and the new wine was tasted.

All the winter festivals were connected in some way with Dionysus, the god of wine, and the Greeks in fact divided the cult-year into two halves, the Dionysiac and the Apollonian, corresponding to winter and summer. A similar division was made by the ancient Hindus, for whom winter was the time for ancestor worship, and summer for the gods of Nature. In other parts of the world, too, winter is the time for appeasing the spirits of the dead. On the third day of the Anthesteria, the celebrations were held within the family circle, with rites in appeasement of ancestors. This festival came at the end of winter in Greece—indeed, it was to celebrate the end of winter marked by the appearance of the year's first flowers—but in northern Europe the cult of the dead was celebrated either in autumn, as among the Saxons, or in early or midwinter, as among the Scandinavians and Celts. In these pre-Christian festivals, bonfires were lighted to represent the waning and waxing sun. The rites were absorbed into Christianity in the guise of All Saints' day on November 1 and All Souls' on November 2. Winter festivals in commemoration of the dead were also celebrated in China until comparatively recent times.

The Last Winter
Connected perhaps with the cult of dead souls, but also with the general harshness of winter, is the widespread notion that the world will come to an end in the middle of a terrible winter. This is the *ftmbul-vetr* of the Icelandic sagas. In one of these poems, Odin, the god of the dead, asks the wise giant Vafthrudnir which of mankind will survive the mighty winter, and is told Lif and Lifthrasir, hidden in Hoddmimir's wood. In a prose saga of the thirteenth century, it is prophesied that winter will precede the great Doom. Snow will drive from all quarters, with sharp frost and cruel wind. The sun will have no power. Three such winters will follow in succession, without an intervening summer. There will be fighting all over the earth, with brother slaying brother.

In Iranian mythology, the rain of Malkosh devastates the earth, and snow and ice cause most of mankind to die of cold and famine. The only men and animals saved from this destructive winter are those who are herded together by one of the gods in a great enclosure. There is a related idea in St. Mark's gospel (chapter

13.18), when Christ, in prophesying the misery and destruction that will precede the Second Coming, urges his disciples to 'pray that it may not happen in winter.' Other verses in the same chapter may have inspired the passage in the Eddie saga about brother slaying brother, but whether the Iranian myth shows Christian influence, or whether even older notions connecting the end of the world with winter underlie both the myth and the gospel prophecy, is impossible to determine.

The Sleep of God

In astronomical terms, winter begins at the solstice on December 21 or 22, and ends at the vernal equinox, on March 20, but in northern latitudes winter begins, in popular estimation, much earlier. In many villages in the Upper Styria region of Austria, it was the custom to 'ring in' the winter as early as August 24, the purpose of the ceremony being to frighten away the malevolent spirits of winter by making a loud noise. According to a saying current at one time in Aachen, Charlemagne goes to his winter quarters on St. Giles's day (September 1) and leaves them on Ascension Day, a reference to the army of ghosts stationed in a magic mountain that Charlemagne still commands. In other parts of northern Europe, winter begins on October 28, November 1, or November 11—St. Martin's day, the saint riding on a white horse as the harbinger of snow. Colder weather is supposed to set in on St. Catherine's day (November 25), but in a warm year when winter is late, St. Andrew's day (November 30) finally marks the real onset of winter.

The day most commonly taken as midwinter is that of the conversion of St. Paul (January 25). In more southerly climates, January and February are regarded as the true winter months.

But it is curious that the Greek and Latin words for 'winter' (*kheimon* and *hiems*) are related to words in prehistoric languages meaning 'snow:' the name Himalaya is cognate. In northern European languages, on the other hand, the words denoting winter are cognate with words meaning

Children are free of the dread of their teachers, and for slaves the festival is as good as a holiday.

'water' and 'wet.' The Greeks probably brought their word with them when they migrated in prehistoric times into their present country. In literature, at any rate, one can find as many references to rain as to snow and ice: 'The winter is past, the rain is over,' says the Song of Solomon (chapter 2.11), words which Chaucer (1343–1400) echoes: 'The winter is goon, with ale his reynes wete.'

In myth and folktale, winter is personified, either in himself, as a storm god (Kari in Nordic legend), or through frost, ice, and snow spirits of one kind or another. There are traces in prehistoric myths of a single god or goddess wielding power over both winter and summer. The Asiatic Nature goddess known to the Greeks as Kubele held the keys of the earth, which she opened in summer and shut in winter. The Teutonic lunar goddess Holda (the Frau Holle or White Woman of German folklore) holds summer captive in her underworld kingdom during winter. When she shakes her bedclothes, it snows.

The idea that Nature is asleep in winter is an ancient one, and the Phrygians believed that the Deity himself was asleep in winter. In primitive belief, winter and death are often

equated, a notion strikingly summed up in an oracle quoted by a Latin author about the time of the birth of Christ: 'The highest God is called Hades in winter.' Here again, there is a link with the winter cults of the dead already mentioned, and with ghosts, which are especially active in winter.

In Nordic myths, winter is the time of the wanderings of Odin, or Wotan, the god of the dead.

The belief that dead ancestors are present in winter explains the practice of the Kwakiutl Indians of British Columbia who change their names at the beginning of winter, when the ghosts arrive, and adopt the names of their ancestors. They also form secret societies in winter, in place of their ordinary summer family life. The practice of exorcizing evil and evil spirits at either the beginning or end of winter is widespread among primitive peoples.

Probably owing to its beautiful, sparkling quality, frost seems to have stimulated the myth-making faculty of man more than either snow or ice. Jack Frost is our own personification of frost, and he seems quite a friendly figure compared with the evil frost giants of the Eddie sagas. These giants, the Hrimthursar, represent snow and ice as well as frost, and were descended from the giant Ymir, who was himself created out of ice. They had been driven out of their ancestral home by Odin and his band of Aesir, and dwelt in Utgard, the outlying world.

Porridge for the Frost Man

Frost is personified in Finnish magic songs, and Frost man appears as the brother of Mist man in a charming Japanese legend. However, the frost spirits were taken most seriously by the Finnish tribes of Russia and Siberia—the Votiaks, the Cheremiss,

Fire-bearers circle figures of The Green Man fighting Jack Frost

the Mordvins, and the Ostiaks. There was a 'Frost woman' as well as a 'Frost man' to whom sacrifices were made. It was the custom among the Mordvins (who live in the district lying between Nizhni Novgorod and Saratov, and who in Byzantine times scored many victories over the Russians) to place porridge for the 'Frost man' in the smoke outlet of their huts on the Thursday before Easter, in order to protect the spring sowings, for although the Mordvins had accepted baptism, they still clung to their ancient mythology and to many pagan beliefs and practices. The Lapps also paid great respect to the 'Frost man,' who was more like a god than a man, as he was believed to govern the weather, the snow, and the ice, and sacrifices were offered to him so that 'the ice should not harm the reindeer and that the blizzard should cease.'

Frost is not the monopoly of the northern hemisphere. A tribe of Australian aborigines have the following myth about the origin of frost. The seven Pleiades (called by them the Meamei) once lived on Earth as seven sisters, whose bodies sparkled with beautiful icicles. Several brothers followed the girls about and tried to seduce them with gifts, but without success. A man stole two of the girls, but could not thaw off the icicles. These two girls flew up to the sky, where they found their five sisters already waiting. Once every year, the sisters break off ice from themselves and throw it down to Earth. Then members of this Australian tribe say, 'The Meamei have not forgotten us.'

When Snow child followed her friends over the glowing embers, she turned into fine vapour, and rose as a cloudlet to heaven.

Snow Maiden

In the mythology of sub-arctic peoples, ice is the original stuff out of which the world is made. Ymir the ice giant has been mentioned already. He is one of many such giants, the personification, perhaps, of icebergs. In the Eddas, the god Buri, grandfather of Odin, was licked into life from a block of ice by the magic cow Aud-humla. A legend of the ice sea was recounted even in the western mountains of Czechoslovakia, which told of twelve ice giants, enemies of the sun. It is these giants, says the legend, that cause eclipses of the sun. The ice wolf, who threatens both sun and moon with his baying, lives with these giants on an island in the ice sea.

In central Europe, ice in winter was connected with good crops the following year, if it came in the period between Christmas and Twelfth Night. Smooth ice in March was taken as a sign that fruit would be plentiful in some places, while elsewhere it was taken to mean the opposite. Long icicles indicated that the flax would grow long in the following year, and again, their appearance in the days following Christmas was especially important. Sometimes the appearance and the time of formation of icicles was taken as a guide as to the best time to sow. If icicles were forked, the flax would also be forked.

Snow is personified in the myths and folktales of many peoples. In Japanese lore, Yuki-onne, the snow woman, is a young woman with a ghastly white complexion, with a slim figure, and a gentle and alluring manner. She appears to any wayfarer caught in a snowstorm and exhausted in the struggle. She soothes him and lulls him to sleep, until he loses consciousness and dies. Sometimes, it is said, she incarnates herself as a beautiful woman and marries a mortal, but she kills her unlucky husband.

Other people picture snow, in personified form, as a man. In Nordic mythology, Snow is an aged king of cold Finland, with the name Snaer, 'the old man.' His father is Iceberg or Frost, and his three daughters are Thick Snow, Snowstorm, and Fine Snow. Snaer is 300 years old, and when people wish one another a long life, they say, 'May you live as long as Snaer.'

Snow is not always personified as a powerful or fearful figure. A Russian folk song tells of an elderly childless couple who made a snow doll in their garden, which a passing stranger blessed, whereupon it became a living child. The blue-eyed, golden-haired little girl was very precocious—she was like a child of fourteen by the time winter had passed. As the snow melted from the fields in spring, little Snow child avoided the sun, in which she wilted, and sought out the shade of the willow trees. Most of all, she liked heavy showers, and if there was a hailstorm she was as gay as if she had found a treasure trove. But on St. John the Baptist's day (June 24) her friends took her on an outing. They were careful to keep her in the shade of the forest, but when night came, they lit a bonfire and leapt back and forth across it. Suddenly they heard a dreadful noise behind them. They could see nothing when they turned to look, but Snow child had disappeared, and though they looked for her for several days, combing the forest tree by tree, they could find no trace of their little pale companion. The old couple were inconsolable, and imagined that a cruel beast had carried Snow child off. But, says the song, it was not a beast. When Snow child followed her friends

over the glowing embers, she turned into fine vapour, and rose as a cloudlet to heaven.

It would be possible to read a symbolic meaning into this apparently very simple story. The Snow child, sweet and innocent as she is, represents the cruel winter, but for all the care she takes to avoid the sun, she is vanquished in the end. It is interesting that it is not the sun itself which melts her, but the bonfire that in pagan times was lit to celebrate the sun god at the height of his power, about the time of the summer solstice.

With the triumph of Christianity, these pagan rites were transferred to the celebration of St. John the Baptist, and in this Russian tale there may also be a barely conscious reference to the triumph of the Son over the powers of darkness, symbolized by the wintry phenomenon of snow.

DAVID PHILLIPS

The Snow Maiden by Vicktor M. Vasnetsov (1848–1926) illustrates the well-known Russian folk song.

Glossary

Ablution   Cleansing of the body, usually as a religious ritual.

Aggregate   The collection of two or more parts taken as a whole.

Antithesis   The exact opposite or contrast.

Appropriate   To take or use without authority or in a way that is unfair or illegal.

Archetype   An original or typical example.

Ascribe   To refer to or regard as a supposed cause.

Attenuate   To make weaker or reduce the value of.

Augur   One who can predict an event, or an official seer of Ancient Rome.

Coalesce   To assemble or come together.

Culminate   To reach a decisive point, often the final result.

Dualism   The state of being or concept divided in two opposing sides.

Edifying   Instructing in a moral or intellectual way.

Embalm   To preserve from decay, usually referring to a corpse.

Grimoire   A book containing spells and incantations, often considered to be magical.

Guise   A presentation, or disguise, usually hiding one's true Nature.

Jaundice   A medical condition often marked by the yellowing of the skin.

Libretto   The text of a musical work, usually opera.

Machination   A scheme or plot.

Manifest   To appear or make evident, to be obvious.

Metaphysical   Abstract, relating to a realm beyond perception.

Motif   A recurring thematic element or idea.

Mummer   An actor in a traditional English play, a merrymaker in disguise.

Obstinate   Stubborn, refusing to change ones ideas, to be difficult.

Ominous   Forboding, to be an ill omen, to imply future misfortune.

Phallic   Resembling or referring to a penis.

Pleiades   In myth, the seven daughters of Atlas, transformed into stars by Zeus.

Portent   A sign that something terrible is about to happen.

Primeval   From or relating to early history.

Propitiate   To gain favour from a diety by doing something to please them.

Sickle   A semicircular blade used for cutting or slicing wheat.

Subterranean   Underground or below the surface.

Tenacious   Determined, persisting, not easily deterred.

Transmigration   When a soul from one body to another, specifically after death.

Torpor   To be inactive, lethargic.

Undine   A female water nymph or spirit.

Wanton   Immodest, also unprovoked and deliberates.

Yarrow   A plant with small white or pink flowers, often used in herbal remedies.

Index

Author List

Contributors to *Man, Myth, and Magic: The Seasons: Natural Rites and Traditions*

Violet Alford is an authority on folklore and folk dance. Her books include *Sword Dance and Drama* and *The Traditional Dance* (with Rodney Gallop).

Ruth Binney Following graduation from the University of Cambridge, England, with a degree in Natural Sciences, Ruth Binney pursued a forty-year editorial career in illustrated non-fiction. Since retiring as Development Editor at Reader's Digest Books, London, she has authored twelve books, including her 'Wise Words' series covering subjects as diverse as the weather, mythology, and country house life.

S. G. F. Brandon (the late) was formerly Professor of Comparative Religion, at Manchester University. Brandon's numerous books include *Man and his Destiny in the Great Religions, Creation Legends of the Ancient Near East, History, Time and Deity, The Judgment of the Dead,* and *The Trial of Jesus of Nazareth.* Brandon also edited the *Dictionary of Comparative Religion* and was a special consultant to *Man, Myth, and Magic.*

C. A. Burland worked previously at the Department of Ethnography at the British Museum. Burland's books include *The Magical Arts; The Ancient Maya; The Aztecs; Man and Art; The Arts of the Alchemists.* Burland was a member of the Editorial Board of *Man, Myth, and Magic.*

Richard Cavendish is the original editor of *Man, Myth, and Magic* and has also written *The Black Arts.*

Tom Driberg, M. P. is the author of *The Best of Both Worlds; The Mystery of Moral Rearmament* and several other titles.

Max Gluckman as the Professor of Social Anthropology at Manchester University, Gluckman has written several books including *Custom and Conflict in Africa; Order and Rebellion in Tribal Africa; Politics,* and *Law and Ritual in Tribal Society.*

Douglas Hill is the author of *Magic and Superstition, Return From the Dead, The Supernatural* (with Pat Williams), *The Opening of the Canadian West; Regency London* amongst others.

J. A. Jackson is the Professor of Social Theory and Institutions, the Queen's University of Belfast, Northern Ireland. He is the author of *The Irish in Britain* and several other titles.

Eric Maple is the author of *The Dark World of Witches, The Realm of Ghosts, The Domain of Devils, Magic, Medicine and Quackery,* and *Superstition and the Superstitious.*

Venetia Newall is a folklorist, traveler, and lecturer. She is honorary secretary of the Folk-Lore Society and the author of *An Egg at Easter.*

David Phillips is a freelance journalist and broadcaster. He was the former head of the BBC Greek service.

Eric J. Sharpe is the senior lecturer in religious studies at Lancaster University. He is the author of *Not to Destroy but to Fulfill.*

Terence Turner is the assistant professor of anthropology at Chicago University.

M. L. West is a Fellow of University College, Oxford and acting editor of Liddell and Scott's *Greek Lexicon.* West has published an edition of Hesiod's *Theogony.*